Hope, Form, and Future in the Work of James Joyce

Hope, Form, and Future in the Work of James Joyce

David P. Rando

BLOOMSBURY ACADEMIC
LONDON • NEW YORK • OXFORD • NEW DELHI • SYDNEY

BLOOMSBURY ACADEMIC
Bloomsbury Publishing Plc
50 Bedford Square, London, WC1B 3DP, UK
1385 Broadway, New York, NY 10018, USA
29 Earlsfort Terrace, Dublin 2, Ireland

BLOOMSBURY, BLOOMSBURY ACADEMIC and the Diana logo are trademarks of
Bloomsbury Publishing Plc

First published in Great Britain 2022
This paperback edition published 2023

Copyright © David P. Rando, 2022

David P. Rando has asserted his right under the Copyright, Designs and Patents Act, 1988,
to be identified as Author of this work.

For legal purposes the Acknowledgments on pp. viii–x constitute an extension
of this copyright page.

Cover design by Eleanor Rose
Cover image: *Into the Penumbra of the Garden* © Elizabeth Wrightman

All rights reserved. No part of this publication may be reproduced or transmitted
in any form or by any means, electronic or mechanical, including photocopying,
recording, or any information storage or retrieval system, without prior
permission in writing from the publishers.

Bloomsbury Publishing Plc does not have any control over, or responsibility for, any
third-party websites referred to or in this book. All internet addresses given in this
book were correct at the time of going to press. The author and publisher regret any
inconvenience caused if addresses have changed or sites have ceased to exist, but can
accept no responsibility for any such changes.

A catalogue record for this book is available from the British Library.

A catalog record for this book is available from the Library of Congress.

ISBN: HB: 978-1-3502-3652-3
PB: 978-1-3502-3656-1
ePDF: 978-1-3502-3653-0
eBook: 978-1-3502-3654-7

Typeset by Newgen KnowledgeWorks Pvt. Ltd., Chennai, India

To find out more about our authors and books visit www.bloomsbury.com
and sign up for our newsletters.

For Walter

Contents

Acknowledgments	viii
Introduction: Hope and Form in Joyce	1
1 Without Paralysis: Hope, Hunger, and Spiritual Liberation in *Dubliners*	29
2 The Future of *A Portrait of the Artist as a Young Man*: The *Künstlerroman* and Hope	55
3 A Humid Nightblue Dot: The Spatialization of Hope in *Ulysses*	77
4 Daydreams of History and Reincarnation in *Finnegans Wake*	109
5 Conclusion: Form, Utopia, and Community	143
Bibliography	157
Index	167

Acknowledgments

A version of Chapter 2 appeared as "The Future of Joyce's *Portrait*: The *Künstlerroman* and Hope" in *Dublin James Joyce Journal* 9 (2016): 47–67. I'm grateful to Luca Crispi and Anne Fogarty for permission to reprint. I want to thank Sean Latham, Carol Kealiher, and the staff at the *James Joyce Quarterly* for permission to reprint a version of Chapter 1 and for being so supportive and generous over the years.

The discussion that followed my lecture on *A Portrait of the Artist as a Young Man* at the 2016 James Joyce Summer School in Dublin showed me that hope might cut freshly through some central and enduring ideas about Joyce's oeuvre. I am grateful to the Summer School students, who came from all over the world to study Joyce together, and to the other lecturers: Valérie Bénéjam, Luca Crispi, Maria-Daniella Dick, Enda Duffy, Anne Fogarty, Luke Gibbons, Margaret Kelleher, Fritz Senn, and Frank Shovlin. As respondent to my paper, Fritz Senn reminded us that hope is the subject of Joyce's first published sentence: "There was no hope for him this time." From his apparently inexhaustible jacket pocket supply, Fritz also kept my two-year-old son Walter generously stocked with Swiss chocolate during the week. Deepest and warmest thanks are due to Anne and Luca for inviting me and for making me and my family feel so at home.

Trinity University supported this book with Summer Research Stipends in 2015 and 2017, funds for travel and accommodation in Dublin in 2016, and academic leave in the Fall of 2018. I am grateful to all of my Trinity colleagues and friends who create such a supportive environment for working, learning, and living. Teaching in the Arts & Ideas FYE with Kyle Gillette, James Ivy, Rachel Joseph, Judith Norman, Nick Reynolds, Zachary Ridgway, Willis Salomon, and Curtis Swope continually challenges my thinking about art. I'm particularly grateful for the support and friendship of Stephanie Velasquez, Ruby Contreras, Coleen Grissom, Willis Salomon, David Liss, and Claudia Stokes.

Thanks are due to Ben Doyle, Lucy Brown, Laura Cope, and to everyone else at Bloomsbury and Newgen who helped to improve and bring this book to print. I'm very grateful to Elizabeth Wrightman for permission to reproduce her painting *Into the Penumbra of the Garden* for my book cover. Her wonderful pictures, including her series inspired by *Ulysses*, can be viewed at wouldgodmilkagoat.com.

This book is the product of classroom, mentoring, and reading group experiences with Joyce's work that go back a quarter century. As an undergraduate at American University, I took classes with Roberta Rubenstein, Richard Sha, and Frank Turaj that included Joyce and made me eager to study him. At University of Texas at Austin, Chuck Rossman, Alan Friedman, and Elizabeth Cullingford warmly welcomed me to the graduate study of Joyce and Irish literature and inspired a *Finnegans Wake* reading group, *onamatterpoetic*, that included Alan Friedman, Eve Dunbar, Rebecca Dyer, Tyler Mabry, and Lee Rumbarger. At Cornell University, I studied modernism with Susan Buck-Morss, Jonathan Culler, Roger Gilbert, Molly Hite, and Douglas Mao. I continued to read Joyce with the Cornell *Wake* group that included Joshua Corey, Christina Dahl, Patrick Foran, Samuel Frederick, Jim LeBlanc, Ari Lieberman, Yoshi Mihara, Angela Naimou, and Ana Rojas. A long-lived *Wake* group in San Antonio included Shannon Mariotti, Paul Myers, Corinne Pache, and Bill and Barbara Sullivan. I'm grateful to my current, virtual *Wake* group that includes Bill Brockman, Sam Frederick, Jim LeBlanc, Lea Pao, and Bill Sullivan. I am also grateful to the Trinity students with whom I've had the privilege of discussing Joyce since 2006. Joyce has always brought me to community and this book is deeply embedded in my communal experiences of reading Joyce.

Since 2012, my writing group has outlasted several restaurants, celebrated publications and promotions, and endured Covid distancing. Thanks to Nicolle Hirschfeld, Tom Jenkins, Tim O'Sullivan, Corinne Pache, and Betsy Tontiplaphol for their weekly support, inspiration, and comradeship. I owe special thanks to Betsy, my department chair and seminar co-teacher, for reading and commenting on these chapters with characteristic incisiveness and thoughtfulness.

The mutual love of Joyce that Sam Frederick and I discovered on our first morning of grad school was the foundation of a friendship that remains a sustaining and most important gift in my life.

This book would not have been possible without my wife, Shannon Mariotti, to whom I owe the most loving thanks. This book of hope and future is for our son, Walter, who delights and amazes us every day.

Introduction: Hope and Form in Joyce

This book paints a picture of James Joyce's fiction in which hope and future assume the primary colors. Critics have insufficiently recognized the extent to which hope animates key aspects of Joyce's approach to both literary content and form. Nor have critics sufficiently acknowledged that hope constitutes a major part of Joyce's textual politics and political vision.[1] While this book certainly does not try to reduce Anna Livia's rich "Plurabilities" (*FW* 104.2) to Polly Anna's naive "pollyfool fiansees" (*FW* 15.14–15), nor does it offer a simplistically gaga or even an especially cheerful Joyce, it does characterize hope as central to Joyce's fiction.

Joyce delineates a complex hope that is oriented toward the future with restlessness, dissatisfaction, and imagination. It is a hope driven by hunger and other resolutely socioeconomic material conditions. Hope for Joyce is linked to materially mediated yet open futures in which the new and the not-yet have a chance to emerge. Joycean hope is thereby capable of envisioning alternatives to the prevailing conventions of hope and of expanding the very range of that for which it seems possible to hope. Above all, Joyce develops a technique of spatializing hope in order to reconceive it from a merely temporally unfolding process to a space that can be grasped and scrutinized as an image. This kind of image-making becomes a technique of discovery for Joyce, a technique capable, at its best, of illuminating and making visible new and open spaces that lie outside of the reigning pictures of both reality and utopia.

Hope and future are not the terms with which Joyce has usually been read. In the classical period of Joyce studies, Joyce was often interpreted as an aesthete who was wary of politics and regarded the future with pessimism, if not outright hopelessness. Within a year of Joyce's death, for instance, Harry Levin canonized Joyce as a would-be maker of "a city of art, a Byzantium,"[2] an artist who sought to inhabit a world of art. For Levin, Joyce represented an aesthetic hermit who was only reluctantly pulled back to the material world, as well as to ties of religion and country, because of the necessarily material medium of language.[3] Within six years of Levin, Richard Kain located Joyce in a pessimistic satirical tradition: "Alienated from homeland, church, bourgeois society, local politics, and Empire allegiance, Joyce centered his masterpiece [*Ulysses*] in the story of two homesick wanderers. The satiric imaginary travels of Gulliver, Candide, and Rasselas have here their modern counterpart."[4] Few subscribe to these precise views now, but the critical approaches that replaced them have not necessarily rehabilitated the place of hope and future in Joyce's fiction.

Under the influence of post-structuralism, critics were more likely to dwell on the subversive features of Joyce's textual representations and politics. Hélène Cixous would come to speak for many when she situated Joyce's work among the "writings whose subversive force is now undermining the world of western discourse."[5] This subversive approach often operated by showing how hopes and wishes in Joyce's fiction are always already undermined or deconstructed. Kevin J. H. Dettmar argues that Joyce represents paralysis in his texts in order to tease out the futility of readers' own desires: "The stories of *Dubliners* are Rorschach inkblots wherein we read the text of our desire in the course of (mis)reading the book of ourselves. *Dubliners* is a text that implicates us in the deadly work of paralysis, and reveals to us our own paralysis."[6] Regarding the sphere of Joycean politics, Colin MacCabe writes, "What is subverted in the writing is the full Cartesian subject and this subversion is a political event of central importance. ... To understand the subject as plural and contradictory is to abandon a conception of politics as a determinate area with its specific discourses and organization."[7] For MacCabe, Joyce's texts combine "subversive force" and "profound political ineffectiveness."[8] As different as the assumptions and reading techniques to which such critics subscribed were from their classical predecessors, their readings were just as and sometimes more likely to offer visions of hopelessness rather than hope.

In recent decades, as this particular form of negative critique has waned, critics have turned toward demonstrating the ways in which Joyce's texts richly reward meticulous and granular placement in history. According to Andrew Gibson and Len Platt, this kind of historicist work, "relies on a practice of historical concretion: particulars take precedence over abstractions. It also relies on a practice of historical saturation: that is, a specifically Joycean historical materialism seeks to support and/or complicate its case by introducing as much historical information as is relevant and practicable. This information has priority over everything else except the texts."[9] This approach increasingly valorizes historical data per se, often at the expense of thinking about questions or theoretical conceptualizations of the future. Indeed, it becomes possible, even probable, to overlook the great extent to which Joyce's texts can and should be seen as machines that generate questions about the future. The reigning historicism also sometimes combines with a stance of critical distance that is skeptical about certain or even all alternative theoretical approaches to Joyce altogether.[10]

This book does not necessarily reject everything in these critical tendencies and habits. In fact, it tries to keep negative and positive critique in their necessary dialectical relationship and within a context of materialism. But the positive side of the dialectic has been ignored for too long and it has distorted our vision of Joyce's fiction and how it operates. This book responds to a critical moment which increasingly recognizes not just the gains but also the limitations of both negative hermeneutics[11] and literary historicism.[12] It offers a picture of what Joyce might look like beyond the limitations of negative critique and perhaps even after the inevitable exhaustion of the current literary historicist project, which often asks us to look back to the past rather than forward to the future. It does so by offering a materialist understanding of hope, one rooted in the branch of materialist critique that has never been content with demystifying art without also attending to art's affirmative and utopian dimensions.[13] From the perspective offered by its primary theorist, Ernst Bloch,[14] hope is the imaginative search for what is missing, and although this search is often driven by utopian impulses, it always unfolds complexly in relation to material forces such as hunger and the ultimate anti-utopia of death.[15] I track this search for what is missing on the level of Joyce's fictional content, where hopes take shape from and against the prevailing material conditions of the world, and also on the level of form, where Joyce's own writing practices are seen in the context of the material constraints, formal opportunities, and exploratory innovations of literary modernism.

In short, this book offers a future-oriented, inventive, and restless Joyce, a Joyce whose hope, expressed both formally and thematically, is mediated through material conditions, with hunger at their core. While Joyce thoroughly demonstrates the material and political resistances to hope in the form of a critique of the poverty that his characters suffer as a consequence of colonialism and capitalism—indeed, as critics have shown, his texts ask readers to recognize the origins and operations of hunger and poverty—Joyce's texts respond to a more hopeful gaze as well. For Joyce, hope is not a means to a specific end, but rather an open-ended wishful, inventive, and emergent process. Joyce's texts, as early as *Dubliners* and *A Portrait of the Artist as a Young Man*, are not directed toward a defined political goal, but are rather open to political futures that cannot necessarily be named or known in advance; Joyce's wishful images reflect a vision of reality that incorporates what Bloch calls "real possibility," futures that are possible given the mediation between present conditions and changing, maturing, emerging, or entirely new tendencies.[16] This book also charts the way in which, in *Ulysses* and *Finnegans Wake*, Joyce increasingly sought to spatialize representations of hope. Joyce's spatial technique removes hope from its customary temporal trajectories and its habitual forms of teleology so that it can be contemplated as an image. Joyce creates new spaces and vistas of hope from which out of the already-known the not-yet might emerge. But Joyce's vision of the new and the not-yet are never prescriptive, only suggestive. Readers must become Joyce's partners in vision and invention. Joyce's wishful images must finally unfold from the literary arena out into the social world.

Stomach Hope

To his parents, James Joyce was the object of much hope, and he gave them many reasons to look forward toward the future. Letters from Mary and John Stanislaus Joyce written in late 1902 and early 1903 convey a hopeful investment in their young son, away in Paris, and their hopeful wishes for his future. Before Christmas, Mary Joyce wrote:

> My dear Jim if you are disappointed in my letter and if as usual I fail to understand what you would wish to explain, believe me it is not from any want of a longing desire to do so and speak the words you want but as you so

often said I am stupid and cannot grasp the great thoughts which are yours much as I desire to do so. Do not wear your soul out with tears but be as usually brave and look hopefully to the future.[17]

In January, John Joyce wrote:

> May *I* be permitted to offer you my best wishes for your future which I, at one time, fancied may have been more rosey [sic] on your attaining your majority but, circumstances alter cases, and as my cases are circumcised I must ask you to forgive me, Jim, for the "might have been." However I hope you will believe me that I am only now, under I may tell you, *very trying* times, endeavouring to do my *little* best, but Jim you are my eldest Son I have always looked up to your being a fitting representative of *our* family one that my father would be proud of. I now only hope that you may carry out *his* ideas through your life and if you do, you may be sure you will not do anything unbecoming a gentleman, but that I am pressed for time I should write you more fully but tomorrow, Jim, I will write to you again.[18]

Each letter, tinged with its own kind of pathos, is premised upon a disappointing present and hope for the future. Mary Joyce believes that she has disappointed her son by failing to respond as he wishes to his ideas, yet she asks him to look past his present disappointments and instead to bravely and hopefully look toward the future. John Joyce regrets that in his straitened circumstances he must disappoint his son by the meager support that he is capable of offering him and by the loss of what "might have been." Not only does the father send the son New Year's wishes for the future, but he also conveys the sense of hope that he has invested in his eldest son for carrying on the pride of the Joyce name.

In these letters the disappointment comes from different sources of poverty: a supposed poverty of mind in Mary's case, and a poverty of the pocket in John's. We might say that even in these letters hope operates in a dialectic with the material conditions from which it emerges, conditions that can be both bodily and socioeconomic. Mary has a "longing desire" to grasp her son's thoughts, yet she apparently believes that grasping them is beyond the capacity of her mind. John fancies that he would have been able to offer his son a "rosier" future, but his circumstances have been "circumcised." The elder Joyce's witticism suggests a phallic circumscription and curtailing, or perhaps, with the hint of being castrated and unable to provide for his son, even a displaced confession of paternal impotence. In these letters, hope for the future emerges within the context of present impoverishments and deprivations. And in each case, the source of impoverishment can be located in material bodies or material contexts. The figurative valences of each letter (circumcised circumstances, the wearing out of the soul) hint that material bodies and contexts interpenetrate. When each parent evokes hope's disappointing context, he or she merges images of the body with extra-bodily properties (friction, wearing out) or with actions (circumcision) that evoke the physical world.

Hope in Joyce's texts is comprised of exactly these kinds of tensions. But it is neither in the brain nor the genitals that we should most fully locate Joycean hope. Instead, Joyce split the difference between his two parents and landed somewhere in between: in the stomach. In Joyce, hope operates in a socioeconomic field and is localized in the body, especially in the experience of bodily deprivation: hunger. It is from the deprivation of hunger that hope emerges. Deficiencies of the mind and of sex are only secondarily important. While many of Joyce's psychoanalytical critics have seen his characters or his texts as motivated by sexual desire and Oedipal anxiety, Joyce's fiction tends to hold with Bloch, who in contradiction to Freud put hunger before the sex drives: "The stomach is the first lamp into which oil must be poured."[19] Rather than sexual longing or Oedipal burdens—"I now only hope that you may carry out *his* ideas through your life"—this book explores physical hunger as the root of hopes in Joyce's fiction.

Joyce's fiction seems motivated by and to offer different ways of hoping from not just those of John Joyce, but also of Mary Joyce, who focuses on the hopes of the intellect. If John Joyce's hope can be characterized as sexual or Oedipal hope, Mary Joyce's intellectual hope might be called idealist hope, hope that evokes a picture or maps out a rationally ideal program or future. This kind of idealism, however, often fails to consider prevailing material conditions or the likelihood of flux in future material conditions. For if genital hope is the stuff of sexual desire and Oedipal burdens, then brain hope would be something like hope shaped through rationality and intellect—"the great thoughts which are yours"—which are rather the static and sometimes stultifying stuff of utopian programs. Although Mary Joyce does not offer a utopian vision of the future, idealism underwrites her exhortation to look bravely and tearlessly toward the future.

In contrast, stomach hope responds fluidly to its environment. It is driven by impulse rather than intellect, but it is not primarily a sexual impulse. Rather, within its material context, it endlessly strives for fulfillment and restlessly seeks out better conditions for achieving fulfillment. Unlike the rationalist scaffolding of a utopian program, stomach hope remains supple and responsive to whatever material conditions present themselves and to however unpredictably they happen to change. This responsiveness and suppleness of the stomach lies at the heart of Joycean transformations and metamorphoses. Indeed, hope and wish are, to borrow a phrase from Joyce's Shaun-like Professor Jones, "both products of our social stomach" (*FW* 163.34). The stomach is neither a utopian nor a libidinous space but rather a space of rumination tied at all points to the conditions of the world.

Hopelessness

Joyce often reserved the word "hopeless" for points of serious nadir in his fiction. In *Stephen Hero*, Stephen observes three clerks playing billiards in the Adelphi Hotel: "The hopeless pretence of those three lives before him, their unredeemable servility, made the back of Stephen's eyes feel burning hot."[20] And then: "—O, hopeless! hopeless! said Stephen clenching his fists." In Father Arnall's awful vision of hell in *A Portrait*, the damned "are helpless and hopeless: it is too late now for repentance."[21] In *Ulysses*, Stephen's Shakespeare theory falters and his hopes of being accepted by Dublin's literary set begin to fade: "—A father, Stephen said, battling against hopelessness, is a necessary evil."[22] And Leopold Bloom, in his dejected mood at the end of the "Nausicaa" chapter, thinks the word "hopeless" two times.[23]

These moods of hopelessness in Joyce have been well documented by critics, especially with respect to *Dubliners*, for which there is a long tradition of coupling hopelessness with the concept of paralysis as a way of articulating one of the story collection's central themes. The first line of *Dubliners*, from "The Sisters," is, after all, "There was no hope for him this time."[24] The introduction to a recent edited collection about *Dubliners* argues, "readers of *Dubliners* are asked to join the author in a scrupulous analysis of the paralysis—rooted in hopelessness."[25] Although critical approaches have shifted dramatically since more classical approaches to Joyce at midcentury, this line of argument is not much different from Hugh Kenner's 1956 claim that "a thematic statement of hopeless paralysis is the first sentence in the book."[26] If *Dubliners* has any relation to hope, it is often said to reside outside of its fictional world, in the possibility that reading *Dubliners* might, as Joyce expressed in a letter, impel readers as "first step towards the spiritual liberation."[27]

Such views of the place of hope and the presence of hopelessness in Joyce's fiction are ripe for contestation and revision, especially in this moment when there is a new openness to critical approaches that might access the more positive or constructive visions of literary texts. This book aims to present an unfamiliar but finally recognizable image of Joyce in relation to hope. In doing so, it runs against the grain of the predominant view of Joyce that was practically ubiquitous until fairly recently: that Joyce was thoroughgoingly, even ruthlessly, subversive and that to even raise the ghost of a hope in relation to his fiction is simultaneously to show how hope is fatally compromised and shot through with inertia and despair.

Non-Hope

It is not only that Joyce's texts are filled with a certain hope. It is also that what might have been interpreted as moments of hopelessness would perhaps be better thought of as moments without hope, or of non-hope. Although Kenner was quick to translate the "no hope" from the first sentence of "The Sisters" into a "statement of hopeless paralysis," Joyce sometimes distinguishes between hopelessness and the conditions of non-hope. Indeed, in certain states of non-hope Joyce finds neither hopelessness nor despair but new possibilities. Non-hope is often linked to death—for example, in the last days of the priest's life in "The Sisters" or in Gabriel's approach to "that region where dwell the vast hosts of the dead" (*D* 194.1595–6) in "The Dead"—because for Joyce the expectation, proximity, or presence of death can liberate hope from its customary and expected paths. Joycean hope operates, as it does for Bloch, not just in relation to hunger but also in relation to hunger's worst outcome: the "harshest non-utopia"[28] of death. In Joyce, proximity to death opens the door to new existences and ways of being. These moments of non-hope resemble hope in their definitiveness and tangibility, but they lack the trajectory and momentum with which hope is historically, culturally, and socially channeled. For Joyce, it is in such spaces between conventional forms of hope and wish that new and unexpected futures emerge. Joyce subverts hope's well-worn paths and parodies utopia's conventional visions, but he does not subvert hope or the utopian impulse altogether. Rather, hope takes us to the heart of Joyce's restless, imaginative, and generative textual practices as well of his vision of politics as it relates to imagined futures.

Hope and Politics

Questions of hope are inseparable from the operations of politics, which are always concerned with imagining and trying to realize different futures. One cannot consider hope in Joyce's texts separately from politics, nor can one address textual politics separately from close attention to hope and wish. But if one takes a dim or fatalistic view of future possibilities, hope and wish can be reduced to pointless, hopeless, or squandered energies. This would be the case, for instance, if one argues that Joyce was a mostly apolitical artist, one who saw art as somehow above the day-to-day fray of politics. This early approach did not recognize the nuances of distance between Joyce and Stephen Dedalus when, for example, Stephen says of McCann's utopian petition for universal peace, "—The affair doesn't interest me in the least" (P 173.835), or when Stephen rejects whole cloth Davin's nationalism and religion: "When the soul of a man is born in this country there are nets flung at it to hold it back from flight. You talk to me about nationality, language, and religion. I shall try to fly by those nets" (P 179.1047–50). This approach saw the political hopes of characters, for example, in "Ivy Day in the Committee Room," as futile and perhaps even pathetic. Such a reading fails to distinguish between Joyce's strong inclination to reject the many well-trodden paths of hope and his abiding allegiance to metamorphic hope itself. For Joyce it is not about hoping less, but rather hoping better; Joyce's fiction seeks to be useful and visionary to readers in just this sense.

Critics have also ignored or dismissed overt expressions of hope and wish in Joyce's narratives and attributed certain alternative hopes rather to Joyce's textual modes. This might be the case, as one sometimes finds in post-structuralist readings, when a critic argues that Joyce practices a textual politics of subversion in which what is directly expressed or indirectly implied in the narrative is negated or overturned by the subversive capabilities of narration or language. This kind of "reading against the grain" might then be said to allow readers to identify a Joycean hope for specific political alternatives somehow independent of or even directly contrary to what characters seem to desire, in the form of an open-ended questioning or subverting of authority. Politically programmatic criticism might treat hope and wish, when it aligns with the critic's preferred program, as mere preconditions for certain political futures or outcomes rather than as energies in Joyce's texts that are valuable to think about in and of themselves. Hopes and wishes that appear counter to the program, of course, are likely under this view to appear to the critic as little more than naivete or false consciousness.

Historicist criticism, especially of the kind that intensely emphasizes historical particularities and information, can knit hope so thoroughly to historical and cultural contexts that hope finds itself perversely hemmed into the past and taking on past orientations. Given the wide reign that historicist criticism enjoys today, it seems especially urgent to guard against isolating hope in the context of the past and historicizing away the life and trajectory of hope's forward momentum. Joyce's texts must be allowed to push "back to the future."

In sum, approaches that regard Joyce's texts as emphasizing a fundamental hopelessness, or as negating its own expressions of hope through textual subversion, or as fundamentally related to and circumscribed by certain past historical or cultural moments not only discount expressions of hope, but they fail to comprehend the properties and workings of hope, which are restless, constantly adapting, and forward-looking. This book demonstrates that when we are oriented toward questions of hope and wish we necessarily have to adopt textual models that differ from those that predominated under classical, post-structuralist, and historicist-materialist critical modes. Thinking about the ways in which hope operates and is posited in Joyce's texts presents the opportunity to reassess basic assumptions about how they work politically.

Enda Duffy, for instance, calls "subversive" a "much overused term in Joyce criticism" and argues that Joyce's textual-political operation is best regarded as a certain "will to visualize," in which "words aspire to the condition of image."[29] Duffy writes, "It is not that Joyce's excessive language in itself, then, is political because it is somehow (for example, satirically) subversive; rather, it is his moments when he strives to let us see through the intensity of his words that, for a politically active aesthetic, are key."[30]

This book extends Duffy's political view of Joyce's visually descriptive images to include Joyce's *wishful images*, moments in his texts when better worlds are conjured or when the future is shown to be fundamentally open to possibility. A reading of this kind focuses less on determinant wishes about the future that Joyce's texts might posit, and more, for example, on the wishful, future-oriented, yet open and undefined condition in which we find Stephen in *A Portrait* in between his current and evolving senses of vocation and purpose. Joyce's texts evidence a remarkable openness to real possibility that has not yet been sufficiently articulated in Joyce criticism.

While this book aims to show how Joyce's writing responds to the categories of hope, wish, and future in ways that have gone unrecognized by critics who prefer the categories of anxiety, paralysis, and history, it also builds on the work of critics who have been able to look beyond memory and anxiety to see Joyce engaging with hope and future. For instance, Emer Nolan contests the view that Irish nationalism as projected in *Ulysses* amounts to a "knowable human community"[31] that can be defined and envisioned in advance. Not only does Nolan focus on the future, rather than on the anxious or nostalgic past, but she also allows that the vision of the future in *Ulysses* is undecided and radically open to real possibility, that it might be quite different from conventional nationalist utopias. Joyce helps readers to envision and to think through such open futures while simultaneously emphasizing the insufficiencies and dissatisfactions of the already-known.

To focus on hope is not wholly to shift away from questions of anxiety in Joyce's fiction; it is rather potentially to redefine the ways in which anxiety about both past and future operates. Reading Joyce through the lens of hope helps to shift one's sense of past and present anxiety out of the anamnestic sphere of Freudian unconsciousness, repression, and memory and into the sphere of present and future material conditions. This book sees the expectant emotions of anxiety and hope in Joyce as similarly rooted in socioeconomic conditions, especially as these emotions relate to physical conditions, hunger, and the ultimate deprivation of death.

In other words, an emphasis on hope does not conduct one into the realm of wild fancy and unlikely utopia, but rather toward the material conditions with which few writers have been able to endow their fiction as richly as Joyce does. Joyce's hope is a particularly insightful form of what Bloch calls *docta spes*,[32] educated or comprehended hope. Joycean hope has been educated in hunger. It is deeply rooted in the material world of Dublin. The poverty, oppressions, and deprivations of Joyce's Dublin are so prevalent that critics often overemphasize the themes of paralysis and defeat. Hope teaches us to read humiliation and defeat in Joyce's characters as inseparable from their hopes of a better world. Joyce's characters, though caught in the grip of anxiety, frustration, defeat, or paralysis, are almost always wishing for something better at the same time. When hope is understood in its fullness and complexity, these wishes do not just serve to add poignancy, insult, or irony to the characters' defeats or tragedies. Rather, they make one more aware of the presence of hope in all elements of daily life, even the most dire and disastrous.

This ubiquity of hope in the daily lives of Joyce's characters is key to recognizing the ways in which Joyce diagnoses misdirected and futile hopes. It is not that Joyce's characters lack hope, but rather, as he shows, that they often hope for the wrong things. His fiction demonstrates the power of redirecting hope through changes of habit as well as by showing the disastrous consequences of failing to hope in more productive and less self-defeating ways. The future is rooted in a dialectic between the material conditions of his characters and their capacities to change their habits of hope.

The unpredictability of this dialectic helps to account for the openness of Joyce's sense of the future. Joyce's hope for or vision of the future is not programmatic. His fiction does not endorse specific solutions, nor does it wish for specific political or utopian outcomes; rather, Joyce's texts are incredibly subtle and sophisticated devices for struggling to imagine, through the dialectical capacities of fiction, forms of liberation that have yet to be imagined. Joyce is not interested in utopian programs, whether social, religious, or nationalist, which he submits to scrutiny and sometimes even to merciless satire;[33] rather, as an artist he is committed to a utopian impulse that searches for the new and the not-yet-conscious.³⁴ This utopian impulse seeks liberation from reigning social, religious, and political utopian programs. Joyce is dissatisfied by all currently conceivable visions of utopia. For Joyce it is never a matter of choosing from among given options; the idea is to "fly past" these options in order to discover that which has not yet found expression. This striving beyond the known in search of the not-yet-known characterizes Joyce's Daedalean artistic impulse. "[T]here being no known method from the known to the unknown" (*U* 17.1140–1), Joyce endeavors to discover the not-yet-known through experiments and struggle with literary form.

Hope and Literary Form

Joyce's modernist formal innovations are part of his dissatisfaction with artistic, religious, social, cultural, and nationalist conventions. His experiments are consistent with a utopian impulse toward discovery. Especially in *Ulysses* and *Finnegans Wake*, Joyce seeks experimental forms for representing hope. Hope is most conventionally understood within the concept of a temporal progression: it emerges from past and present conditions. It is forward-looking and anticipates the future. However, Joyce's experiments increasingly tend to represent hope in the context of space rather than solely in time. Joyce spatializes hope, taking it out of time, in order to scrutinize it from detached and parallactic perspectives. Whereas Joyce's tendency in *Dubliners* and *A Portrait* is to represent hope as it is misdirected or thwarted within the temporal and narrative contexts of his characters' lives, in *Ulysses* and *Finnegans Wake* Joyce invites readers to contemplate complex images of hope at a standstill. Joyce offers constellations of hope that emerge when one widens to the cosmic perspective of the "Ithaca" episode in *Ulysses* or to the mythic-historical framework of *Finnegans Wake*. Rather than only representing hope as it moves forward toward the future, these later works bring hope to a halt and invite readers to investigate hope from multiple perspectives.

In other words, Joyce offers both an anatomy and an astronomy of hope. Readers see misdirected and thwarted hopes up close and unfolding temporally but also spatially, when hope has reached its limits and become circumscribed and finite. By scrutinizing hope in the form of a defined and finite image, Joyce represents hope not when it is merely hopeless but also when it is futureless. *Ulysses* and *Finnegans Wake* invite readers to envision temporal hope startlingly reduced to spatial hope and to recognize the point at which the very perspective from which we wish has become a vanishing point. Joyce's spatialization of hope transforms hope into remembrance; the image of hope becomes a memento. Joyce's readers are charged with herculean tasks of remembering the things for which characters hoped and strived but did not receive.

Joyce's technique of spatializing hope should not be understood as a retreat from time, history, or futurity. His spatial technique brackets time "temporarily" so that it is not the immediate future, but a wider future that can come into view. *Ulysses*, to play on Lenehan's quip in "Aeolus" about John F. Taylor's death, leaves the great future of its characters behind it, so that a wider one may open ahead. The technique shifts the question of the future away from the logistics of tomorrow morning's breakfast to more distant and less easily imaginable futures. Joyce opens a space for the visionary and the revisionary; it is his readers' task to take up the creative project of imagining different futures.

The Dark Matter of Hope: *Giacomo Joyce*

Open-ended hope is something like the dark matter of Joyce's fiction; it lives in the interstices between the grand, memorable, and much commented-upon acts and deflations of specific hopes by which Joyce's characters live and die. One text that makes these spaces especially visible is Joyce's posthumously published prose poem, *Giacomo Joyce*. *Giacomo Joyce* plays an interstitial role in Joyce's *oeuvre*.[35] Rarely ever numbered among the sequence of Joyce's great or major achievements,[36] *Giacomo Joyce* is nonetheless recognized by critics as a generative and imaginative space out of which emerged specific images, phrases, preoccupations, and techniques that found their way into *A Portrait*, *Ulysses*, and later poems. *Giacomo Joyce* is at once, as Fritz Senn notes, something of the culmination of Joyce's earlier phase, and also, as Vicki Mahaffey emphasizes, an important step in Joyce's evolution.[37]

Giacomo Joyce exemplifies the way in which hope functions as connective tissue in Joyce. It represents Joyce's tendency to nudge hope out of time and into space. *Giacomo Joyce* is a text about adulterous desire—a species of hope—that does not come to fruition. As Senn says, it "is deeply involved in events, longings and fantasies of [Joyce's] Trieste years."[38] John McCourt calls it "libidinally driven."[39] Mahaffey regards *Giacomo Joyce* as "an experiment with fantasy," and writes, "It traces the course of secret love from desire to imagined satisfaction, betrayal, and emotional crucifixion."[40] *Giacomo Joyce* alternates between specific wishes and hopes and more ambiguous matters of wishing and hoping. *Giacomo Joyce* visualizes interstitial or liminal spaces of hope via its blank spaces that are irregularly laid out on the page. McCourt calls it a "shadowy and multi-liminal text"[41] with "scattered paragraphs divided by surprisingly large and uneven bridges of white space, its words 'betwixt and between' significant blank gaps."[42] While Joyce's concise prose poems represent specific instances of specular and voyeuristic desire, the blank spaces represent rather an unspecified wishfulness, a generative and surprising hopefulness out of which almost anything might emerge.

Critics have noticed that there is something static about the work. Richard Brown notes that *Giacomo Joyce* operates in a primarily imagistic mode, and that "rather than being a work which develops toward an end, *Giacomo Joyce* seems to be a work which is profoundly static."[43] For Brown, the text is driven by "desire and loathing,"[44] yet rather than exploring these feelings through narrative progression *Giacomo Joyce* works through apposition or juxtaposition. The passage set in the Jewish cemetery in Trieste exemplifies this juxtaposition and the way in which Joyce finds hope emerging from in-between spaces like the liminal cemetery:[45]

> Corpses of Jews lie about me rotting in the mould of their holy field. Here is the tomb of her people, black stone, silence without hope .... Pimply Meissel brought me here. He is beyond those trees standing with covered head at the grave of his suicide wife, wondering how the woman who slept in his bed has come to this end .... The tomb of her people and hers: black stone, silence without hope: and all is ready. Do not die![46]

Joyce juxtaposes tomb and bed imagery. The image of the black stone of the tombs is put twice in apposition, across a comma, with the phrase "silence without hope." Not only does this passage represent the way in which the text operates imagistically, but it also shows some ways in which hope and form interrelate. Hope may propel desire, but desire is balanced against hope's absence. This absence of hope in the cemetery facilitates a shift from the temporal modality of desire to the spatial modality of tomb, stone, and image. The stony lack of hope in the cemetery makes a space outside of the speaker's sexual desire for his beloved, and out of this space a new and unanticipated awareness of her future tomb and hope for her continued life emerges. This unanticipated concern for the beloved's very life emerges suddenly to subtend libidinal desire. The new solicitude for the beloved's mere existence represents a more utopian, if platonic, form of love than does the sexual interest that the speaker has heretofore shown. Critics have seized on the many scenes of libidinal desire, but they have tended not to notice this unanticipated and liminal desire for the beloved's life. In this little scene the new and unanticipated emerge from the very space where hope loses its libidinal and temporal trajectory and comes to a standstill: the deathly and stony cemetery. The dead as represented in this cemetery are not hopeless; rather, they are "without hope." But for Joyce it is precisely the space of non-hope, between the end of the specific hopes of quotidian life and life's end, from which new hopes can emerge, new worlds can be imagined, and the specific hopes that guide characters' lives can be reinflected or transformed.

The sudden concern for the beloved's body beyond its ability to be sexually possessed reflects Joyce's materialist approach to hope. Sexual desire gives way to a hunger at the site of the beloved's body. That body, though it is the body of a wealthy "young person of quality" (*GJ* 1), is consistently represented as small and underfed, vulnerable, and perhaps hungry. Her face is "pale" (1), with "grey wheyhued shadows under her jawbone" (2). The speaker thinks, "Her face, how grey and grave!" (14). The speaker also observes her "slim and shapely haunches, the meek supple tendonous neck, the fine-boned skull" (3). She has "a lithe smooth naked body" with "slender buttocks" (7). Her knees are twice referred to as knobby (4, 15) and her elbow is thin (10). She has a "cold frail hand" and "cold fingers" (13). Seen in furs (1) or under "a plaid cloak shielding from chills her sinking shoulders" (14), she seems in danger of freezing. When the speaker hears her "Small witless helpless and thin breath," he likens her to, "A sparrow under the wheels of Juggernaut" (7), consistent with the text's pattern of associating the beloved with bird imagery. She is a "frail blue-veined child" (3), marked by "weariness" (13).

While these descriptions in part describe the young woman's nubility—she is also "Rounded and ripened" (2)—libidinal desire clearly crosses paths with physical emaciation, hunger, and the specter of death in *Giacomo Joyce*. Critics are fond of finding genital imagery in the beloved's furs and flowers, but they have been less attuned to the sexual imagery surrounding her belly when she needs emergency surgery:

> Operated. The surgeon's knife has probed in her entrails and withdrawn, leaving the raw jagged gash of its passage on her belly. I see her full dark suffering eyes, beautiful as the eyes of an antelope. O cruel wound! Libidinous God! (11)

Libidinous desire is unmistakably crossed with and even literally cut through by the flesh of the material body, the belly. The beloved's brush with death actualizes the fear and solicitude for the beloved's life that the speaker first felt in the cemetery's space of non-hope. While the beloved remains the object of the speaker's sexual impulses (genital hope) and the subject of his utopian sexual fantasies (intellectual hope), it is finally her belly that must be fluidly responded to, adjusted to, operated upon, penetrated, and sutured shut. The belly, and not the genitals, is the threshold of her body and operates as the irreducible locus of hope.

Near the end of *Giacomo Joyce*, Joyce widens to a more cosmic perspective. Hope slides out of its temporal frame and becomes spatial, something that can be grasped at a glance rather than experienced as it unfolds through time:

> "Why?"
>
> "Because otherwise I could not see you."
>
> Sliding—space—ages—foliage of stars—and waning heaven—stillness—and stillness deeper—stillness of annihilation—and her voice. (16)

From a sequence that proceeds temporally from "why" to "because," we arrive upon a static vision of "space" and "stillness," a word that Joyce repeats three times. The wide lens required to comprehend a vision of "ages" stretches the temporal frame beyond the immediate longings of the narrator, beyond their infinitely shorter duration compared to the longevity of stars. Dashes accentuate the sense of space, and "Sliding," "waning," and "annihilation" deepen the sensation that the speaker's intimate exchange with the beloved is now in dizzying relation to the cosmic scale. "[H]er voice" seems more plausibly a flattened figure in space than a response to a question in a time-bound conversation.

This moment invites comparison to the vision in "Ithaca" that greets Bloom and Stephen when they enter the backyard of 7 Eccles Street:

> What spectacle confronted them when they, first the host, then the guest, emerged silently, doubly dark, from obscurity by a passage from the rere of the house into the penumbra of the garden?
>
> The heaventree of stars hung with humid nightblue fruit. (*U* 17.1036–40)

The "heaventree of stars" recalls "the foliage of stars" in *Giacomo Joyce*. Both signal a narrative shift from a human-temporal scale to a spatial-cosmic one. Both show the Shem-tree (heaventree, foliage) and the Shaun-stone (stars) as "everintermutuomergent" (*FW* 55.11–12). Chapter 3 details other techniques by which "Ithaca" inserts Bloom and Stephen into temporal and spatial contexts so far in excess of their temporally bound lives and hopes that their lives can finally only be regarded spatially, in the form of the speck or dot that ends the chapter, but in *Giacomo Joyce* the effect is similar.

Giacomo Joyce meditates self-reflexively on temporal versus spatial representations of hope. The "Why?" passage is preceded directly by a section in which the speaker contemplates his fruitless and hopeless desire for his beloved:

> Youth has an end: the end is here. It will never be. You know that well. What then? Write it, damn you, write it! What else are you good for? (*GJ* 16)

Along with the end of youth comes the impossibility of the specific future that the speaker has imagined and longed for. Temporal hope is at an end: the speaker recognizes in this epiphanic moment that his no-longer unfolding hope must now be sublimated into writing, into form. A subsequent blank space on the page then leads to the cosmic vision that we have just examined, one that abandons the temporalities of youth as well as the imagined utopian consummations with which the speaker has tortured himself. The moment resembles many in *Dubliners* in which characters or readers realize that characters have been hoping for the wrong things. But generally unlike in these stories, libidinal desire in *Giacomo Joyce* is successfully sublimated or even bravely abandoned in favor of the space of writing. The text of *Giacomo Joyce* itself represents the speaker's own transformed desire.

Giacomo Joyce might be thought of as a little modernist fable about how the alluring arms of the beloved, which are objects of desire in the speaker's unfolding yearning, become by the end of the tale a static spatial image: a coat of arms. Her arms appear first in the course of the speaker's fantasy of dressing and undressing the beloved's "lithe smooth naked body":

> She raises her arms in an effort to hook at the nape of her neck a gown of black veiling. She cannot: no, she cannot. She moves backwards towards me mutely. I raise my arms to help her: her arms fall. (7)

These are arms in motion, his and hers, rising and falling. The arms perform a sequence of actions that unfold in time and are animated in space. This sequence is a sliver of the speaker's fantasy of seduction, a set of actions that signify his hope and desire and their potential realization. But when the beloved's "arms" return in the penultimate sentence of *Giacomo Joyce*, they are no longer the flesh-and-blood arms of the desired body, but rather a still image of her "red-flowered" hat and umbrella, which the speaker imagines as her coat of arms: "Her arms: a casque, gules, and blunt spear on a field, sable" (16). Critics have noted the pictorial quality of this description. McCourt likens the objects to an arrangement for a still-life painting and notes that the way in which Joyce represents them resembles *ekphrasis*.[47] Mahaffey calls this description of the coat of arms a "pictorial epitaph for his 'dead' love,"[48] a characterization that emphasizes the finally spatial form of the speaker's love. The arms become an image of monument or even of embalmment. Much has been made of the umbrella and the red flower as alternately masculine or feminine sexual images. But if they are sexual images, they have become static ones, poised without the expectation of change or movement. Similarly to the way in which the beloved's voice had earlier better resembled the concluding dot of "Ithaca" than it had the continuation of a temporally progressing conversation, here even music, the temporal art *par excellence*, becomes a space, a dead one: "A long black piano: coffin of music" (16).

While *Giacomo Joyce* is obviously libidinally driven, it is also crucial to appreciate that the text's irregular blank spaces leave room for more open-ended kinds of desire to emerge. These liminal spaces ultimately become the socle and pedestal for the text's final spatialization of hope: "Envoy: Love me, love my umbrella" (*GJ* 16). "Love me," an imperative expression of temporal and dynamic sexual desire, becomes "love my umbrella," the static love for an object stilled in space. Mahaffey notes of the beloved that "her umbrella, or protective shield, is part of her."[49] To love this beloved is to love the very protective barrier that puts a stop on libidinal love; it is to love the space that freezes desire and takes it out of time. It is fitting that this moment of spatialization halts the temporal progress of Joyce's narrative and concludes the text itself. Or, rather, the narrative gives way to one final recurrence of irregular blank space, which is the true ending of the text.

Giacomo Joyce, which has been seen as a point of culmination, threshold, and future projection, exemplifies Joyce's technique of representing non-specific hope as a kind of binding tissue, his proclivity to root hope in hunger rather than in intellectual or idealized utopias or libidinal impulses, and his increasing tendency to spatialize representations of hope. The following chapters take up these questions of hope and future in relation to representation and literary form in Joyce's four major works of fiction.

Chapter 1 challenges the consensus that *Dubliners* is best understood as an expression of paralysis or hopelessness. Seen through Bloch's critical theory, hope emerges as a forward-looking process in Joyce's stories, one that is tied to historical conditions such as hunger and is wary of apotheosis. What emerges is a new way of regarding the political operation of Joyce's texts as adaptive, anticipatory, and unfolding. From this perspective, Joyce's work is drenched in hopeful and even utopian impulses that force us to reevaluate the place of hope in *Dubliners*. While Joyce never underestimates the material and political resistances to hope posed by the poverty and hunger that his characters suffer under colonialism and capitalism—in fact, his texts invite readers to scrutinize these conditions—Chapter 1 shows that *Dubliners*, while not directed toward a specific political goal, is fundamentally open to what Bloch calls "real possibility," or to social and political futures that are possible given prevailing and maturing material conditions but which cannot necessarily be named or known in advance.

Chapter 2 aims to capture the future effects that result from the way in which *A Portrait* manipulates the artist novel or *Künstlerroman* genre. Seen in terms of Bloch's distinctions between the detective and the artist novel genres, *A Portrait* is a hybrid of genres, at once obsessed with detective fiction's "darkness at the beginning" (as emblematized by Stephen's anxiety surrounding the *Fœtus* inscription) and the artist novel's not-yet (as emblematized by the wish image of Stephen's green rose). *A Portrait*'s status as an artist novel is complicated by Stephen's reprisal in *Ulysses*, but despite its deflationary view of Stephen's earlier aspirations for flight and artistry, *Ulysses* does not exhaust the hope potential in the earlier novel. *A Portrait*'s anxiety about the past is seen in material and historical terms. Through a reading of the novel's often overlooked wishful tissue, Chapter 2 argues that *A Portrait* is a novel fundamentally oriented toward the future and open to unanticipated possibility.

Chapter 3 builds upon the idea that *Ulysses* offers both an anatomy and an astronomy of hope. The novel invests readers in the hopes of characters on June 16, 1904 by focusing minutely on their interior worlds, but it also increasingly distances readers from these hopes as the narrative expands outward to encompass cosmic perspectives. The cosmic perspective reveals hope as a constellation, at once dwarfing hopes and spatializing them. Seen through the theme of the dying or deathbed wish in *Ulysses*, Joyce's encyclopedic novel charges readers with the task of remembrance, not only of its minutiae and events, but also of what characters hoped for but did not achieve. By bracketing the immediate future, Joyce's spatialization of hope in *Ulysses* creates the opportunity to imagine a wider and transformative future.

Chapter 4 revises the dream approach to *Finnegans Wake*, so persistent in the critical history, by understanding the book not as a representation of nightdreaming and unconscious desire, but rather as an expression of daydreaming, of clear-eyed and conscious wish dreams about history and the future. These wish dreams manifest as the magnificent and continuously metamorphizing historical juxtapositions offered in the *Wake*. Through the lens of reincarnation and metempsychosis, Chapter 4 understands *Finnegans Wake* as motivated by a wish dream that seeks to compensate for the brevity of life relative to history. But reincarnation and metempsychosis are not just wish dreams of overcoming the finitude of individual life, but also of overcoming the violence and sufferings of history and of grasping history spatially as a "being-present." The conceptual and compositional principles of reincarnation and metempsychosis in *Finnegans Wake* express the desire to crystallize and to be present at the utopian moment itself, which always necessarily fails to come in one's lifetime.

The conclusion moves from the wishful forms of Joyce's texts to the wishful communities of Joyce's readers. Beginning with Bloom and Stephen's exchange about utopia in the "Eumaeus" episode, the conclusion calls for carefully delineating utopian programs from utopian impulses in Joyce, and it examines a range of ways that each kind of utopianism is viewed in Joyce criticism. Returning to the topic of Joyce's wishful designs for his audience (as explored in Chapter 1), the conclusion examines the ways in which Joyce's utopianly striving forms create communities of readers. This tangible effect of Joyce's writing, in which we might locate a hunger or striving for the communal itself, can be seen in classrooms, in reading groups, and at academic gatherings and conferences. The conclusion views Joycean reading communities as conscious or unconscious responses to the formal hoping and striving to be found in Joyce's forms. The conclusion argues that when we can recognize the connection between the utopian impulses reflected in Joyce's forms and the communities of readers that coalesce around Joyce's work, we can harness those impulses in order to refine, attend to, and more purposefully to direct our own interpretive and communal goals and needs.

Notes

1 While some scholars have significantly begun to examine Joyce's work in the light of utopia studies, see Wolfgang Wicht, *Utopianism in James Joyce's Ulysses* (Heidelberg: Universitätverlag Winter, 2000); Hugo Azérad, "'Negative Utopia' in James Joyce, Walter Benjamin, and Ernst Bloch," in *Joyce in Trieste: An Album of Risky Readings*, ed. Sebastian D. G. Knowles, Geert Lernout, and John McCourt (Gainesville: University Press of Florida, 2007), 102–16; and Alec Charles, "The Meta-Utopian Metatext: The Deconstructive Dreams of *Ulysses* and *Finnegans Wake*," *Utopian Studies* 23.2 (2012): 472–503—none has shown the importance of hope not only to Joyce's vision of the future but also to the literary form of all four of his major works. I discuss these and other utopian readings of Joyce in the conclusion.

2 Harry Levin, *James Joyce: A Critical Introduction* (Norfolk: New Directions, 1941), 20.
3 Levin writes,

> The artist is an exile from the city. He has renounced his ties with friends and family, church and country. In isolation, he seeks to cultivate the traditions and techniques of his craft, to recreate life artificially through the medium of words. But words—means of communication as well as expression—have an independent life which is active and gregarious, which derives its velocity from the lips of men. With each successive work, like carrier pigeons from abroad, they come home to roost in Dublin. (20)

The vision of an aesthete Joyce was finally put to rest by Dominic Manganiello's *Joyce's Politics* (Boston, MA: Routledge and Kegan Paul, 1980).

4 Richard M. Kain, *Fabulous Voyager: James Joyce's Ulysses* (Chicago: Chicago University Press, 1947), 17.
5 Hélène Cixous, "Joyce: The (R)use of Writing," in *Post-structuralist Joyce: Essays from the French*, ed. Derek Attridge and Daniel Ferrer, trans. Judith Still (Cambridge: Cambridge University Press, 1984), 15.
6 Kevin J. H. Dettmar, *The Illicit Joyce of Postmodernism: Reading against the Grain* (Madison: University of Wisconsin Press, 1996), 104.
7 Colin MacCabe, *James Joyce and the Revolution of the Word* (London: Macmillan, 1979), 152, 153.
8 Ibid., 153.
9 Andrew Gibson and Len Platt, "Introduction," in *Joyce, Ireland, Britain*, ed. Andrew Gibson and Len Platt (Gainesville: University Press of Florida, 2006), 18.
10 For example, Gibson and Platt write,

> Historical materialism ... administers the coup de grace to the universalism from which Joyce studies might be thought of as having fitfully worked themselves away. It does so in two respects: it insists on extremely specific historical factors in understanding Joyce; and it implicitly turns aside from the myth of universal explicability, the idea that any and every theoretical template or critical approach is of equal usefulness in interpreting Joyce's writings. (19)

Gibson and Platt are quick to see earlier phases of Joyce criticism as historically determined, but they are perhaps less aware of how their prioritizing of information and particularities in 2006 reflected the emergence of a period in information history in which the reluctance or failure to abstract, theorize, and synthesize particulars, and even to distinguish between fact and fake, has contributed to political catastrophe.

11 This position is perhaps most prominently articulated in Rita Felski, *The Limits of Critique* (Chicago: University of Chicago Press, 2017). See also the forum on *The Limits of Critique* in *PMLA* 132.2 (2017); Bruno Latour, "Why Has Critique Run Out of Steam?" *Critical Inquiry* 30 (Winter 2004): 225–48; and Eve Kosofsky Sedgwick, *Touching Feeling: Affect, Pedagogy, Performativity* (Durham, NC: Duke University Press, 2003).

12 See, for instance, Allen Dunn and Thomas Haddox, eds., *The Limits of Literary Historicism* (Knoxville: University of Tennessee Press, 2012).

13 In the words of Fredric Jameson, "Such a view dictates an enlarged perspective for any Marxist analysis of culture, which can no longer be content with its demystifying vocation to unmask and to demonstrate the ways in which a cultural artifact fulfills a specific ideological mission … but must also seek … to project its simultaneously Utopian power," Fredric Jameson, *The Political Unconscious: Narrative as a Socially Symbolic Act* (Ithaca, NY: Cornell University Press, 1981), 291.

14 Ernst Bloch, a contemporary of Theodor Adorno and Walter Benjamin, with philosophical affinities with the Frankfurt School, is usually overlooked in Joyce criticism and in Anglophone modernist studies more broadly. However, as interest in post-structuralist conceptualizations of identity, power, and subversion continue to wane in literary studies, there is a renewed interest in alternate ways of reading modernists such as Joyce politically. *Hope, Form, and Future in the Work of James Joyce* is the first book to put the work of Joyce into extended conversation with Bloch, a thinker whose ideas have seen a resurgence of interest as scholars look to liberate their sense of hope, future, and utopia from the reigning critical paradigms. It is characteristic of Bloch's forward-looking work that his time in Anglophone criticism seems always just about to arrive. For evidence of recent interest in Bloch, see the essays in *The Privatization of Hope: Ernst Bloch and the Future of Utopia*, ed. Peter Thompson and Slavoj Žižek (Durham, NC: Duke University Press, 2013) and, earlier, *Not Yet: Reconsidering Ernst Bloch*, ed. Jamie Owen Daniel and Tom Moylan (London: Verso, 1997). See also José Esteban Muñoz, *Cruising Utopia: The Then and There of Queer Futurity* (New York: New York University Press, 2009); and Fredric Jameson, *Archaeologies of the Future* (New York: Verso, 2005).

15 Peter Thompson writes,

> Hope, for Bloch, was the way in which our desire to fill in the gaps and to find something that is missing took shape. But this sense of something missing, of desire, and of hope was not something which had a quasimystical character. For Bloch it started with simple physical material hunger, and yet he maintained a commitment to a dialectical understanding of the unfolding

of human interaction with these material forces that give rise to desire and consequently to hope.

Peter Thompson, "Introduction: The Privatization of Hope and the Crisis of Negation," in *The Privatization of Hope: Ernst Bloch and the Future of Utopia* (Durham, NC: Duke University Press, 2013), 3.

16 Bloch writes,

> Here we must of course distinguish between the merely cognitively or objectively Possible and the Real-Possible, the only one that matters in the given context. Objectively possible is everything whose entry, on the basis of a mere partial-cognition of its existing conditions, is scientifically to be expected, or at least cannot be discounted. Whereas really possible is everything whose conditions in the sphere of the object itself are not yet fully assembled; whether because they are still maturing, or above all because new conditions—though mediated with the existing ones—arise for the entry of a new Real. Mobile, changing, changeable Being, presenting itself as dialectical-material, has this unclosed capability of becoming, this Not-Yet-Closedness both in its ground and in its horizon. So that we may deduce from this: the really Possible *of sufficiently mediated, i.e. dialectically, materialistically mediated newness* gives utopian imagination its *second, its concrete correlate*: one outside a mere fermenting, effervescing in the inner circle of consciousness. And as long as the reality has not become a completely determined one, as long as it possesses still unclosed possibilities, in the shape of new shoots and new spaces for development, then no absolute objection to utopia can be raised by merely factual reality.

Ernst Bloch, *The Principle of Hope*, 3 vols., trans. Neville Plaice, Stephen Plaice, and Paul Knight (Cambridge, MA: MIT Press, 1986), 196–7, emphases in original.

17 Letter from Mary Joyce, December 1902 (*Letters II*, 22).
18 Letter from John Stanislaus Joyce, January 31, 1903 (*Letters II*, 26), emphases in original.
19 Bloch, *The Principle of Hope*, 65. Bloch gives a class-based account of why Freud might have been insufficiently sensitive to hunger:

> But no matter how loud hunger bellows, it is seldom mentioned by the doctors here. This omission shows that it is always only the better class of sufferers who have been and are treated psychoanalytically. The problem of finding nourishment was the most groundless of worries for Freud and his visitors. The psychoanalytical doctor and above all his patient come from a middle class which until recently had to worry little about its stomach. (65–6)

Needless to say, for Joyce's Dubliners, the problem of finding nourishment, the hunger drive, often takes priority over the sex drive.
20 Joyce, *Stephen Hero*, 218.
21 Joyce, *A Portrait of the Artist as a Young Man*, 108.749–50.
22 Joyce, *Ulysses*, 9.828.
23 Joyce, *Ulysses*, 13.1233, 13.1266.
24 Joyce, *Dubliners*, 3.1.
25 Vicki Mahaffey and Jill Shashaty, "Introduction," in *Collaborative Dubliners: Joyce in Dialogue*, ed. Vicki Mahaffey (Syracuse: Syracuse University Press, 2012), 9.
26 Hugh Kenner, *Dublin's Joyce* (Bloomington, IN: Indiana University Press, 1956), 51.
27 Letter to Grant Richards, May 20, 1906 (*Letters I*, 63).
28 Bloch, *Principle of Hope*, 1097.
29 Enda Duffy, "The Happy Ring House," *European Joyce Studies 21: Joyce, Benjamin and Magical Urbanism*, ed. Maurizia Boscagli and Enda Duffy (Amsterdam: Rodopi, 2011), 176.
30 Ibid., 176–7.
31 Nolan writes,

> It may remain difficult to abstract ... an image of a knowable human community from the novel, but in the light of my reading we may at least be in a position to interrogate more fully what is at stake if it is allowed that Bloom represents "the voice of the future," in specific opposition to an actually existing community, and also to describe those elements in the representation of the present which point towards the possibility of the future creation of such an authentic community. Otherwise this lingers merely in the form of a nostalgic memory of a past which is forever lost, or else, as Joyce writes of Bloom's meditations in "Ithaca," an unattainable Utopia, "there being no known method from the known to the unknown."

   Emer Nolan, *James Joyce and Nationalism* (New York: Routledge, 1995), 87.
32 Bloch, *The Principle of Hope*, 7.
33 Wolfgang Wicht's *Utopianism in James Joyce's Ulysses* establishes Joyce's negating approach to utopian programs in *Ulysses* at length.
34 For Fredric Jameson's distinction between utopian program and impulse, see "Varieties of the Utopian," in *Archaeologies of the Future: The Desire Called Utopia and Other Science Fictions* (New York: Verso, 2005), 1–9.
35 Senn justly says that *Giacomo Joyce* "retains [a] position in-between," Fritz Senn, "On Not Coming to Terms with *Giacomo Joyce*," in *Giacomo Joyce: Envoys of the Other*, ed. Louis Armand and Clare Wallace (Prague: Litteraria Pragensia, 2006), 20.

36 Louis Armand highlights "the otherness of the text itself, as fugitive, subordinated, bastardised, suppressed," Louis Armand, "Through a Glass Darkly: Reflections on the Other Joyce," in *Giacomo Joyce: Envoys of the Other*, ed. Louis Armand and Clare Wallace (Prague: Litteraria Pragensia, 2006), 5.

37 "Somehow Joyce's early phase came to a minute climax in *Giacomo Joyce* and perhaps the path was cleared for new arts as yet unknown, but already prefigured," Senn, "On Not Coming to Terms with *Giacomo Joyce*," 25. Mahaffey writes, "The evolution of Giacomo's lady into Molly Bloom, like the displacement of Stephen Dedalus by Leopold Bloom, reflects a profound change of attitude, an acceptance of imperfection and human mutability as part of the larger human comedy," Vicki Mahaffey, "Giacomo Joyce," in *Giacomo Joyce: Envoys of the Other*, ed. Louis Armand and Clare Wallace (Prague: Litteraria Pragensia, 2006), 67.

38 Senn, "On Not Coming to Terms with *Giacomo Joyce*," 22.

39 John McCourt, "Epiphanies of Language, Longing, Liminality in *Giacomo Joyce*," in *Giacomo Joyce: Envoys of the Other*, ed. Louis Armand and Clare Wallace (Prague: Litteraria Pragensia, 2006), 236.

40 Mahaffey, "Giacomo Joyce," 33, 41.

41 McCourt, "Epiphanies of Language, Longing, Liminality in *Giacomo Joyce*," 248.

42 Ibid., 240.

43 Richard Brown, "Eros and Apposition," in *Giacomo Joyce: Envoys of the Other*, ed. Louis Armand and Clare Wallace (Prague: Litteraria Pragensia, 2006), 307.

44 Ibid.

45 Michel Foucault, for instance, numbers cemeteries among spaces that he called "heterotopias": "The cemetery is certainly a different place compared with ordinary cultural spaces, and yet it is a space that is connected to all the other emplacements of the city or the society or the village, since every individual, every family happens to have relatives in the cemetery." "The heterotopia begins to function fully when men are in a kind of absolute break with their traditional time; thus, the cemetery is indeed a highly heterotopian place, seeing that the cemetery begins with that strange heterochronia that loss of life constitutes for an individual, and that quasi eternity in which he perpetually dissolves and fades away," Michel Foucault, "Different Spaces," in *Aesthetics, Method, and Epistemology*, ed. James D. Faubion (New York: The New Press, 1998), 180, 182.

46 James Joyce, *Giacomo Joyce*, with an introduction and notes by Richard Ellmann (London: Faber & Faber, 1968), 6. Subsequent page references are given in parentheses within the text.

47 McCourt, "Epiphanies of Language, Longing, Liminality in *Giacomo Joyce*," 245.

48 Mahffey, "Giacomo Joyce," 43.

49 Ibid., 44.

1

Without Paralysis: Hope, Hunger, and Spiritual Liberation in *Dubliners*

Hope, as articulated in the work of Ernst Bloch, is a historical, forward-looking process, open to possibilities not necessarily imaginable in advance, resistant to apotheosis, and linked to the socioeconomic conditions of hunger. Through this lens, this chapter departs from both classical and post-structuralist "paralysis" readings of Joyce and reconceives the politics of spiritual liberation in *Dubliners* as a dialectic between hope and hunger. It argues that the many moments of humiliation and defeat in Joyce's *Dubliners* are also moments in which characters hope for something better than is offered by the present world. It dissociates epiphany from both the classical function of narrative closure and the post-structuralist model of textual impasse and argues for the productive role of simony in mediating between the material and spiritual worlds. Finally, it concludes with a new view of spiritual liberation in *Dubliners*, one that envisions the "journey westward" as a searching, restless, and future-oriented negation of received and prevailing utopias of liberation.

Dubliners depicts characters in states of paralysis: this is perhaps the only idea in the critical history of Joyce's stories to have endured virtually every shift in methodology. Whether through attention to the stories' formal patterns or structures, their gaps and silences, characters' psychology, or through depictions of Irish culture and history, readers with many different critical allegiances have variously affirmed a fundamental paralysis at the heart of *Dubliners*.[1] Early in the critical tradition, for example, Hugh Kenner argued that *Dubliners* presents characters in a state of "living death."[2] Later, Morris Beja found a formalist pattern of "bondage and escape" in the stories, emphasizing "the frustration and fears, as well as the hopes"[3] of the characters. More recently, Trevor Williams, looking through a political lens, views the hopelessness that derives from Ireland's domination by England and the Catholic Church as leading to "the way of paralysis."[4] Luke Gibbons, from an Irish historical perspective, connects the early twentieth-century discourse of post-Famine Irish "enervation" to paralysis in *Dubliners*.[5] And in their introduction to *Collaborative Dubliners*, a recent collection of critical essays on the stories, Vicki Mahaffey and Jill Shashaty argue, "readers of *Dubliners* are asked to join the author in a scrupulous analysis of the paralysis—rooted in hopelessness—that precludes characters (like many of the readers they mirror) from seeing themselves accurately, and from acting with a greater degree of freedom."[6] Although recent scholarship reflects a vast range of concerns, these pursuits are often built on the bedrock of paralysis.

Such consistency across critical periods and methods suggests that the paralysis thesis is probably here to stay in some form. Joyce himself, in a letter to his reluctant publisher Grant Richards, described Dublin as Ireland's "centre of paralysis."[7] Nor is this view perversely to be discredited, as each of the mentioned readings accesses something true about the stories. But paralysis is only part of the story of *Dubliners* and to overemphasize paralysis is to distort the stories. For the situation has always been most complex. For one thing, as Anne Fogarty reminds us, although Joyce's authorial comments about *Dubliners* in his letters to Richards have been made to carry considerable critical weight in Joyce studies, the extent to which they reflect what Joyce intended has probably been inflated in critical practice.[8]

In addition, even when we entertain them in context, Joyce's authorial pronouncements still imply a mode of reception whose operation is far from self-evident. For instance, Joyce refers to *Dubliners* as the "first step towards the spiritual liberation"[9] of Ireland, suggesting that his stories could have a salutary effect on the population about which he wrote. But how are we to move from literary text to spiritual liberation? To Richards, Joyce offers only metaphor: "I seriously believe that you will retard the course of civilisation in Ireland by preventing the Irish people from having one good look at themselves in my nicely polished looking-glass."[10] But how can a literary reflection move Irish readers toward spiritual liberation? Are readers supposed to absorb the paralysis depicted in the stories, identify with it, and then reform their lives? Stage a rebellion? The mirror is foggy at best. Critics of *Dubliners* have thus always been called upon to square representations of paralysis with hopes for spiritual liberation via an implied theory of literary representation or reflection, a challenge that goes to the heart of the way we view the spiritual and political meaning and operations of literature.

When Joyce evokes spiritual liberation, he signals that paralysis exists in a dialectical relationship with three categories that have too often gone unrecognized in the critical history of *Dubliners*: hope, wish, and future. All critics agree that paralysis exerts tremendous pressure in the stories against any trace of hope, wish, and future: characters lose and then lose some more. Their hopes, wishes, and ideal futures are dashed with sometimes cruel swiftness. Yet we miss something crucial about Joyce's textual politics and his sense of spiritual liberation if we dismiss the wishful side of this dialectic. To understand *Dubliners* through a dialectic of paralysis with hope, wish, and future is to open a political alternative to a whole spectrum of conclusions about *Dubliners* that range from the early days of Joyce criticism, when Joyce was styled as an apolitical aesthete or as a political defeatist of the "We-can't-change-the-country-Let-us-change-the-subject" variety,[11] to the more recent tendency to see Joyce's work as directed against and politically subversive of specific oppressive authorities.

Exemplifying the latter view, Mahaffey and Shashaty argue that *Dubliners* invites readers into "frustrated, paralyzed lives in order to bring the psychic, social, and political structures of frustration and paralysis to light. The hope is that understanding may produce motivation: the motivation to try to dismantle such structures—not in the fictional world, but in the reader's."[12] This approach is fairly typical of the way Joyce's textual politics were understood to work during the post-structuralist era. The then-dominant model of how *Dubliners* might achieve a spiritual effect was through subversive representation. Although the exact mechanism of subversion varies from critic to critic, the consistent idea is that while Joyce's stories depict paralysis, they also function textually to undermine or resist the colonial, political, or religious authority that causes paralysis.[13] A critic might read the stories as representing characters paralyzed by ideological and institutional oppression, but he or she might also argue that because of the force with which Joyce depicts paralysis the stories take on political, subversive potential against these oppressors.[14] Or, more subtly, a critic might demonstrate that the gaps and indeterminacies of the stories train readers to brush the texts against the grain and to distrust the authority of the narrative voice. In this way, the text passes on oppositional and potentially subversive modes of thinking to the audience. Here, the argument is that *Dubliners* makes rebels out of readers.[15]

It would be incorrect to suggest that there is nothing subversive in Joyce or that these views do not capture something typical of him. After all, the modernist aesthetic itself is premised at least in part on subverting earlier aesthetic ideologies and taboos through innovation and formal defiance, and Joyce often approaches literary, religious, and colonial authorities critically, or even with an irreverence that in *Finnegans Wake* he calls "general thumbtonosery" (253.28). However, as Enda Duffy observes, in Joyce's critical history the subversive hand has been overplayed. As noted in the introduction, Duffy calls subversion "that much overused term in Joyce criticism," and argues, "It is not that Joyce's excessive language in itself ... is political because it is somehow (for example, satirically) subversive; rather, it is his moments when he strives to let us see through the intensity of his words that, for a politically active aesthetic, are key."[16] As the preoccupations and modes of reading associated with post-structuralism continue to wane in literary studies, we have an opportunity to reassess basic assumptions about the ways in which Joyce's texts function politically and spiritually. Specifically, it is a ripe time to rethink the connection between *Dubliners* and spiritual liberation, especially the politically active literary mechanisms through which we imagine that liberation might be achieved. How might our sense of Joyce's innovations and operations in fiction expand if we begin, for instance, with the premise that paralysis and subversion are only parts, more modest than previously thought, of the larger political operation of Joyce's texts?

Such a shift would reveal a Joyce whose relationship to future possibility is richer than previously understood. Fritz Senn suggests something of this possibility when he argues that *Dubliners* derives its complexity through "unforeseen augmentations that can be disruptive and unsettling."[17] In Joyce, the future hardly ever arrives in the manner predicted or in the political form desired in advance. Instead, the kind of futures that *Dubliners* implies are unpredictable ones that are born from daily wishing, changes of habit, redirections of hope, and from Joyce's resilient sense of the profound openness of the future. Joyce's hope is rooted in the material conditions of daily Dublin life, especially in the conditions of poverty and hunger. In

Dubliners Joyce creates characters whose lives are saturated at all points with hunger and hopes, hopes that are usually poisonously vain or fatally misdirected. Yet Joyce's posited vision of the future in *Dubliners* is one in which characters and readers recognize the unpredictable and productive power of rechanneling self-destructive hopes in new directions. For Joyce, the future will not arrive down a political and spiritual path of the already-known, but rather by directing wish toward unknown or even unnamable political and spiritual paths. In this view, Joycean liberation is less a matter of naïve hope or doomed hopelessness, salvation or subversion, but more one of struggling to imagine forms of liberation that have yet to be imagined, which therefore can only be mediated through fiction in relation to the future as a state of emergence.

Two Hungry Gallants

For Bloch, hope is an expectant emotion born from hunger, which he posits as the fundamental human drive of self-preservation.[18] Unlike Freud's materialism, which privileges the sex drive, Bloch's materialism is resolutely socioeconomic and historical. Here, hope is politics felt in the body in the form of hunger. Rather than the person looking for love, Bloch's quintessential subject is the unemployed person (65). And hunger itself is a historical matter, changing its aspect as "the mode of production and exchange" (69) changes. Moreover, because hope and hunger are inextricable, Bloch suggests that self-preservation is not tied to conservatism, as we might intuitively suspect, but rather to an appetite always ready for "more appropriate and more authentic states for our unfolding self" (69). Because hunger "seeks to change the situation which has caused its empty stomach" (75), it relates to transformation, revolution, and, most distantly, to utopia. Bloch also insists that we approach cultural expressions and the future through a combination of "militant optimism,"[19] and *docta spes*, or educated hope (7). Accordingly, readers must risk an educated credulity and take the gambit of reading Joyce through the framework of hope. After all, Bloch may be right when he says, "pessimism is paralysis per se, whereas even the most rotten optimism can still be the stupefaction from which there is an awakening" (446).

If hope is historical, forward-looking, open to the Not-Yet-Become, resistant to culmination, and linked to the material conditions of hunger, then it is possible to return to *Dubliners* with a renewed sense of politics, the spiritual, and the future. Joyce gives us everyday stories of characters whose routines are embroidered from moment to moment with hope. Some hopes are vain or futile, and many hopes come to nothing, bound as they are by self-destructive habits or by an inhospitable and oppressive colonized world, yet there is hardly a moment in *Dubliners* in which a character cannot be found hoping for something better than what is given.[20]

"Two Gallants," for example, suggests something about the intersections of class, hope, and hunger in *Dubliners*; it is a story about all that fills the mouths and stomachs of Dubliners instead of food: beer, cigars and cigarettes, and above all, talk. Instead of being used for eating, Lenehan's tongue is "tired for he had been talking all afternoon" (*D* 39.35). As Lily asserts in "The Dead" of the "men that is now," Lenehan is similarly "all palaver" (154.93). We learn, "He was hungry for, except some biscuits which he had asked two grudging curates to bring him, he had eaten nothing since breakfast-time" (45.261–46.263). We see, retrospectively, that Lenehan's twice-repeated comment on Corley's narrated exploits with women—"That takes the biscuit" (39.29, 40.67)—refers not just to the sleazy content of Corley's tales but also to Lenehan's last meal, which must unconsciously weigh on his thoughts. When Corley accuses Lenehan of trying to interfere with his seduction of the servant, Lenehan claims, perhaps with a certain regret, "All I want is to have a look at her. I'm not going to eat her" (43.184). Food is also evoked when Corley characterizes the cigars he has received from a woman as "the real cheese" (40.58), and Corley refers to two different women as "a fine tart" (40.49, 43.157). In each of these instances, the language of food and hunger creeps into the characters' discourse about other kinds of desire, especially of sexual desire. Lenehan and Corley give substance to Bloch, who, arguing against Freud's ahistorical privileging of Eros, argues for the historicity of the drives, with hunger as their origin. As we have seen, Bloch asserts, "The stomach is the first lamp into which oil must be poured" (65).

This language of food and deprivation is gendered in "Two Gallants." Although Lenehan's "figure fell into rotundity at the waist" (*D* 39.23–4), his plumpness suggests an unhealthy beer belly rather than a well-fed one. After all, Lenehan is skilled at insinuating himself at a pub "until he was included in a *round*" (39.41, emphasis added). Images of roundness in the story that actually do suggest nourishment or plentitude are reserved for the women, who are often figured as full, nourished, or nourishing. Lenehan's "rotundity" is mentioned when on Rutland (now Parnell) Square he passes the Rotunda maternity hospital, where pregnant women may be seen entering and emerging. Joyce describes Corley's prey in terms that reinforce the association of women and health: "Frank rude health glowed in her face, on her fat red cheeks" (44.216–17). The gold coin that Corley wheedles from her[21] is another part of the inventory of round images that contrasts with images of thinness, like Lenehan's "scant and grey" (39.24) hair and his face's "ravaged look" (39.26).[22] Yet the servant is also described in terms that emphasize her thinness: "The great silver buckle of her belt seemed to depress the centre of her body" (44.209–10). In fact, all Dubliners seem subtly underfed: "The crowd of girls and young men had thinned" (47.315–16).

So far there seems little justification for hope in the story, and certainly not for political or spiritual hope. However, on Kildare Street Lenehan, Corley, and listeners in a "ring" (43.161) hear a harpist's mournful song, Thomas Moore's "Silent, O Moyle," and the narrator describes the instrument in a curious way: "His harp, too, heedless that her coverings had fallen about her knees, seemed weary alike of the eyes of strangers and of her master's hands" (43.164–6). It has been noted that Joyce indulges in the pathetic fallacy here, a fact that Warren Beck attributes to "Joyce's stream of sentimentality, too strong to be always repressed."[23] The sentimental reading sees the harp as a symbol of Ireland exploited by its English masters. However, Margot Norris sees this moment as a "blind," arguing that its "blunt and obvious pathos ... distracts the reader's attention from the more trenchant and unsentimentalized degradation in the story to which both narrator and reader may remain 'blind.'"[24]

Both the classical and the post-structuralist readings seem plausible: the moment can be read as a sentimental lament about Irish exploitation and can also be resisted to focus on a broader social critique. However, what has been missed in this moment is its forward-looking tendency. This tendency links hunger and history and suggests a wishful dimension that offers something more than sentimental pathos or subversive critique. The forward-looking tendency inheres in the way in which Joyce uses the pathetic fallacy, which according to M. H. Abrams's *A Glossary of Literary Terms* is a "representation of inanimate natural objects that ascribes to them human capabilities, sensations, and emotions."[25] John Ruskin objected to the pathetic fallacy's subjectivity, in which the object is forced to share the thoughts, feelings, or emotions of the subject. Rather than its projected subjectivity, however, what we might notice is the pathetic fallacy's intersubjectivity between subject and object and the possibilities that lie there. Under the Marxist theory of estranged labor, alienation between subject and object appears as a fundamental condition of capitalism because workers are alienated from their products and thus from the fruits of their own labor. Bloch, however, finds a utopian charge in all wishful images that represent an overcoming of alienation between subject and object: "And precisely the world of this final real possibility ... presents itself in exemplary form as: harmony of the unreified object with the manifested subject, of the unreified subject with the manifested object. These are—turned towards a near and distant future—the basic proportions of human development" (248). Joyce describes a moment of shared subjectivity between object and subject that hints at the wishful possibility of overcoming alienation.[26]

But the relationship between subject and object is finally important because it connects to the relationship between subjects. Bloch also argues, "the hinge in human history is its producer—working man, who is finally no longer dispossessed, alienated, reified, subjugated for the profit of his exploiters" (249). The moment that has been described as sentimental or as a narrative ruse appears rather like a hint of a better, less alienated world, expressed precisely through a lament about the concrete material conditions of Dublin. These conditions not only divide subjects and objects but also result in degrading and destructive relationships between subjects, nowhere better exemplified in the story than by Corley's exploitation of the servant.

However, the hopeful content of this scene is quite disembodied. Joyce's hope is usually more bodily, as when Lenehan, pausing before the ham and plum pudding in the *Refreshment Bar* window, "eyed this food earnestly for some time" (*D* 45.58-9), and, after determining the price of a plate of peas, "ate his food greedily" (46.276). Then, like Leopold Bloom after he eats in the "Lestrygonians" episode of *Ulysses*,[27] Lenehan's mood changes. Although he still wishes for money, a steady job, and a home with "a warm fire to sit by and a good dinner to sit down to" (46.287–8), a sated Lenehan becomes reflective and hopeful:

> Experience had embittered his heart against the world. But all *hope* had not left him. He felt better after having *eaten* than he had felt before, less weary of life, less vanquished in *spirit*. He might yet be able to settle down in some snug corner and live happily if he could only come across some good simpleminded girl with a little of the ready. (46.290–6, emphasis added)

The italicized words here bring together Joyce's care for the spirit with hope and hunger. Lenehan's changed mood demonstrates the way in which Joyce links the body and hope. Because human drives are historical, hunger has transformative potential. Change begins in the stomach: "The body-ego ... seeks to change the situation which has caused its empty stomach. ... The No to the bad situation which exists, the Yes to the better life that hovers ahead, is incorporated into *revolutionary interest*" (75, emphasis in original). Like Bloch, Joyce suggests a historical process that is best described as a dialectic of hope and hunger.

"After the Race" provides a telling contrast with "Two Gallants" in this regard; this story demonstrates what happens to the spirit when hope detaches from hunger. The hopes and desires of the story's wealthy young men have little to do with food, of which there is plenty. Joyce depicts the men overeating, as when, on the American's yacht, "A man brought in a light supper, and the young men sat down to it for form' sake" (*D* 37.181–2), even though they have recently enjoyed an "excellent, exquisite" (35.123) dinner in a Dublin hotel. Before dinner, even Villona, the poorest of the young men, "was in good humour because he had had a very satisfactory luncheon; and besides he was an optimist by nature" (33.28).[28] Notably, Jimmy Doyle's father "had made his money as a butcher" (33.34), a seller rather than a buyer of food.

Wealth detaches hope from food and attaches it to money schemes. Doyle plans to invest capital with Ségouin. Doyle also gambles, an exercise similar to capital investment: money is risked for the sole purpose of returning more money. Gambling has a different relationship to hope than hunger does, however.[29] Of the gambler, Walter Benjamin writes, "his desire to win and make money cannot really be termed a 'wish' in the strict sense of the word. ... [H]is frame of mind is such that he cannot make much use of experience.

A wish, however, appertains to an order of experience."[30] For Benjamin, because gambling is an isolated activity—the last bet perfectly disconnected from the next—it "nullifies the lessons of experience."[31] Opposed to such an activity, then, are hopes and wishes that *can* be integrated with experience: Benjamin writes, "a wish fulfilled is the crowning of experience."[32] Doyle's gambling contrasts with the experiences of hunger and deprivation that Joyce describes elsewhere in *Dubliners*, when experience and wish do not have the luxury of separation. In Lenehan's case the food remains on the table and attaches bodily to his wishes for a better life, while in Doyle's the cards literally displace the light supper: "Cards! Cards! The table was cleared" (*D* 37.190).

Doyle's epiphany will come under the harsh light of morning, when it becomes clear that his vain desire to emulate and be accepted by continental elites has invited financial ruin. But to be sure, Doyle does not have a monopoly on bad choices. Corley's use of the servant woman, Joyce lets us understand, is particularly vile; Lenehan's desire for a "simpleminded girl with a little of the ready" is another misdirected wish. Joyce's characters often wish for the wrong things, and the moment of epiphany often revolves around recognizing this. Their wishes usually have little to do with spiritual or political liberation.

Epiphany and the Process of History

Because moments of epiphany in *Dubliners* tend to highlight poor wishes and choices, traditional and post-structuralist critics both use epiphany to advance a paralysis thesis that tells only part of the story. Joycean epiphany is usually understood through the definition offered in *Stephen Hero*: the moment when an object's "soul, its whatness, leaps to us from the vestment of its appearance" (*SH* 213). This is traditionally understood as the foundation of the aesthetic theory underlying *Dubliners*. For instance, in an early book-length consideration of *Dubliners*, well representative of a classical view, Warren Beck argued that in a *Dubliners* story, "at an epiphanal point it may be discovered that all along some not yet identified realization was being sought, or at least skirted, and its factors had been taken in without clear foresight of a relevance they were to assume in the vision, the completed construct and overflow of knowledge."[33] Here, the stories seem teleologically tilted toward a moment of culmination and completion. Such a view understands the stories as fundamentally oriented toward a scene of clarity or realization, which has been covered over or ignored up until the crucial moment when the veil drops. Seen this way, the stories are rather funnel-shaped: the object may resist but yet revolves around and finally succumbs to the center with the inexorability of gravity.

Post-structuralist critics of *Dubliners* posed serious challenges to the presumption of unity implicit in this view of Joycean epiphany, teaching readers to be wary of apparent moments of illumination. These challenges put a permanent dent in the classical view of epiphany formulated by critics such as Beck, Beja, and others.[34] For example, Kevin J. H. Dettmar proposes the term "epi*phony*" (false epiphany) to describe misguided critical attempts to satisfy "the desire for narrative closure" through the supposedly unifying power of the epiphany.[35] According to Dettmar, the stories enjoin readers to "[g]ive up the flattering project of interpretation; give in to the mystery which is life."[36] Margot Norris reads *Dubliners* in a similar spirit of indeterminacy in order to challenge the truth content of the supposed epiphany. When, after his dispiriting mission to the bazaar, the young narrator of "Araby" concludes, "Gazing up into the darkness I saw myself as a creature driven and derided by vanity; and my eyes burned with anguish and anger" (*D* 26.218–20), he seems to experience an epiphany. However, Norris reads this not as a moment of genuine illumination, but rather as yet another expression of the narrator's adolescent romanticism and narcissism, which the story subtly invites readers to unmask.[37]

But post-structuralist readings are subject to their own forms of culmination or apotheosis, in the form of the predictable point of impasse or stasis. For example, Dettmar writes, "Indeed this is the final epiphany of the most powerful stories in *Dubliners*: *our* realization, as readers, that the characters have not had *their* epiphany. Believing that they have transcended, believing themselves finally to be free, characters like the narrator of 'Araby' and Gabriel Conroy pathetically verify their prison—this is perhaps the most bitter paralysis in all of *Dubliners*."[38] Plainly, the content of the epiphany may be deconstructed while yet affirming paralysis.

But coupling paralysis with epiphany tends to obscure the ways in which hope mediates between hunger and the spirit in the stories. The fact that hopes are often misdirected under colonized and capitalist life negates neither the wishful energy that animates Joyce's stories nor the potential that Joyce represents for redirecting hope toward spiritual or political liberation. Hope can reframe the place and function of epiphany in Joyce's stories because hope, understood seriously, is incompatible with apotheosis, climax, anti-climax, or impasse. Against both the apotheosis of the classical reading and the impasse of the post-structuralist one, hope suggests a restless process at work in *Dubliners*. Endlessly dynamic, hope always changes relative to a given endpoint. Bloch proposes several ways in which this is true. For instance, sometimes there is hope left over after fulfillment (186). Even "sufficiently perfect" realization of a hope can be accompanied by a "melancholy of fulfillment" (193). Or perfect realization is revealed never to be perfect because even if the object is attained, the hope, which had taken on a life of its own, "will not die with fulfillment" (184). Or, after fulfillment, a possible "Being-even-better" comes into focus when "A new peak appears behind the previously attained one" (189). But most importantly, even perfect realizations of hope lie within a "process of history," which is still "undecided" (193).[39] Fulfilled wishes deny culmination because they remain vulnerable to an ongoing, unpredictable history. In Bloch's words, "hope makes us mistrustful—justly and with precision, in fact with the highest kind of conscience: that of the goal—of every realization that offers itself all too plumply" (183).

To dissociate the concept of epiphany from apotheosis, impasse, paralysis, destiny, and stasis is to liberate it into the historical process, where hope and change are the constants. Epiphany emerges as the opportunity to redirect misdirected hope because hope's restlessness, its resistance to satisfaction, is the origin of its productiveness. Seen in these terms, "Two Gallants" not only leaves open the possibilities that emerge from the connection between hope and hunger, but also posits a situation in which the conditions of hunger could possibly animate hope in the direction of change. Paul K. Saint-Amour and Karen R. Lawrence articulate something similar to this in their reading of "A Painful Case." Although they see Joyce as diagnosing Mr. Duffy and all of Dublin with "a terse and scornful diagnosis," they also argue that the story "stages the crisis produced by such habits of mind, taking them to the end of the line as if to exhaust them and perhaps to glimpse what lies beyond their terminus."[40] This glimpse beyond the terminus suggests a way to move past the traditional and post-structuralist models. The stories set patterns of hope and frustration, rooted in the hungers of the material world, in history; they perhaps do not permit us to imagine a radical and liberating break for the characters after the stories end, but we recognize that the dialectic of hope and hunger continues unabated, perhaps taking new and unanticipated turns toward a future unnamable in advance.

Even the stories that seem most hopeless and whose characters' lives, choices, and efforts seem most ineffectual—for instance, Mr. Duffy in "A Painful Case" or Maria in "Clay"—do not negate this hope content. For one thing, *Dubliners* does not operate through a mechanical and rote structure that is entirely uniform or predictable; nor should we expect each story tediously to demonstrate the same point, whatever it is said to be, over and over again. Joyce's art is too subtle to confirm either hope or paralysis in a clumsily repetitive fashion. Part of Joyce's method consists of alerting us to the constant hopefulness of his characters' lives, while nonetheless showing us the painful cases and contexts within which hope and wish prove to be futile, feeble, powerless, or even fatal. But if characters reach a point at which change is impossible, Joyce shows us that their hopes were not impotent, but misrecognized and misdirected. Within the cultural, material, and oppressed contexts of their lives, his characters do not hope less, but wrongly. Some stories, especially "The Dead," open new paths or possibilities for hope, new habits adopted, while others seem to record moments in which these possibilities have narrowed definitively or been foreclosed upon entirely. As such, it is inadequate to argue that hope, when present in *Dubliners*, is impotent and futile, amounting to something worse than hopelessness.

Spiritual Liberation and Simony

Even if it is possible to say that hope amends the paralysis thesis, certain stubborn questions remain: How do we get from the all-too-earthly or the historical to the spiritual in *Dubliners*? And how is "spiritual liberation" finally to be defined in Joyce's terms? It is a start to say that liberation may come when readers identify themselves in a literary mirror. But it is not enough for readers to recognize themselves in Joyce's frustrated lives, which might only reproduce paralysis. Nor are they necessarily spurred into specific forms of ideology or rebellion. Rather, readers must grasp that habit is mutable in relation to hope and hunger. When readers observe the presence and misdirection of hope in the characters' lives, *Dubliners* instructs them about the places, uses, and misuses of hope in daily life. In this model readers are not only able to recognize their own paralysis but also to identify the saturation of their lives with misdirected hope and, accordingly, the very near and profound power to wish for better things.[41]

However, in order to define spiritual liberation more concretely it is necessary to reimagine another term from what Bernard Benstock called the "time-honored trinity"[42] of italicized words in "The Sisters": *simony* (*D* 3.12). At the conclusion of "Grace," Father Purdon, ostensibly adapting his sermon to his audience of worldly businessmen, asks his listeners to conduct a spiritual self-accounting: "he was their spiritual accountant; and he wished each and every one of his hearers to open his books, the books of his spiritual life, and see if they tallied accurately with conscience" (*D* 151.797–800). The obvious interpretation is that Father Purdon is a kind of simoniac, a trader of things of the spirit for things of the material world. As R. Brandon Kershner and Mary Lowe-Evans write, "Undoubtedly, the indulging of devotional practices contributed to Joyce's interest in simony, an important thematic concern in 'Grace' where abuses of ecclesiastical power become associated with their secular counterparts in the world of commerce."[43] And Mahaffey writes, "simony … depends upon a hungry materialism that sees everything as something that can be bought or traded. The simoniac is, by implication, greedy, eager to profit personally from supplicants' desires for love or forgiveness or knowledge."[44]

The abuses of simony are surely central to Joyce's diagnosis of his paralyzed Dubliners. However, the currency and circulation that simony establishes between the material and spiritual worlds is nonetheless something like the very precondition, to an artist like Joyce, for the possibility of a literary work to act as a "first step towards the spiritual liberation." The possibility of circulation between material and spirit that simony can open serves as the very precondition for art to touch the spirit. How else can the worldly artist do so unless he were, "a priest of eternal imagination, transmuting the daily bread of experience into the radiant body of everliving life" (*P* 195.1677–9)?

This formulation from *A Portrait* imagines an artist who negotiates between material and spirit in ways that reflect Joyce's own profane artistic ambitions and practices, as well as his comments about spiritual liberation to Richards that express an intention to touch and grow the spirit of his country.

Instances of simony can quite easily invite satire of the kind that Joyce offers when Stephen Dedalus, again in *A Portrait*, "seemed to feel his soul in devotion pressing like fingers the keyboard of a great cash register and to see the amount of his purchase start forth immediately in heaven" (P 129.35–7). And, as Mahaffey argues, simony surely diagnoses the prevailing economic climate that drives characters to exploit one another.[45] Yet simony might also be said to name the dynamic technique of Joyce's art in *Dubliners*. When Father Purdon offers himself as "spiritual accountant" for his flock, Joyce evokes something similar to Stephen's pietistic cash register and suggests one reason for Joyce's own principled rejection of the Eucharist. But he does not rule out, and in fact invokes, the idea of traffic and transmutation between the material and spiritual worlds. It might be too simple to say that Joyce longs to be the "spiritual accountant" for Ireland, but there is surely some truth in the idea that in writing *Dubliners* Joyce was laying Dublin's books open and tallying them according to his standards of conscience. Simony would then become something like the condition for spiritual hope in the profane world, not just the route to pietistic illusions of transcendence, but also toward transmutation and transformation.

Liberation from Spiritual Liberation

The semiotic square in Figure 1 schematizes what spiritual liberation might mean for Joyce and *Dubliners*.[46] The square suggests, *pace* Kenner[47] and others, that hope's contradiction is not hopelessness, but rather non-hope, just as satisfaction's contradiction is not dissatisfaction, but non-satisfaction. Further, hope implies non-satisfaction and satisfaction implies non-hope. The synthesis of the two terms at the top of the semiotic square, what A. J. Greimas calls the "complex" term,[48] is a state of hope with satisfaction. This position represents an utterly conventional, illusory, and unattainable "spiritual liberation," little more than the stuff of flimsy utopias, which Joyce could never but subvert

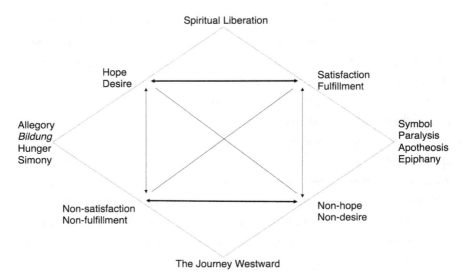

Figure 1 Spiritual liberation versus the journey westward in *Dubliners*.

and parody. However, the square also identifies an alternative, represented by the combination of the two bottom terms, or what Greimas calls the "neutral" term. This neutral term, comprised as it is of two negations, is difficult, if not impossible to conceptualize, but it resonates best with Joycean hope. If the complex term of spiritual liberation represents a positive utopian ideal, which can only be approached skeptically, then the negative term represents something else. Fredric Jameson has identified the semiotic square's neutral term as the position that most usefully keeps utopian possibility open because it fails to generate a positive vision: the two bottom terms that comprise the neutral term, "must neither be combined in some humanist organic synthesis, nor effaced and abandoned altogether: but retained and sharpened, made more virulent, their incompatibility and indeed their incommensurability a scandal for the mind, but a scandal that remains vivid and alive, and that cannot be thought away, either by resolving it or eliminating it."[49]

This alternative in *Dubliners* is not as easy to name as the conventional kinds of spiritual liberation that are advertised in the marketplace or preached from the altar, which promise to combine the states of hope and satisfaction, to conflate desire and fulfillment. Rather, the combined states of non-hope and non-satisfaction would be aligned with, though not identical to, one of

Dubliners' most pervasive themes: death. The neutral term makes visible an overlooked possibility in the opening line of *Dubliners*. Instead of representing "a thematic statement of hopeless paralysis," as Kenner argues, the first line of "The Sisters"—"There was no hope for him this time"—might represent a state of non-hope. The priest is not yet dead, but close to it. He is not so much hopeless as quiescent, though still within an ongoing process. The priest possesses neither the satisfactions of life nor has he yet attained the privative state of death. Hope and hunger have become nearly irrelevant for him, as have growth or becoming (*Bildung*) or even simony, his implied sin. Instead, we might say in the words of "The Dead," "His soul had approached that region where dwell the vast hosts of the dead" (*D* 194.1595–6).

Dubliners begins and ends by evoking this enigmatic state of non-hope and non-satisfaction that frames and conditions the collection's dialectic of hope and hunger and its pursuit of spiritual liberation more broadly. The dialectic between hope and hunger is ultimately a dialectic between hope and the anti-utopian privation of death. Like the priest in "The Sisters," Gabriel Conroy of "The Dead" becomes unhinged from his hopes and desires and from the allegorical process of personal becoming more broadly. As Gretta tells Gabriel about Michael Furey's self-sacrificing love for her, Gabriel "caught sight of himself in full length" in the "cheval glass" (*D* 190.1432–3). The hotel room's mirror perhaps serves Gabriel as a version of Joyce's own "nicely polished looking-glass." Processing Gretta's revelation, Gabriel soon reevaluates the hopes and desires that have motivated him during the whole evening and, indeed, during most of his married life. The desires that had up until only minutes ago driven and defined him now appear to him "ludicrous" (191.1482), "clownish" (191.1484), and "fatuous" (191.1485). Repelled by this vision of himself, Gabriel can no longer take up the hopes that once drove him, gave meaning to his life, and shored up his identity. Yet the absence of his hopes and desires has culminated in neither hopelessness nor paralysis. Instead, Gabriel finds himself open to pity for Gretta ("a strange friendly pity for her entered his soul" (193.1558–9)), for his aunt Julia ("Poor aunt Julia! She too would soon be a shade" (193.1571–2)), and finally for everyone at the gathering that night and perhaps for humanity more generally ("One by one they were all becoming shades" (194.1584)). As in the cemetery scene in *Giacomo Joyce*, proximity to death generates new and unforeseen feeling and states of being. Gabriel's lust for and anger at Gretta have been rechanneled into an unexpected "strange friendly pity" that is then transferred to others. Gabriel's "Generous tears" (194.1590) come less from his own shattered illusions than from the collective concerns that are implied in the etymological root of "generous": *genus*, stock or race. Gabriel transitions from his individual ego-desires to a more generalized, personally disinterested, and collective perspective: "His own identity was fading out into a grey impalpable world: the solid world itself which these dead had one time reared and lived in was dissolving and dwindling" (194.1597–600). Difficult to conceptualize, this state is like the snow that falls "upon all the living and the dead" (194.1614–15) at the end of the story; a distinctive descent, a trajectory determined by gravity, it is yet removed from hope and satisfaction. It is not a state of paralysis, but of movement and change. Just as it would be ridiculous to speak of falling snow as hopeless, this state similarly cannot be called hopeless; it is only a state of non-hope, a negation of hope that is not hopelessness.

As Gabriel watches the distinct but unmotivated movement of the snow "falling obliquely" (194.1603), the narrator comments, "The time had come for him to set out on his journey westward" (194.1604). The journey westward seems to occur to Gabriel because of the way in which flakes fall "obliquely": not in a straight or direct way, yet simultaneously disinterested and kinetic. As with the falling snow, it is impossible to think of this journey in personalized terms of hope, desire, or satisfaction. It is a tangible and definite movement that culminates in an unmistakable if unpredictable arrival. It is closely related to death but not identical to it. It is comprised only of the negation of hope and desire: non-hope and non-satisfaction. This is why I have labeled the neutral term in the figure, comprised of two negations, the "journey westward" (*D* 194.1604). Gabriel contemplates this journey, but it is never given a final positive content.

Although "westward" contains undeniable resonances of both death and the west of Ireland,[50] it is nonetheless impossible to find a final determinism in the word that would delimit its meaning to these or that could diminish its ability to signify open-endedly. Moreover, whereas spiritual liberation is limited because it is a namable state in which hope combines utopianly with satisfaction, the journey westward, comprised of two negations rather than two positive terms, seems open and unlimited. The journey westward eludes a concept, which marks the reason for its centrality to *Dubliners*. A kind of no-man's land between life and death, the journey westward represents an alternative pull in the stories, a veering away from both positively defined spiritual liberation and from paralysis and toward a strange state that negates the collection's key oppositions and limitations. In a state of non-hope there is no allegory or *Bildung*, while in a state of non-satisfaction, there can be no symbol or culmination. Here the oppositions of allegory and symbol, and *Bildung* and paralysis, fade into impalpability, suggesting liberation from the concept of spiritual liberation itself.

For Joyce hope is an essentially historical experience as well as an index to history. The hope content of *Dubliners*, more profoundly than its precise, naturalistic detail or its painstaking attention to the sources and effects of paralysis, is the key to its historicity. By representing the ongoing process of hope and hunger within their historical conditions, Joyce's stories point forward to a wishful future, however undefined. But the more undefined we see this future the better we understand Joyce's vision of possibility, for *Dubliners* does not offer specific images of spiritual or political liberation; rather it represents a wider wishful impulse that, open to contingency and possibility, looks to a better future. And while Joyce's characters often wish for the wrong things or fail to overcome (or even to recognize) their regressive habits, spiritual liberation begins implicitly by recognizing the abiding presence of and then channeling "infant hope" (to borrow a phrase from "A Little Cloud" (*D* 60.106)). Indeed, because Joyce imbricates his characters' mundane, vain, and futile wishes with detailed accounts of the historical conditions of their hunger, he gives a physical and potentially political charge to every such wish.

Yet while *Dubliners* represents its characters as they are impelled by a dialectic of hope and hunger toward or away from spiritual liberation, the journey westward acknowledges the limitations of conventional liberation, of the characters' and readers' limited ability to imagine what is not already given in the preexisting political, social, and religious imagination. It may be the case, as Jameson argues, that the ability to conceive utopia is always frustratingly limited to the already-known,[51] but Joyce's westward journey gestures to the new and unknown, to what Bloch calls "the Not-Yet-Become" (6). This journey is consistent with Joyce's vision of *Dubliners* as a first step toward spiritual liberation. After all, who ever imagined that by spiritual liberation Joyce meant anything that could fit within a Catholic context or, for that matter, within any other conventional and preexisting positive vision of spiritual liberation?

Rather, the spiritual liberation that Joyce imagines is better defined as liberation *from* the utopian constructs and paths to liberation offered by the reigning religious, social, and political paradigms. And while Joyce's dialectic of hope and hunger recognizes these paradigms as the source of paralysis and the sphere of potential subversion and real struggle, a struggle of the greatest consequence for the lives of his characters and their horizons of possibility, the journey westward finally points toward new states of becoming that in their opposition to conventional spiritual liberation are all the more vital for the spirit as such, even as it falls back, as it always must, into the flux of becoming and history.

Notes

1 Recent exceptions may be found in John Hobbs, "Are Joyce's Dubliners Paralyzed? A Second Opinion," *Papers on Joyce* 15 (2009): 17–29, and Kathleen Heininge, "The Way Out of Paralysis: Joyce and the Habitual Present Tense," *James Joyce Quarterly* 57.3–4 (Spring–Summer 2020): 263–73. Hobbs concludes that Joyce's irony prevents us from seeing his characters as paralyzed. He argues, "the didactic intent of Joyce the social critic has thankfully been subverted by the achievement of Joyce the artist who brings an ironic sympathy to each of his characters and their situations" (28). Heininge finds a way out of paralysis through Joyce's grammatical forms, arguing, "Joyce ironically employs Irish grammatical forms, particularly the habitual present tense, to suggest that the paralysis he laments was but a temporary stasis, a way-point to something different, and that there was a way out through the exercise of language" (263–4). For recent essays that see Joyce's stories as not just about paralysis but also about movement of various kinds ("flipping the traditional approach to *Dubliners* and reading the text as preoccupied with momentum and progress rather than overt stagnation"), see Claire A. Culleton and Ellen Scheible, "Introduction: Rethinking *Dubliners*: A Case for What Happens in Joyce's Stories," in *Rethinking Joyce's Dubliners*, ed. Claire A. Culleton and Ellen Scheible (New York: Palgrave Macmillan, 2017), 3. While "movement" is perhaps too limited a term to evoke the sense of hope and future that I wish to argue for, Jim LeBlanc's formulation of "the dialectic between paralysis and liberation that Joyce sought to enact," in his essay in that volume

is productively resonant with my purpose here. See Jim LeBlanc, "A 'Sensation of Freedom' and the Rejection of Possibility in *Dubliners*," in *Rethinking Joyce's Dubliners*, ed. Claire A. Culleton and Ellen Scheible (New York: Palgrave Macmillan, 2017), 64.
2 Hugh Kenner, *Dublin's Joyce* (Bloomington, IN: Indiana University Press, 1956), 58.
3 Morris Beja, "One Good Look at Themselves: Epiphanies in *Dubliners*," in *Work in Progress: Joyce Centenary Essays*, ed. Richard F. Peterson, Alan M. Cohen, and Edmund L. Epstein (Carbondale: Southern Illinois University Press, 1983), 6. Beja concludes more hopefully than Kenner does, arguing that Mahony of "An Encounter" achieves some "genuine moral progress," and that Gabriel Conroy of "The Dead" shows signs of "growth, maturation, and a new perception about himself and others" (13).
4 Trevor L. Williams, "No Cheer for 'the Gratefully Oppressed': Ideology in Joyce's *Dubliners*," in *ReJoycing: New Readings of Dubliners* (Lexington: University Press of Kentucky, 1998), 99.
5 See Luke Gibbons, "'Have you no homes to go to?': James Joyce and the Politics of Paralysis," in *Semicolonial Joyce*, ed. Derek Attridge and Marjorie Howes (Cambridge: Cambridge University Press, 2000), 150–69.
6 Vicki Mahaffey and Jill Shashaty, "Introduction," in *Collaborative Dubliners: Joyce in Dialogue*, ed. Vicki Mahaffey (Syracuse: Syracuse University Press, 2012), 9.
7 Letter to Grant Richards, May 5, 1906 (*Letters II*, 134).
8 Fogarty offers a qualifying and tempering view of the purpose of Joyce's correspondence with Richards: "These authorial pronouncements have become so familiar and have acquired such currency as the basis for analyzing *Dubliners* that they have lost the rhetorical bravado and provisionality with which they were once uttered. … On closer inspection, it must be recognized that Joyce's confidences to his would-be publisher were tactical, monitory, and deliberately self-aggrandizing," Derek Attridge and Anne Fogarty, "'Eveline' at Home," in *Collaborative Dubliners: Joyce in Dialogue*, ed. Vicki Mahaffey (Syracuse: Syracuse University Press, 2012), 98.
9 Letter to Grant Richards, May 20, 1906 (*Letters I*, 63).
10 Letter to Grant Richards, June 23, 1906 (*Letters I*, 64).
11 I refer here, of course, to Stephen's bitter response to Bloom's utopianism in "Eumaeus," a scene that I take up in the conclusion.
12 Mahaffey and Shashaty, "Introduction," 19.
13 For example, Kevin J. H. Dettmar describes, "the radically subversive spirit of Joyce's style(s)," Kevin J. H. Dettmar, *The Illicit Joyce of Postmodernism: Reading against the Grain* (Madison: University of Wisconsin Press, 1996), 6. Garry Leonard argues that Joyce "undermines the mythic ideology of unified consciousness," or the "self," Garry M. Leonard, *Reading Dubliners Again: A*

Lacanian Perspective (Syracuse: Syracuse University Press, 1993), 4, and Sonja Bašić links uncertainty in the stories to subversion, arguing that because "closures are either inconclusive or elided by gaps and sudden interruptions" they therefore "end in a subversive way," Sonja Bašić, "A Book of Many Uncertainties: Joyce's *Dubliners*," in *ReJoycing: New Readings of Dubliners*, ed. Rosa M. Bollettieri Bosinelli and Harold F. Mosher Jr. (Lexington: University Press of Kentucky, 1998), 24.

14 Trevor L. Williams gives a particularly compelling example of such a reading when he argues, "Joyce ... was choosing to resist ideological domination" and that "paralysis is ultimately determined by the particular form of government these characters labor under ... and that the church through its pervasive ideological domination, is complicit with the dominating state force, both having a vested interest in controlling the visions of the future available to the people." Because church and state force characters to feel somehow "without a future," they are paralyzed. Williams, "No Cheer for 'the Gratefully Oppressed,' " 91, 95–6.

15 This is the approach offered by Margot Norris in the aptly titled, *Suspicious Readings of Dubliners*, which argues that *Dubliners* is designed to train readers to question and resist the information that the narrators of the stories would deceptively try to make them complicit with. She writes, "In reading *Dubliners* it is as important to attend to everything that is outside the narration—outside it in a determinate rather than an indeterminate sense—and to treat these extra-narrational elements as expressive and, therefore, as silent discourses that supplement, interrogate, and frequently, dispute the narration." Norris's hope is that "learning how to read *Dubliners* oppositionally could enhance student skill and confidence in dealing with situations where there are limitations to their knowledge, and yet where they may be obliged to act," Margot Norris, *Suspicious Readings of Joyce's Dubliners* (Philadelphia: University of Pennsylvania Press, 2003), 9, 14.

16 Enda Duffy, "The Happy Ring House," in *European Joyce Studies 21: Joyce, Benjamin and Magical Urbanism*, ed. Maurizia Boscagli and Enda Duffy (Amsterdam: Rodopi, 2011), 176–7.

17 Fritz Senn, "Gnomon Inverted," in *ReJoycing: New Readings of Dubliners* (Lexington: University Press of Kentucky, 1998), 250.

18 See Ernst Bloch, *The Principle of Hope*, 3 vols., trans. Neville Plaice, Stephen Plaice, and Paul Knight (Cambridge: MIT Press, 1986), 11, 67. Subsequent references are given in parentheses in the text.

19 For more on the concept of "militant optimism," see Bloch, *The Principle of Hope*, 198–205.

20 Bloch finds not only oppression but also hope in habit and repetition. See Bloch, *The Principle of Hope*, 339–40.

21 Corley confirms the second half of Lily's insight about the men of her day: "all palaver and what they can get out of you" (*D* 154.93–4).
22 "Ravaged" is a word that Joyce also uses in *A Portrait of the Artist as a Young Man* in association with hunger, as when Stephen sees evidence of the "ravaged turnover" that his siblings have presumably devoured from hunger (*P* 142.567).
23 Warren Beck, *Joyce's Dubliners: Substance, Vision, and Art* (Durham, NC: Duke University Press, 1969), 140.
24 Norris, *Suspicious Readings of Joyce's Dubliners*, 82.
25 M. H. Abrams and Geoffrey Galt Harpham, *A Glossary of Literary Terms*, Tenth Edition (Boston, MA: Wadsworth, 2012), 269–70.
26 It is also worth noting that the musical emphasis of the harp performance—"The notes of the air throbbed deep and full" (*D* 43.168–9)—contributes a potential affective charge to the hope content in Joyce's pathetic fallacy. Indeed, Bloch credits the music of lament with a consolatory, hopeful purpose: "a sound can express better than any colour or words that transition where we no longer know whether it is a lament or a consolation." He continues, "[Music] has a totally lonely but long-drawn-out, undying light in the pain it states, and for seriousness it has a song which covers even the hardest step of the grave as one towards hope" (827).
27 See, in particular, *U* 8.854–6.
28 Significantly, amid all of this abundant food, "After the Race" is the *Dubliners* story that most involves the concept of "taste" as a form of cultural discernment, detached from the actual taste of food. We are told, "Ségouin, Jimmy decided, had a very refined taste" (*D* 35.124), and "The five young men had various tastes" 36.132–3). With the exception of the decidedly "common tastes" of Mrs. Mooney's lodgers in "The Boarding House" (50.31), the other instances of "taste" in the collection refer to the physical taste of food and drink.
29 Walter Benjamin and Bloch agree that the prevailing mood of bourgeois capitalist life is boredom. For Benjamin, capitalism tries to cover its own stasis with the endless novelty of commodities. The gambler is a capitalist type because the gambler's intoxication comes from the twin though ultimately futile desires of passing the time and of summoning "a thoroughly new, original reaction," Walter Benjamin, *The Arcades Project*, ed. Rolf Tiedemann, trans. Howard Eiland and Kevin McLaughlin (Cambridge: Harvard University Press, 1999), 513. See also *Arcades*, 512. For Bloch, the bourgeoisie can only be indifferent or openly hostile to the new, because "capitalist society senses itself negated by the future" (137). Whereas the boredom of capitalist life is evident enough to the factory worker or the unemployed person, "The rich man … sees to it that boredom is at least made interesting," as Bloch puts it, with luxuries of all kinds. Yet "even the excitements of gambling go stale eventually" (34).

30. Walter Benjamin, "On Some Motifs in Baudelaire," in *Selected Writings, Volume 4, 1938-1940*, ed. Howard Eiland and Michael W. Jennings (Cambridge: Harvard University Press, 2003), 331.
31. Ibid., 351 n.54.
32. Ibid., 331.
33. Beck, *Joyce's Dubliners*, 25.
34. For more traditional treatments of epiphany in addition to those already cited, see Zach Bowen, "Joyce and the Epiphany Concept: A New Approach," *Journal of Modern Literature* 9.1 (1981–2): 103–14; Harry Levin, *James Joyce: A Critical Introduction* (Norfolk: New Directions, 1960); William York Tindall, *A Reader's Guide to James Joyce* (New York: Farrar, Straus & Giroux, 1969); Florence L. Walzl, "The Liturgy of the Epiphany Season and the Epiphanies of Joyce," *PMLA* 80.4 (Sept. 1965): 436–50.
35. Dettmar argues that an entire critical tradition has worn "rose-colored glasses, the result inevitably being rose-colored glosses." *Dubliners* catches its readers as they project their own narrative desires or "*misty*readings," on the text and "implicates us in the deadly work of paralysis, and reveals to us our own paralysis." See Dettmar, *The Illicit Joyce of Postmodernism*, 100, 104, emphasis in original.
36. Ibid., 104.
37. Norris writes, "The question is whether the closing self-allegorization indeed constitutes an epiphany—a moment of illuminated enlightenment or the transcendent self-recognition we call *anagnorisis*. Or does the parabolic gesture in the story enfold other philosophical maneuvers that offer knowledge and insight as reversible or retractable: an ocular voyeurism that turns upon itself as a 'gaze' and recognizes its own quest for self-knowledge as merely another species of narcissism?" Norris, *Suspicious Readings of Joyce's Dubliners*, 46.
38. Dettmar, *The Illicit Joyce of Postmodernism*, 92, emphasis in original.
39. Bloch warns, "Every mortal danger belongs to it and every individual death, the millions of young people who fell in the World Wars belong to it and the pervasive imbecility which has learnt nothing from them" (194).
40. Paul K. Saint-Amour and Karen R. Lawrence, "Reopening 'A Painful Case,'" in *Collaborative Dubliners: Joyce in Dialogue*, ed. Vicki Mahaffey (Syracuse: Syracuse University Press, 2012), 260.
41. One of Bloch's key claims in the face of political inertia, regression, or paralysis is that there is enough hope present in daily life right now to change the world for the better. The problem is that hope, when misdirected and channeled into unproductive, regressive, or self-destructive wishes, prevents either political or spiritual remediation. Joyce's stories operate through a similar insight.

42 Bernard Benstock, *Narrative Con/Texts in Dubliners* (Urbana: University of Illinois Press, 1994), 3. The other keywords italicized on the first page of *Dubliners*, of course, are *paralysis* and *gnomon* (D 3.10, 3.11).
43 R. Brandon Kershner and Mary Lowe-Evans, "'Grace': Spirited Discourses," in *Collaborative Dubliners: Joyce in Dialogue*, ed. Vicki Mahaffey (Syracuse: Syracuse University Press, 2012), 326.
44 Vicki Mahaffey, "*Dubliners*: Surprised by Chance," in *A Companion to James Joyce*, ed. Richard Brown (Malden, MA: Wiley-Blackwell, 2011), 22.
45 See ibid.
46 It is farthest from my intention to reduce *Dubliners* to a structuralist system at this point; rather, the semiotic square helps to visualize a set of elastic possibilities that my argument has been trying to draw out in the stories.
47 Kenner writes, "a thematic statement of hopeless paralysis is the first sentence in the book." "There was no hope for him this time," is, of course, the line in question (D 3.1). See Kenner, *Dublin's Joyce*, 51.
48 On the semiotic square, see Algirdas Julien Greimas, "The Interaction of Semiotic Constraints," in *On Meaning: Selected Writings in Semiotic Theory*, trans. Paul J. Perron and Frank H. Collins (Minneapolis: University of Minnesota Press, 1987), 48–62.
49 Fredric Jameson, *Archaeologies of the Future: The Desire Called Utopia and Other Science Fictions* (New York: Verso, 2005), 180.
50 For the latter, see especially, Frank Shovlin, *Journey Westward: Joyce, Dubliners and the Literary Revival* (Liverpool: Liverpool University Press, 2012).
51 Jameson writes that throughout his discussion of utopia, "we have been plagued by the perpetual reversion of difference and otherness into the same, and the discovery that our most energetic imaginative leaps into radical alternatives were little more than the projections of our own social moment and historical or subjective situation," Jameson, *Archaeologies of the Future*, 211.

2

The Future of *A Portrait of the Artist as a Young Man:* The *Künstlerroman* and Hope

Joyce's *A Portrait of the Artist as a Young Man* generates a number of questions about the future, as any good *Bildungsroman* and *Künstlerroman* should do. These genres, which depict, respectively, the way in which a young hero is educated, matures, and assimilates into his or her society, and the way in which a nascent artist is formed, cause readers to wonder about the fate of the budding aspirant in whom they have become invested. Among the many other coordinates that the novel interests readers in tracking is whether Stephen Dedalus will fail or succeed as an artist. Can or will he mature into the kind of artist capable of writing a book like *A Portrait*? Can or will he forge an art capable of affecting the Irish "racial" conscience or the nationalist politics of Ireland? This chapter aims to capture some of the future effects that are the consequence of the way in which *A Portrait* manipulates the artist novel genre.

The twentieth century's most exhaustive theorist of hope and future, Ernst Bloch can help to access some of these future effects. Bloch offers a refined mode of detecting political hopes in daily life and practices and of incorporating such hopes, as well as the possibilities they give rise to, into our picture of past and present reality. Under Bloch's gaze the world comes to seem drenched in wishful images and hopes that, however misdirected or misrecognized at present, are nonetheless politically vital to the calculation of possible futures. At the end of his encyclopedic *The Principle of Hope*, Bloch concludes, "man everywhere is still living in prehistory, indeed all and everything still stands before the creation of the world, of a right world."[1] One justification for this extraordinary view is Bloch's conviction that descriptions of reality that omit real possibility (things that *could* happen, however remote or unlikely they seem) are incomplete. Accordingly he writes, "*Concrete utopia stands on the horizon of every reality; real possibility surrounds the open dialectical tendencies and latencies to the very last.*"[2] Fredric Jameson captures Bloch's vision in this way: "little by little wherever we look everything in the world becomes ... a manifestation of that primordial movement toward the future and toward ... Utopia, and whose vital presence, behind whatever distortions, beneath whatever layers of repression, may always be detected, no matter how faintly, by the instruments and apparatus of hope itself."[3] It is to just such a hopeful gaze that *A Portrait* responds.

Bloch's concept of hope and his analysis of the artist novel and detective novel genres help to access the precise future qualities of *A Portrait*. In a set of paired essays written in the early 1960s—"A Philosophical View of the Detective Novel [*Detektivromans*]" and "A Philosophical View of the Novel of the Artist [*Künstlerromans*]"—Bloch views the genres of the detective novel and the artist novel as essentially opposed. The detective novel, according to Bloch, has an Oedipal form, modeled on Oedipus's encounter with the Sphinx in Sophocles; detective fiction begins with an enigma rooted in the past—what Bloch calls "the darkness at the beginning"[4]—and the role of the detective (and thus the desire of the reader) is to shine a light on the past, bringing it into ever more perfect recollection until the true nature of the crime is revealed. Detective fiction is a fundamentally anamnestic genre, concerned above all with the recollection of the past and modeled upon the way in which the tragic past of Oedipus is eventually remembered and its consequences made manifest.[5]

The novel of the artist, by contrast, interests readers in a creative person who longs to bring something new into the world, which Bloch calls a "*portrayal of the desire to articulate that which has never yet been heard in Apollo.*"[6] For Bloch, the *Künstlerroman* fundamentally "requires recognition of and interest in the creative person who brings out something new instead of something past."[7] In this way the novel of the artist invests readers in the production of the yet-unseen masterwork that the aspiring artist seeks to create. Bloch writes, "The detective story depends on penetrating and digging up material, while the inventive story depends on revealing and shaping it in the not-yet and out of the not-yet that arises before us as that of the work."[8] Because it leads readers to anticipate and even to welcome the new and the not-yet, the artist novel is organized prospectively where detective fiction is oriented retrospectively.

But while the *Künstlerroman* may give readers a *desire* for the new masterpiece, it cannot quite satisfy them with the new masterpiece *itself*, because the longed-for artwork cannot or at least does not typically appear within the *Künstlerroman* narrative. It is usually posited as the great but undefined artwork that the aspiring artist will go on to create in the future. Sometimes, as is potentially the case with *A Portrait*, the novel itself could stand as the culmination of the artist-hero's ambition and skill—if, that is, *A Portrait* could be interpreted as the fine artwork that Stephen Dedalus will go on to write—but even in such cases the fictional artwork itself cannot be said to reside *within* the *Künstlerroman* narrative, and the longed-for work may still inhabit that wishful space between the character-artist's will and desire and the author's product. It is almost inevitable that precisely on the ground where readers are conditioned by the generic conventions of the artist novel to train their hopes for the new that an open space will persist. As Jameson puts it, "this emptiness of the work within the work, this blank canvas at the center, is [for Bloch] the very locus of the not-yet-existent itself."[9] As readers await the artist's masterpiece, the *Künstlerroman* transmits to them the impulse to "make it new," to break from the past. But because this desired artwork cannot appear within the novel *about* the artist and also is not exactly identical to the novel itself, readers return from the world of fiction with a distinct sense of what Bloch calls the not-yet,[10] with what we might call an undischarged longing for the new. For Bloch, there are utopian implications that issue from this feature of the *Künstlerroman*. Having brought readers to anticipate and to value the not-yet, the *Künstlerroman* is fundamentally a genre of hope. It is especially important to Bloch because it is a genre preoccupied with the ontological openness of the future, the future that tends to arrive in forms we cannot exactly anticipate.

In an early section of *The Principle of Hope*, Bloch catalogs the character of wishes that typify various stages of human development. The "little daydreams" that Bloch attributes to children, adolescents, and young adults often mirror the wishes and daydreams of Stephen Dedalus, and the resemblance suggests the extent to which hope motivates Stephen and propels the narrative. Bloch especially attributes many creative and artistic wishful impulses to youth. These youthful hopes and wishes would doubtless sound some familiar chords in readers of *A Portrait*.[11] One of them seems particularly resonant for Stephen, who as a nascent artist can theorize at length about art, but as yet can produce only a modest villanelle. Bloch argues that at this age art is always easier to talk about than to achieve: "Adolescents of this kind know the feeling of a fire burning inside them, of art being close, but when they try to grasp its being, it becomes dry, it shrinks so much that they cannot even fill a page. Talking at this time is common and easy, writing hard."[12]

For Bloch, however, none of Stephen's daydreams and wish images of childhood, adolescence, and young adulthood would be particularly exceptional. On the contrary, he sees such wishes as typical of immature bourgeois youth.[13] But if these wishes are typical of bourgeois youth, then the wishes that are characteristic of bourgeois adulthood and middle age, according to Bloch, are especially impoverished, revolving almost exclusively around sex and money. He writes, "wishing does not decrease later on, only what is wished for diminishes."[14] Along with these wishes for sex and money come regrets about the past, missed financial or sexual opportunities, and sometimes a desire for revenge: more Simon Dedalus than Stephen. Bloch's point is to show how each stage of life is saturated with hope, but that in their bourgeois forms, hope is directed into selfish and sometimes destructive pursuits. The remedy is to recognize the constant current of hope that charges virtually every moment of human life and to direct it toward creating a better world rather than reproducing the bourgeois world and its desiccated or catastrophic pursuits. Reading his encyclopedic *The Principle of Hope*, in which (to modify the narrator of "Araby") wishful images accompany one into even those places most hostile to hope, one is impressed with two thoughts: first, that hope is the most abundant and most decisively future-oriented, or "expectant" emotion; and, second, that it is tragically, even catastrophically narrowed and misdirected under capitalism. It is therefore precisely within the impoverished hope-worlds of middle-class readers that the *Künstlerroman* form has an important role to play. Bloch writes, "Instead of the so-called higher echelons of society, the life of the artist seems to be more attractive—the successful artist and accordingly his novel of the artist."[15] In spite of Stephen's callowness, his anxiety, and his mistakes, the important fact is that—unlike his friends, who mostly choose among the (admittedly meager) options available to them for aspiring to bourgeois success—civil and colonial service, medical school, and so on—Stephen is represented on the cusp of maturity with wishes for a better world still intact, and this hope that diverges from the bourgeois wishes of middle age helps to characterize the cultural and political work that the artist novel can do, as well, perhaps, as the genre's enduring appeal to bourgeois readers.

But *A Portrait* is not an entirely conventional *Künstlerroman*, for at least two reasons. First, the question of the future in Joyce's artist novel is complicated by Joyce's reprisal of Stephen in *Ulysses*. Robert Scholes represents the approach of many subsequent critics when he argues, "If the Stephen in *Ulysses* is the same person as the Stephen in *A Portrait*—and there seems to be no question about this—then we must consider *Ulysses* in interpreting *Portrait*."[16] More recently, Gregory Castle refers to *Ulysses* as *A Portrait*'s "dangerous supplement,"[17] a poststructuralist term that evokes the curious situation in which something that is ostensibly whole and self-sufficient nonetheless seems to require completion by something external to it. However different *A Portrait* and *Ulysses* are as novels, and however greatly their narrative ambitions and intentions may vary, the two have become almost inexorably hermeneutically linked. This makes *A Portrait*'s relation to the future quite different from artist novels whose heroes walk off into eternity at the end, long before they ever have a chance to do so on Sandymount strand.[18]

On the one hand, the routine frequency with which critics turn to *Ulysses* in order to answer specific questions raised by *A Portrait* only substantiates the extent to which the idea of the future is somehow central to *A Portrait*. Yet, on the other hand, as sensible as Scholes's claim that critics must consider *Ulysses* when interpreting *A Portrait* is, unreflective or automatic recourse to *Ulysses* can distort interpretations of *A Portrait*. The simplest reason for this, it seems to me, has to do with genre: *A Portrait* is primarily a *Künstlerroman* and *Ulysses*, whatever it may be, is primarily not one. We can see some of this generic distortion in Hugh Kenner's criticism when he makes what he calls "the crushing ironies of *Ulysses*"[19] central to his influential reading of Stephen in *A Portrait* as an unwitting "victim being prepared for a sacrifice."[20] Even were we to agree with Kenner that *Ulysses* is a book of crushing ironies, it still seems unfitting to apply those ironies to *A Portrait*, which remains to the last open toward the future: "Welcome, O life! I go to encounter for the millionth time the reality of experience and to forge in the smithy of my soul the uncreated conscience of my race" (*P* 224.2788–90). While there is certainly a repeating structural pattern in the novel of highs followed by lows, and while we can recognize many features of Stephen's national, cultural, and personal worlds that seem likely to inhibit his artistic ambition, nothing in *A Portrait* proper necessarily crushes the ontological openness of the future, its real possibility.

Now, it is true that Joyce seems first to have conceived of *Ulysses* as an extension of the loosely autobiographical story that he was telling in *Stephen Hero* and in what later became *A Portrait*. As he wrote to Ezra Pound in 1915, "[*Ulysses*] is a continuation of *A Portrait of the Artist as a Young Man* after three years' interval."[21] A late fragment from the manuscript of *A Portrait*, referred to as the "Doherty fragment," after the name given there to Buck Mulligan's precursor, seems to show that Joyce once considered ending *A Portrait* with Stephen leaving Ireland as a result of the Martello tower quarrel, which, of course, he later used as the starting point for *Ulysses*.[22] The genesis of *Ulysses* is thus fully imbricated with Joyce's composition of *A Portrait*, which is consistent with Joyce's habit, as A. Walton Litz describes it, in which "Phrases, characters, and long passages are deleted from one manuscript only to appear later in a different context."[23] This general compositional practice, the narrative and temporal continuity between *A Portrait* and *Ulysses*, and Joyce's specific reworking of the Doherty fragment make it reasonable to say that *Ulysses* is a kind of "sequel" to *A Portrait*, at least according to the conventional definition of the term: "a literary work that, although complete in itself, forms a continuation of a preceding one" (*OED*). But the inadequacy of the word "sequel" only helps to show that the distortion cuts both ways: to define *Ulysses* as a "continuation" of *A Portrait* is to make one of the most comical understatements available to literary history; it is to underestimate radically the ambitions and means of a novel that might have begun as a continuation of *A Portrait*, but which then grew to epic proportions. We could even say that *Ulysses* challenges the limits of the concept of a sequel because, although it in part continues a preceding story, its method and purpose of telling differ so dramatically from the preceding story as to render the two more than a little alien from each other.

Even if *Ulysses* were *a* sequel, it is far from *the* sequel to *A Portrait*. In other words, the present represented in *Ulysses* is not and could not be exactly identical to the future as it is *posited* by *A Portrait*. It is not that the two take place in slightly different fictional worlds, although that may well be true, but rather because as a *Künstlerroman A Portrait* necessarily has a generic commitment to the future of a kind that the epic *Ulysses* need not have. Specifically, to too quickly swallow the supplement of *Ulysses* is to deny the hopeful and even hopefully utopian work that *A Portrait* does through the ways in which it negotiates the generic form of the artist novel. As a *Künstlerroman A Portrait* naturally has a number of future effects, some of which may have been obscured because of the "accident" of Stephen's later appearance in *Ulysses*, but which the later novel, however it represents Stephen, cannot retrospectively negate.

If the first reason that *A Portrait* departs from the conventional *Künstlerroman* has to do with the future represented by *Ulysses*, then the second reason involves *A Portrait*'s relationship to the past, in the form of its obsession with origins. Joyce's pattern of charting present progress and forward growth as they are enmeshed with origins dates back at least as far as the work to which *A Portrait* is itself a kind of "sequel": Joyce's 1904 essay, "A Portrait of the Artist." There Joyce wrote, "the past assuredly implies a fluid succession of presents, the development of an entity of which our actual present is a phase only."[24] The past mediates the succession of presents and also determines the trajectory or curve of the subject's future course. However, in that essay Joyce also acknowledges that the earliest past has a mysterious or perhaps inaccessible quality, because the portrait itself can only start after the subject has achieved "use of reason."[25] Similarly, we might say that one of the defining aspects of *A Portrait* is that there is a curious "darkness at the beginning" of this novel of the not-yet. Bloch argues that the detective and artist genres are essentially opposed, yet one of the most distinctive features of *A Portrait* is the strange way that it smuggles the detective form and its orientation toward obscure origins into the artist novel. At the risk of oversimplifying, for schematic purposes I am going to associate *A Portrait*'s not-yet with the green rose that Stephen imagines during his sums lesson—"But you could not have a green rose. But perhaps somewhere in the world you could" (*P* 10.197–8)—and associate the "darkness at the beginning" with the word, *Fœtus*, which Stephen finds carved into a desk of the anatomy theater in Cork when he searches for his father's initials—"A vision of their life, which his father's words had been powerless to evoke, sprang up before him out of the word cut in the desk" (78.1053–5).

Each image marks a horizon or a vanishing point, but one looks forward to the not-yet and the other looks backward to the darkness at the beginning.

Maud Ellmann notes that when Stephen searches the desks in the Queen's College anatomy theater for his father's initials—the father's phallic signature—he discovers instead the carved *Fœtus*—the mother's umbilical scar. She writes, "Both the timing and the meaning of the word suggest the *Fœtus* represents the navel of the novel: the founding scar that marks the primordial attachment of the fetus to the mother."[26] The *Fœtus* scene is one that looks back to Stephen's origins, both paternal and maternal. Yet it remains a puzzle; the word itself is a Sphinx whose riddle could only be unraveled by a return to the source, to the darkness at the beginning. But to unravel the navel would be to reopen the maternal scar that marks the end of umbilical attachment between the mother and child and the beginning of individual identity itself. Because, as Ellmann argues, the navel, "is the central plughole through which language and identity go down the drain,"[27] we cannot unravel the *Fœtus* back to a point of origin. *Fœtus* is therefore the best image in the novel for a kind of endless anxiety about identity and origins, an anxiety that makes it on some level impossible *not* to read Joyce's artist novel as detective fiction.

So *A Portrait* defies Bloch's definition of the detective novel as fundamentally anamnestic and the *Künstlerroman* as primarily oriented toward the future to the extent that it can be read as though it were a detective novel, under the mark of the *Fœtus,* as readily as it can be read as an artist novel, under the name of the green rose.[28] Many of the most enduring debates about *A Portrait* have tended to locate critical interest in the past of the narration rather than in the novel's orientation toward the future. For instance, the intractably enduring problem of assessing the relationship between author and character, narrator and protagonist—what Mark Wollaeger calls the "irony crux"[29]—turns the critic into a detective for a crime in the past that can only be described as the author's ambivalence toward the hero. The clues by which the critic-detective attempts to determine the precise quality of the Sphinx-like author's ambivalence are read in the act of writing, the growing or narrowing gulf of ironic distance, and in the narrative texture itself. In this case, what Bloch calls "that 'X' that precedes the beginning"[30] in detective fiction is Joyce's attitude toward Stephen prior to or during his act or acts of writing. This becomes *A Portrait*'s primordial and immemorial element, its original sin and fall from grace. No reading emblematizes this orientation toward the clues of the past more than Kenner's bravura act of literary detection that shines a critical light on the darkness of the novel's beginning, arguing that *A Portrait*'s "first two pages ... enact the entire action in microcosm."[31] If, as Bloch writes, "every last investigation of origins is related to the Oedipal form, which treats the incognito basically not just as an unknown of the logical variety, but also as something uncanny, unknown even to itself,"[32] then Kenner's reading is an investigative reaction *par excellence* to the novel's darkness before the event and to its uncanny origins.

Not surprisingly, the novel has also invited psychoanalytical readings that tend to be persistently anamnestic, viewing Stephen's early Oedipal coordinates as determinant of his subsequent course. Typically, the movement of the novel is described as a series of compulsive and neurotic repetitions and returns to Oedipal origins, a preoccupation that tends to obscure or even to discount *A Portrait*'s movement toward the new and the unknown.[33] Indeed, psychoanalytical critics often, though not always, regard the new with knowing pessimism or even cynicism.[34]

The novel has also invited critical detection of Stephen's development, which diagnoses the roots of his inadequacies, failures, or his lack of understanding. These critics are often pessimistic about Stephen's potential, although some find cause for cautious optimism.[35] Diagnostic interpretations are, of course, central to the *Bildungsroman* genre because they involve questions of education and learning. Moreover, the novel's ambiguity about Stephen as artist allows for and even demands that the novel be read as detective fiction, to trace the roots of potential failure. The artist novel genre has a tradition of depicting those who fail to become artists, though this is generally unambiguous. As Bloch comments: many are called, but few are chosen.[36] The difficulty is that we cannot quite tell if this is the case for Stephen, so we scrutinize his roots all the more carefully. At the same time, interpretations that see Stephen's many shortcomings as definitive evidence of his permanent failure to become an artist deplete the *Künstlerroman*'s native stock of hope that Joyce's narrative relies on. If anxiety may be seen as the dominant anticipatory emotion of the detective form—the crime committed in the past becomes the anxious exigency of the present, from the ground of which the detective seeks its future revelation and resolution—then we can characterize readings of *A Portrait* in the mold of detective fiction as practicing a hermeneutic of anxiety. We might also conclude that one of the distinctive features of Joyce's *Künstlerroman* is that it invites and to some extent relies upon this kind of anxiety.

But as much as *A Portrait* has elicited interest in the "darkness at the beginning," it has also produced readings that evoke and evaluate specific hopes for the future that are aligned with the *Künstlerroman*'s not-yet and with Stephen's green rose. At the beginning of the novel, Stephen sings, "*O, the geen wothe botheth*" (P 5.12), which is his childish conflation of, "*O, the wild rose blossoms / On the little green place*" (5.9–10). In this, Stephen's first artistic transfiguration, accidental as it might be, he begins to bring a new thing—a green rose—into existence just as the novel begins. The green rose has a range of meanings, all of which attach to hopes about the future. Most obviously, the green rose signifies Stephen's desire to be an artist and to create something that the world has not seen before: "I desire to press in my arms the loveliness which has not yet come into the world" (222.2726–7), he says. The green rose is the not-yet of artistic genesis.[37]

Many critics find something genuine in Stephen's intention to forge the conscience of the Irish race in not just hopeful but even potentially utopian ways. For Marian Eide, sexual and moral freedom are inseparable from Joyce's nationalism, and she argues that Joyce intends "to reconcile physical and intellectual creation," an arch-utopian goal if there ever was one.[38] Emer Nolan argues that *A Portrait* is invested in "the creation of the ideal national community, in a projected future and a collective freedom."[39] Pericles Lewis sees Stephen as striving for "moral unity" with the conscience of his race, arguing that "Joyce's narrative technique seems to offer some hope that Stephen will succeed in achieving this mystical union."[40] Vincent Cheng goes even further by viewing the potentiality contained in Stephen's image of the "green rose" not just as representing Irish independence, but specifically "Irish nationhood within the world community," aligning Joyce's values not entirely with those of Stephen but also with the internationalist and utopian values of MacCann.[41]

But what Bloch can really teach us in this case is that all of these readings of the green rose, while true, are also finally *too* determinant, that they limit our comprehension of the political potential of the novel through their determinacy. Just as critics cannot be satisfied with *A Portrait* as a detective novel that leads backward into the darkness of the *Fœtus*, so is it inadequate to follow the sign of the green rose to interpretations that find a point of *fixed* hope the desire for which the novel organizes. And just as the *Fœtus* attaches to specific parental and Oedipal anxieties but also signifies, in an inexhaustible manner, a generalized and perhaps insoluble anxiety rooted in and pertaining to the past, so does the green rose exceed the specific hopes to which it can attach by signifying a generalized hopefulness and a genuine openness to the future. It is in this free-floating openness and hopefulness that *A Portrait of the Artist as a Young Man* assumes its most political and utopian dimension.

Because it would be too simple to say that it merely *symbolizes* Stephen's personal freedom or Ireland's political freedom, let us posit that this green rose represents an elusive kind of freedom yet unknown in the world. Even more, let us say that Joyce's green rose *allegorizes* freedom (in Benjamin's transitory sense of allegory in contrast to what Bloch calls the symbol's "*Unitas of one sense*")[42] across a shifting array of senses, from artistic to national to international, but especially in this final sense: absolute and unalienated freedom. One way of articulating this imaginary and utopian state would be as the young Karl Marx did, locating such freedom in nothing short of "the *genuine* resolution of the conflict between man and nature and between man and man."[43] Like the green rose, this freedom has never existed in the world, but through the new artwork that the novel posits but cannot produce, Joyce's *Künstlerroman* makes its audience desire precisely that which has never yet been seen or known: the highest good.

Notoriously, the future does not always arrive in the forms that we can anticipate. The future is more radically open to possibility than any of the specific questions that emerge from *A Portrait* can account for. Yet this openness to possibilities that cannot be named in advance is a crucial component of the *Künstlerroman*, whose central generic investment in the Not-Yet-Conscious—which Bloch defines as "the psychological birthplace of the New"[44]—has not yet sufficiently found articulation within political criticism of Joyce's novel. Bloch helps to reconceive the revolutionary quality of *A Portrait* as fundamentally open to the future, but not always to a specific future and not always in forms that we can easily hope for or even ask about. For example, Stephen's decision to reject the priesthood is followed by his epiphanic vision of the bird-girl, which confirms for Stephen his vocation as artist. Both of these scenes have generated enormous critical attention, and for good reason: they are major turning points in the way in which Stephen imagines potential concrete futures for himself. His visions of religious and artistic futures guide the decisions he makes in the present and these decisions will have much to do with the succession of events in the future. There are, however, less concrete but no less important ways in which *A Portrait* is oriented toward the future.

A good example of undefined openness and hope occurs precisely in the connective tissue between Stephen's rejection of the priesthood and his artistic epiphany in the next section. The end of the priesthood section comes at a special point in the novel because Stephen has rejected a religious career but has not yet embraced an artistic one. Stephen is open to the future, but he does not yet have a specific future in mind. The section culminates with a scene in which Stephen and his siblings, on the verge of yet another change of address because of the family's descent into poverty, sing Thomas Moore's "Oft in the Stilly Night" together. Stephen recognizes the weariness in the voices of his young brothers and sisters, having already begun to be ground down by poverty, yet their voices also remind him of Newman, who found in the weariness of children an accompanying hope. This little scene tells us something, but it is not something that we have necessarily been trained to want to know: the family singing scene has generated little critical attention, probably because it falls right between two of Stephen's most weighty concrete decisions about his future. It does not seem to say anything at all about the specific questions about the future that the novel poses, or at least it seems to speak to these specific questions with so much less muscle than other celebrated passages that it is usually confidently overlooked. However, the scene could be an emblem of the tough and sinewy sort of hope-stuff that comprises and holds the scenes of *A Portrait* together as it ambles toward specific futures with a generally wishful sense of futurity. We should look closely at this connective wishful tissue to see what it can yield for a generic reading of Joyce's novel.

Coming after Stephen rejects the priesthood but before he embraces a vocation as an artist, the family singing passage evokes hope before it becomes channeled into a specific hope, whether about the artist, the nation, the Irish people, or even about the family's most pressing financial troubles. Just after one of Stephen's sisters reveals that the landlord is on the verge of putting the family out, the song begins:

> The voice of his youngest brother from the farther side of the fireplace began to sing the air *Oft in the Stilly Night*. One by one the others took up the air until a full choir of voices was singing. They would sing so for hours, melody after melody, glee after glee, till the last pale light died down on the horizon, till the first dark nightclouds came forth and night fell. (P 143.586-91)

Moore's "Oft in the Stilly Night" is an appropriately crepuscular choice of song for the hour of the day. Moore's sleepless, solitary speaker reflects sadly on better days and departed friends, and he likens himself to the only person remaining in a deserted banquet hall. The air's yearning for better days chimes with the happier and more affluent past of the declining Dedalus family. But the song also presents several ironic or even comic contrasts to the setting. The siblings are too young for all their friends to have died, and far from being sole survivors, they are instead represented as part of a family choir, one tightly knit enough to sing for hours together and to speak in a distinctively jokey family vernacular ("Goneboro toboro lookboro atboro aboro houseboro" (143.576)) that further suggests their close community. Even if the siblings are unfortunately experienced enough to be able to look back on more secure and prosperous times, the fact that it is the youngest brother who takes up the song only heightens the contrast between the song's strong nostalgia and the scanty store of years available to the children as fodder for wistful recollection.

Stephen notices the painful contrast between youth and fatigue in "the overtone of weariness behind their frail fresh innocent voices" (143.593-4), but he dwells less on the past and more on what his siblings' singing voices signal about their attitude toward the future: "Even before they set out on life's journey they seemed weary already of the way" (143.595-6). This idea leads Stephen to further meditation:

> He heard the choir of voices in the kitchen echoed and multiplied through an endless reverberation of the choirs of endless generations of children: and heard in all the echoes an echo also of the recurring note of weariness and pain. All seemed weary of life even before entering upon it. And he remembered that Newman had heard this note also in the broken lines of Virgil *giving utterance, like the voice of Nature herself, to that pain and weariness yet hope of better things which has been the experience of her children in every time.* (143.597-605, emphasis in original)

Stephen's instinct to abstract and universalize his siblings' voices ("the choirs of endless generations of children") may deny to them some of the particularities of their situation, but the abstracting move also enables him, through John Henry Newman, to identify and articulate the hope of better things to come that Stephen also recognizes in their song alongside their anxiety about the future. The passage from Newman's *An Essay in the Aid of a Grammar of Assent* that Stephen remembers (more or less accurately) comes as part of a series of examples that Newman gives of what he calls "real assent" to, or belief in, given propositions. In this example, Newman imagines a young boy who, learning Horace or Homer, may initially be unable to distinguish their verses from those of any number of merely clever writers. Real assent to or faith in the propositions contained in the passages of classic authors eludes the inexperienced boy, but it comes later to the more experienced adult: "at length [these passages] come home to him, when long years have passed, and he has had experience of life, and pierce him, as if he had never before known them, with their sad earnestness and vivid exactness."[45]

The Newman comparison suggests that Stephen believes that his siblings will come to understand the sad and nostalgic verses of Moore only after gathering more experience of life, yet their past and present experiences of poverty and hunger already help them to intuit the weariness of life's journey to come, even if they cannot yet experience real assent to Moore's propositions about the passage of time, vanished youth, lost love, and dead friends. Yet Stephen, too, is still a young man, as the title of the novel emphasizes, and as Joyce emphasized to Frank Budgen.[46] Much of what his comparison to Newman implies about the limited experience and intuition of his siblings applies equally well to Stephen. Moreover, the prospective weariness that Stephen attributes to his siblings and that readers may attribute to Stephen is inseparable from hope: children may regard the journey of life to come with reluctance and weariness when they encounter verses like those of Moore that spell out the perhaps inevitable losses to come, yet because by definition these children lack the experience that could confirm Moore's melancholy in the form of real assent, there is an inescapable anticipatory character in their singing that also leaves a space for hope. The weariness about what is to come combines with inexperience to create a strange formula for hope.

Just prior to the family singing scene is another emblematic wishful image, also a musical one. As Stephen's conversation with the priest about a potential vocation ends, "a quartet of young men" passes, singing: "The music passed in an instant, as the first bars of sudden music always did, over the fantastic fabrics of his mind, dissolving them painlessly and noiselessly as a sudden wave dissolves the sandbuilt turrets of children" (*P* 140.469–72). The image of music dissolving the fabrics of his mind just as a wave dissolves children's sandcastles looks back to the novel's nadir of hopelessness: Father Arnall's description of the eternal spiritual pains of Hell. In Father Arnall's punishing and hopeless vision of Hell a little bird carries away one grain of sand every million years, and even after it shuttles away the entire mountain, and then mountain after mountain, "eternity would have scarcely begun" (115.1087). Yet here the quartet's song seems to wash away in a single wave the sand that in Father Arnall's Hell would have had to be removed grain by grain for eternity. The sudden wave that music creates in Stephen's mind is an image of artistic abundance or surplus. It is an antidote to hopelessness. Perhaps to say that Joyce's writing strives toward the condition of music is not so much to claim that it aspires toward a musical rhythm or tone, although it is often incredibly musical in these ways, but rather that it seeks to share in what Bloch hears in music: the surplus of hope-material that points toward the future without naming a specific future.[47] *A Portrait*'s moments of definitive futurity are actually the exception; wishful tissue of this kind is the rule.

Joyce's images of real possibility, of the openness of the future, and of its movement toward a utopian resolution of conflict and genuine freedom—especially in the wishful tissue of the novel—constitute an overlooked political function of *A Portrait*. It is not only through its representations of hope, but also through its variegated impulses toward the not-yet that the novel can transmit a political sense of openness to readers. At the same time, *A Portrait*'s distinctive alignment of the detective and artist novel genres works in such a way that the future horizon of the novel melts into the vanishing point of its obscure beginnings. Its openness to the future meets the novel's darkness at the beginning. Hope and anxiety are entwined, and it may be that part of what is enduring about the novel is the way in which the *Fœtus* gestates into the green rose and the green rose blooms into the *Fœtus* in a distinctively Joycean transformation of the kind that Fritz Senn and others have helped us to see organizing Joyce's metamorphic texts.[48]

How, finally, do the detective story elements that *A Portrait* exhibits distinguish Joyce's novel from other novels of the artist and how do they affect its political meaning? In order to answer, we need to redefine our understanding of the type of anxiety that circulates through *A Portrait*'s detective form. As we have seen, critics tend to define this anxiety in sexual and especially Oedipal terms. But here again Bloch can offer a useful modification. Unlike Freud, who sees the sexual drive as the root of anxiety, Bloch, following Marx, sees hunger in the context of the social environment as the foundation of anxiety, including "subsistence worries, economic despair, and existential anxiety."[49] Therefore things such as socioeconomic concerns, world wars, and fascism lie at the root of anxiety. Psychoanalytical readings that overlook the socioeconomic roots of anxiety misidentify the novel's Sphinx, whose riddle poses the problem not of sex but of hunger. Irish hunger has been well historicized, of course. For a person of Joyce's generation, the Famine, like the *Fœtus*, would have represented an irreducible anxiety that precedes even the ancient Oedipal dramas of individuation. The *Fœtus* may be a consequence of sex, but its only exigency is hunger. As we have seen, Bloch writes, "The stomach is the first lamp into which oil must be poured."[50] In *A Portrait*, the detective impulse leads finally to the digging out of the material conditions of hunger, which is as ever-present in the novel's connective tissue as its wishful content. Hunger is there at the beginning of the family singing scene, in the "latchless door" (*P* 142.558), in the "naked hallway" (142.559) of the Dedalus house, in the "second watered tea" (142.561), and in "the small glassjars and jampots which did service for teacups" (142.562-3). Hunger is especially present in the "turnover" that his siblings have just eaten, which is described as "ravaged" (142.567).

As a detective novel *A Portrait* uncovers a persistent socioeconomic anxiety that manifests itself in hunger and in other forms throughout the text, while as an artist novel it points toward a better future by investing readers in the creation of the new and by supporting this impulse by wishful images of real possibility woven into otherwise harsh and privative material reality. *A Portrait* therefore combines hope and anxiety, possibility and hunger, horizon and vanishing point, green rose and *Fœtus*, even dissolved sandcastle and ravaged turnover, in order to orient readers toward detecting and uncovering the material conditions of anxiety, but also, within those material conditions, to recognize real possibility and the ontological openness of the future. Joyce's artist novel is, to borrow two more phrases from Bloch, an "art for hope's sake,"[51] but it is always an "educated hope,"[52] a hope whose *Bildung* has been in hunger. As we have seen, sometimes Joyce's images evoke concrete possibilities, but more often they take the form of a wishful impulse toward a better future that can hardly be named in advance. Unlike what readers of *Ulysses* might suppose, the future of *A Portrait* cannot be known in advance. To read *A Portrait*, rather, is to keep awaiting the masterpiece it posits (not just the masterpieces that Joyce actually wrote), to remain attuned to its hopeful and anxious impulses, to feel its real possibilities and its irreducible socioeconomic anxieties, and to nurture its wishful images of determinate, indeterminate, and, at its most distant horizon, utopian futures.

Notes

1 Ernst Bloch, *The Principle of Hope*, 3 vols., trans. Neville Plaice, Stephen Plaice, and Paul Knight (Cambridge: MIT Press, 1986), 1375.
2 Ibid., 223, emphasis in original.
3 Fredric Jameson, *Marxism and Form* (Princeton, NJ: Princeton University Press, 1971), 120.
4 Ernst Bloch, "A Philosophical View of the Detective Novel," in *The Utopian Function of Art and Literature: Selected Essays*, trans. Jack Zipes and Frank Mecklenburg (Cambridge: MIT Press, 1988), 256.
5 For more on the way in which Bloch links Freudian psychoanalysis with anamnesis, see Bloch, *The Principle of Hope*, 51–113.
6 Ernst Bloch, "A Philosophical View of the Novel of the Artist," in *The Utopian Function of Art and Literature*, 274, emphasis in original.
7 Ibid., 267.
8 Ibid., 276.
9 Jameson, *Marxism and Form*, 132.
10 Perhaps even, "not yet, though venisoon after" (*FW* 3.10).
11 For instance, about children Bloch writes, "The hidden boy is also breaking out, in a shy way. He is searching for what is far away, even though he shuts himself in,

it is just that in breaking free he has girded himself round and round with walls," Bloch, *The Principle of Hope*, 23. About adolescents Bloch writes, "Even later on this combination of narrowness and beautiful foreign lands does not disappear. In other words: from this time the wishful land is an island," and "Around the thirteenth year, the fellow-travelling ego is discovered. That is the reason why dreams of a better life grow so luxuriantly around this time," (24). At the time of young adulthood, the nature of wishes begins to change: "Loneliness is no longer sought after and spun out in fantasies, but is intolerable, it is the most intolerable aspect of the life that begins at seventeen," and "The young person torments himself with the enjoyable prospect of this future, he wants to induce it all at once, even with storms, suffering, thunder and lightning, as long as it is just life, real life that has so far not yet become," (26, 27).

12 Ibid., 27.
13 Bloch even associates such dreams and dreamers with potentially catastrophic outcomes, such as a susceptibility to fascism:

> The often invoked streak of blue in the bourgeois sky became of course a streak of blood: the stupid or stupefied had their own strong man called Hitler. But the greyness of a young mediocrity has never shone without capricious figures; the wish itself puts them on his arm. At this time, between the March and June of life, there is not a break, either love fills it up, or the prospect of a kind of stormy dignity. (Bloch, *The Principle of Hope*, 29)

14 Ibid.
15 Bloch, "A Philosophical View of the Novel of the Artist," 265.
16 Robert Scholes, "Stephen Dedalus: Poet or Esthete?," in James Joyce, *A Portrait of the Artist as a Young Man: Text, Criticism, and Notes*, ed. Chester G. Anderson (New York: Viking Press, 1968), 468–9. Making a similar point, Wayne Booth claims that ironic readings of Stephen occurred to nobody at least until *Ulysses* was published. Wayne Booth, *The Rhetoric of Fiction* (Chicago: University of Chicago Press, 1961), 333.
17 Gregory Castle, "Coming of Age in the Age of Empire: Joyce's Modernist Bildungsroman," *James Joyce Quarterly* 50.1–2 (Fall 2012–Winter 2013), 379.
18 In *Ulysses*, Stephen wonders, "Am I walking into eternity along Sandymount strand?" (*U* 3.18–19).
19 Hugh Kenner, "The *Portrait* in Perspective," in *James Joyce's A Portrait of the Artist as a Young Man: A Casebook*, ed. Mark A. Wollaeger (New York: Oxford University Press, 2003), 39. Kenner also points out Joyce's comment to Frank Budgen that in *Ulysses* Stephen "has a shape that can't be changed." See Frank Budgen, *James Joyce and the Making of Ulysses, and Other Writings* (London: Oxford University Press, 1972), 107.

20 Kenner, "The *Portrait* in Perspective," 55. Kenner also understands *A Portrait* in relation to *Dubliners* in a manner that potentially distorts *A Portrait*, as when he argues that *A Portrait* is an extended *Dubliners* story of "paralysis, frustration, or a sorry, endlessly painful, coming to terms." See Kenner, "Joyce's *Portrait*—A Reconsideration," in James Joyce, *A Portrait of the Artist as a Young Man: Authoritative Text, Backgrounds and Contexts, Criticism*, ed. John Paul Riquelme (New York: W.W. Norton, 2007), 361.

21 Quoted in Richard Ellmann, *James Joyce*, New and Revised Edition (New York: Oxford University Press, 1982), 383.

22 This is BL Add MS 49975. The fragment appears with commentary in A. Walton Litz, *Method and Design in Ulysses and Finnegans Wake* (New York: Oxford University Press, 1964), 132–41, and in *The Workshop of Daedalus: James Joyce and the Raw Materials for A Portrait of the Artist as a Young Man*, ed. Robert Scholes and Richard M. Kain (Evanston, IL: Northwestern University Press, 1965), 106–8. Litz points to internal evidence to call the fragment a "late draft" and argues, "in the original plan of his autobiographical novel ... the Martello tower episode was intended to be the cause for Stephen's leaving Ireland" (136, 137). Similarly, Scholes and Kain comment, "Fragment 2 indicates that Joyce's intention in *A Portrait* was to have Stephen's departure into exile be the result of his expulsion from the Martello Tower by the Gogarty-figure called Doherty in this fragment and in the Pola notebook but Mulligan in *Ulysses*" (106).

23 Litz, *Method and Design*, 132.

24 Richard Ellmann, A. Walton Litz, and John Whittier Ferguson, eds., *James Joyce: Poems and Shorter Writings* (London: Faber & Faber 1991), 211.

25 Ibid.

26 Maud Ellmann, "The Name and the Scar: Identity in *The Odyssey* and *A Portrait of the Artist as a Young Man*," in *James Joyce's A Portrait of the Artist as a Young Man: A Casebook*, 169.

27 Ellmann, "The Name and the Scar," 172.

28 Lise Jaillant notes that in 1928 *A Portrait* was published in the Modern Library series contemporaneously with *Fourteen Great Detective Stories*. She writes, "Not only did the two books share a similar physical format, but they were displayed in the same way. Indeed, *Fourteen Great Detective Stories* was number 144 in the series, and *A Portrait*, number 145. As booksellers generally arranged Modern Library books by numbers on a special display rack," she continues, "most consumers would have encountered the two texts simultaneously," Lise Jaillant, "Blurring the Boundaries: *Fourteen Great Detective Stories* and Joyce's *A Portrait of the Artist as a Young Man* in the Modern Library Series," *James Joyce Quarterly* 50.3 (Spring 2013), 769.

29 Mark A. Wollaeger, "Introduction," in *James Joyce's A Portrait of the Artist as a Young Man: A Casebook*, 21.
30 Bloch, "A Philosophical View of the Detective Novel," 256.
31 Kenner, "The *Portrait* in Perspective," 33.
32 Bloch, "A Philosophical View of the Detective Novel," 260.
33 Chester G. Anderson exemplifies this approach in rhetorically dramatic fashion when he argues of the novel's hopeful ending, "Even if we had forgotten Stephen's castration fears, his phobias and fetishes, his paranoia, his morbid guilt feelings and obsessions, his homosexual wishes and strong desire to be female, his coprophilia and mild masochism, the rhetoric itself might help us guess that this manic crest will have its trough." While it is reasonable to guess that Stephen's hopeful road will be a long one because the chapters of the novel spell out an alternating pattern of elevation and deflation, and *Ulysses* could even be seen as the trough to come, Anderson's psychoanalytical coordinates deplete the obvious interest that the novel determinedly builds in what is to come in favor of the darkness of the unconscious past. Chester G. Anderson, "Baby Tuckoo: Joyce's 'Features of Infancy,'" in *Approaches to Joyce's Portrait: Ten Essays*, ed. Thomas F. Staley and Bernard Benstock (Pittsburgh, PA: University of Pittsburgh Press, 1976), 135.
34 Sheldon Brivic, for example, reads Stephen from a psychoanalytical perspective in which, even though the structure of the novel, like Stephen himself, is seen as compulsively repetitive, Stephen is yet able to recognize his repeating pattern as a preparation for changing it. Interestingly, Brivic argues that Stephen's intention "to re-form human consciousness by bringing a new awareness of the mind through self-exploration" is an idea that has not only spread since the novel was published but, by inspiring other writers, has even advanced human freedom "in a way that may be critical and lasting." Out of this largely anamnestic vision of the novel, then, emerges a distinct orientation toward the new and the future in the form of the novel's subsequent effects in the world. Sheldon Brivic, "The Disjunctive Structure of Joyce's *Portrait*," in James Joyce, *A Portrait of the Artist as a Young Man: Case Studies in Contemporary Criticism*, Second Edition, ed. R. Brandon Kershner (Boston, MA: Bedford/St. Martin's, 2006), 297.
35 For instance, Vicki Mahaffey argues, "although [Stephen] grandly says no to God in the tradition of Lucifer, he has not learned to say no to the phallic function, to experience and accept his own insufficiency and self-division," Vicki Mahaffey, "Père-version and Im-mère-sion: Idealized Corruption in *A Portrait of the Artist as a Young Man* and *The Picture of Dorian Gray*," *James Joyce Quarterly* 50.1–2 (Fall 2012–Winter 2013), 245. Other critics argue that Joyce intended for readers to diagnose the precise developmental hurdles that an ironically or satirically drawn Stephen must overcome before he can self-actualize as an artist or as a mature adult. For instance, Suzette Henke writes, "In a tone of gentle

mockery, Joyce makes clear to his audience that Stephen's fear of women and his contempt for sensuous life are among the many inhibitions that stifle this young man's creativity," Suzette Henke, *James Joyce and the Politics of Desire* (New York: Routledge, 1990), 84. Michael Levenson balances anamnesis with what Bloch would call the Not-Yet-Become when he argues that the burden of Joycean character is to "be all that it has been and all that it might become," Michael Levenson, "Stephen's Diary in Joyce's *Portrait*—The Shape of Life," *ELH* 52.4 (Winter 1985), 1034.

36 Bloch, "A Philosophical View of the Novel of the Artist," 270.
37 Stephen contrasts this prospective desire with Yeats's retrospective Michael Robartes, who "remembers forgotten beauty" and "presses in his arms the loveliness which has long faded from the world." Stephen's response to Yeats's anamnestic beauty is "Not this. Not at all" (*P* 222.2725–6). Critics have also noted that the green rose links Stephen to other creators. For instance, Kenner ominously associates the green rose with Daedalus who did violence to nature by trying to improve upon it, while Joseph Valente, through the "wild" rose blossoms and the characteristic green carnation, links the green rose to Oscar Wilde. See Kenner, "The *Portrait* in Perspective," 41 and Valente, "Thrilled by His Touch: The Aestheticizing of Homosexual Panic in *A Portrait of the Artist as a Young Man*," in *James Joyce's A Portrait of the Artist as a Young Man: A Casebook*, 251–2. Valente reads *A Portrait* according to the anxiety approach: "Instead of unfolding on the latency model, which neatly conforms with the linear, quasi-organic development typical of the *Künstlerroman*, Stephen's homoerotic affects emerge in a knot or fold known, in Freudian parlance, as a 'deferred action,' in this case the retroactive generation of a subsequently phobic desire" (252). Here I link the green rose to Wilde not to stress Stephen's anxiety but rather to emphasize the not-yet of artistic creation.
38 Marian Eide, "The Woman of the Ballyhoura Hills: James Joyce and the Politics of Creativity," *Twentieth-Century Literature* 44.4 (Winter 1998), 388, 390.
39 Emer Nolan, *James Joyce and Nationalism* (New York: Routledge, 1995), 47.
40 Pericles Lewis, "The Conscience of the Race: The Nation as Church of the Modern Age," in *Joyce through the Ages: A Nonlinear View*, ed. Michael Patrick Gillespie (Gainesville: University Press of Florida, 1999), 102.
41 Vincent Cheng, *Joyce, Race, and Empire* (Cambridge: Cambridge University Press, 1995), 72.
42 Bloch, *The Principle of Hope*, 176.
43 Karl Marx, "Private Property and Communism" section of "Economic and Philosophic Manuscripts of 1844," in *The Marx-Engels Reader*, ed. Robert C. Tucker (New York: W.W. Norton, 1978), 84, emphasis in original.
44 Bloch, *The Principle of Hope*, 116.

45 John Henry Newman, *An Essay in the Aid of a Grammar of Assent*, ed. I. T. Ker (Oxford: Clarendon Press, 1985), 56–7.
46 "Some people who read my book, *A Portrait of the Artist* forget that it is called *A Portrait of the Artist as a Young Man*," Frank Budgen, *James Joyce and the Making of Ulysses, and Other Writings* (London: Oxford University Press, 1972), 61.
47 Although music, like all art, is deeply conditioned by the dominant ideology, for Bloch there also inheres within artworks, but especially music, a certain amount of "*surplus over and above their mere ideology there and then*" that points over the horizon toward the utopian (Bloch, *The Principle of Hope*, 56–7, emphasis in original).
48 See, for instance, Fritz Senn, "Book of Many Turns," in *Ulysses: Fifty Years*, ed. Thomas F. Staley (Bloomington, IN: Indiana University Press, 1974), 29–46.
49 Bloch, *The Principle of Hope*, 84.
50 Ibid., 65.
51 "*l'art pour l'espoir*," ibid., 173.
52 "*docta spes*," ibid., 7.

3

A Humid Nightblue Dot: The Spatialization of Hope in *Ulysses*

Dubliners and *A Portrait of the Artist as a Young Man* represent models of hope and present visions of the future that are open to real possibility. As we have seen, in these earlier works Joyce represents the restless search for new and unexpected alternatives to the prevailing visions of the better world and utopia. This chapter demonstrates that in *Ulysses* Joyce develops a technique of spatializing hope that enables him to expand on these earlier representations while also scrutinizing hope from a variety of different, or parallactic, angles. In *Ulysses*, hope is no longer just a temporal and gradually unfolding phenomenon. Hope also becomes an image and a point in space that can be grasped at once in its forms of finitude and completion. To use terms from "Proteus," hope is no longer represented as only *Nacheinander* (one after another, or temporally), but also as *Nebeneinander* (side by side, or spatially) (*U* 3.13, 15). Although Joyce does not abandon his earlier practice of representing hope intimately and minutely as it unfolds in time, he also begins to telescope out to perspectives that alienate readers from the minutiae of characters' hopes. This more spatial, even astronomical and cosmic perspective on hope transforms all varieties of living hope into a species of dying wish: hopes whose limits and finitude have become all-too self-evident. From *Ulysses*' distanced and spatialized perspectives, hope is always as it appears on the deathbed: fragile, finite, and finally circumscribed. One result is that instead of merely observing the ways in which the characters' hopes and wishes unfold or are foiled in temporal succession, readers can also grasp these hopes as shapes and spaces. Just as Bloom and Stephen remember the dying wishes of their respective parent, *Ulysses* prompts readers to regard these spatialized hopes as a form of *remembrance*. While the spatial and cosmic perspective emphasizes the frailty and finitude of hope, it simultaneously suggests vast fields of hope and open futures that lie outside of the range of conventional hopes and visions of the better world. These open fields of hope put pressure on readings, most formidably posed by Fredric Jameson, that see *Ulysses* as too totalized in structure, too depersonalizing in narrative perspective, and too autonomous in style to be capable of imagining a future. Once we reconceive Joyce's experiments in structure, perspective, and style as innovations on the representation of hope, *Ulysses* becomes remarkable in its potential to think the future.

As in *A Portrait* and *Dubliners*, the future that *Ulysses* supposes is an open one. Unlike those earlier works, however, *Ulysses*' future comes less out of characters' hopes and more from the distance that it creates between readers and these hopes. While the emotional hopes of characters sustain the narratives of *A Portrait* and *Dubliners* and point to their open futures, in *Ulysses* it is a more distant, and consequently more open, spatial perspective on these hopes that finally offers a capacious sense of future.[1] In distinction from Joyce's practice in *Dubliners* and *A Portrait*, *Ulysses* breaks character off from the ability to calculate or imagine the future in ways that will only intensify in *Finnegans Wake*, where characters and their temporal hopes are all but reduced to exchangeable character-positions so that a wider sense of past, present, and future might emerge.

Hope in a Cosmic Perspective

In Homeric epic there are two basic narrative trajectories: the quest or voyage out, which characterizes the Greek's Trojan campaign, and the *nostos* or homecoming, which describes Odysseus' arduous return to Ithaca. We are highly accustomed to think of Joyce's *Ulysses* in terms of homecoming, but the cosmic scale of the "Ithaca" episode makes the novel something of a journey out as well, even a kind of space odyssey that runs all the way from 7 Eccles Street in Dublin to "The cold of interstellar space, thousands of degrees below freezing" (*U* 17.1246). *Ulysses*, particularly "Ithaca," gives both microscopic detail of human life and a larger cosmic perspective, as when Leopold Bloom, viewing "The heaventree of stars hung with humid nightblue fruit"

(17.1039) in his backyard with Stephen Dedalus, contemplates "the parallax or parallactic drift of socalled fixed stars, in reality evermoving wanderers from immeasurably remote eons to infinitely remote futures in comparison with which the years, threescore and ten, of allotted human life formed a parenthesis of infinitesimal brevity" (17.1052–6). If the seventy years of average human life form a parenthesis of infinitesimal brevity, this passage implicitly asks, to what could a single day such as June 16, 1904 amount, even if it is a day that Joyce has created and cataloged so minutely, carefully, and lovingly? Nor is this cosmic view in "Ithaca" the first appearance of a scale that dwarfs the individual life: the narrative experiments of the middle chapters of *Ulysses* have already prepared readers for a stance of dispassionate distance from the very characters whose thoughts, feelings, and experiences were rendered so immediately in the early episodes and then again in "Penelope." *Ulysses* is unrivaled in the way in which it combines intimate knowledge of characters with a boldly intrepid narrative perspective that ultimately regards these characters as cosmic stardust. Richard Kain makes a related point when he argues that the "Ithaca" episode projects June 16 "against the great backdrop of infinity."[2] Bloom is transformed in this parallactic process of rescaling. Near the end of a novel "devoted to placing Bloom socially, psychologically, temporally, geographically, and cosmically," Kain writes, "The paragon of animals has indeed been reduced to the quintessence of dust" by "a large black dot."[3]

The dot that concludes the "Ithaca" episode to which Kain refers has generated controversy ever since it first appeared in typescript. Joyce instructed his French printers, "*La réponse à la dernière demande est un point*," and he wrote on the page proofs, "*le point doit être plus visible*."[4] In different editions of *Ulysses*, the dot has been printed bigger or smaller, rounder or squarer, and it has sometimes disappeared altogether.[5] Nor is it at all agreed upon how this rather ambiguous typographical feature should be understood. When Austin Briggs surveyed published interpretations of the point's form and meaning (in French, *point* can signify both full stop and point), a very partial list of his findings included an aperture, an outer limit, a black hole, the head of a nail, a mark of closure, a parody of closure, a smudge, a scruple, a star, a seed, a womb, an egg, a period (both punctuational and menstrual), and an anus.[6]

Confirming this ambiguity and flexibility, when *Ulysses* is grasped as simultaneously voyage home and voyage out, the curious dot may be construed as egg and star at once—"the childman weary, the manchild in the womb" (*U* 17.2317–9)—perhaps something like a precursor to the star child who shines down on Earth in the final frames of Stanley Kubrick's *2001: A Space Odyssey*. The "Ithaca" dot can suggest at once Bloom's return to the bed, the womb, or the ovum, while it can also mark the distant goal of his weary avatar, Sinbad the Sailor, as he takes off over the horizon for unknown and unimaginable adventures.[7] Joyce's dark dot combines *nostos* with cosmos. The dot is given as the answer to "Where?" (*U* 17.2331), but instead of responding with words to this question, Joyce's narrator simply offers a visual mark, a sign that speaks nothing and yet seems to contain everything. It is almost as if everything that has unfolded temporally in *Ulysses*, minute by minute and hour by hour, is offered here as a spatial image, one that recedes in the distance and shifts the scale of our comprehension so dramatically that time gives way to space (a "where"). Joyce's instruction to the printer to make the point more visible or evident reinforces this sense of the dot's "whereness," its presence in and as space. Bending time into a spatial form, the final punctum in "Ithaca" may be the most modernist dot in all of literature.

The cosmic visions of "Ithaca" and the dark black dot, which hovers so silently in its blank white space, may evoke another intrepid journey and modern quest as well, another analogue for Sinbad the Sailor setting off for the unknown: *Voyager 1*. *Voyager* was launched fifty-five years after *Ulysses* was published, sent by NASA on a mission to fly past the planets of our solar system and finally to wander forever in "the cold of interstellar space." *Voyager* eventually became the most distant human-made object to travel away from Earth, billions of miles removed from the warmth of the Sun. Like *Ulysses*, *Voyager* expressed human hopes and aspirations and captured the images and sounds of Earth, as etched into its famous golden record, while also putting an astronomical distance between itself and these subjects. Before leaving the solar system for good, in 1990 *Voyager* turned its camera around to take one last look at a certain "pale blue dot," as astronomer Carl Sagan then characterized Earth. That final image revealed Earth as a little speck of light in the band of a sunbeam, just as small as the dot in "Ithaca," and, coincidentally, just as humid and nightblue as the color of the first edition of *Ulysses*. Three decades before NASA's fabulous *Voyager* left Earth, Kain's *Fabulous Voyager* made the case that with "Ithaca" *Ulysses* finally reaches "the cosmic plain."[8] And nearly two decades before *Voyager*'s image from the cusp of our solar system made the Earth "*plus visible*" in this way for the first time, Richard Ellmann remarked that the "Ithaca" dot "may be taken as the earth itself as seen from interstellar space."[9] Two years after the publication of Sagan's *The Pale Blue Dot*, Briggs made explicit the resonances between Joyce's micro- and macrocosmic dot and Sagan's eloquent phrase.[10]

As the parallactic *Ulysses* does, the pale blue dot moves our perspective outward until it encapsulates the gradual unfolding of time and experience into a small mark in space. In Sagan's well-remembered comment on the image, he emphasizes that the spatial mark contains all of the historical or temporal content of which we can conceive, all in a single point. Sagan stresses that the image of the dot in space encompasses the totality of human hopes and aspirations. Although we habitually represent these hopes to ourselves temporally, as experienced and unfolding through time and in history, the dot now makes it possible to grasp them in a spectacular instant of space:

> Look again at that dot. That's here. That's home. That's us. On it everyone you love, everyone you know, everyone you ever heard of, every human being who ever was, lived out their lives. The aggregate of our joy and suffering, thousands of confident religions, ideologies, and economic doctrines, every hunter and forager, every hero and coward, every creator and destroyer of civilization, every king and peasant, every young couple in love, every mother and father, hopeful child, inventor and explorer, every teacher of morals, every corrupt politician, every "superstar," every "supreme leader," every saint and sinner in the history of our species lived there—on a mote of dust suspended in a sunbeam.[11]

In Sagan's reading of *Voyager*'s image, human hopes, usually experienced and conceptualized temporally and set within the stream of historical narrative, are now startlingly reorganized in space, glimpsed and recognized at a single and vertiginously scale-altering glance. *Voyager*'s quintessentially modernist perspectival shock only works because we are intimate with hope as it is experienced and unfolds over time and from the ground level. But the spatial view now opens up the possibility of a double vision of hope, or perhaps, to use a favorite concept from Joyce's *Ulysses*, a kind of parallax on hope. First it is seen in one, familiar way (unfolding in time) and now in another, new perspective (as an image grasped all at once). As temporal experience cedes way to the spatial image, time collapses into space.

On the cosmic scale, *Ulysses* represents hope as a spatial constellation in the distance, even as it represents hope as it unfolds up close. Through interior monologue and dramatic narrative distances, *Ulysses* is part unfolding mental stream and part enfolding Milky Way. Or, to return to the terms of my introduction, *Ulysses* conducts both an anatomy and an astronomy of hope: hope is examined in its complexity at very close range, but as Joyce's narrative experimentation increases the novel begins to pull out to alienating distances and turns around for a wide, even cosmic, view of the field of hope as a fragile mote of dust.

Ulysses and the Totalization of Hope

In contrast to *Dubliners* and *A Portrait*, which relentlessly posit future challenges, *Ulysses* seems more like a perfected structure, a finished encyclopedia or a Book of the World to which it would be redundant, controversial, or even sacrilegious to add a single word.[12] Rather than radiating hope in the direction of the future, *Ulysses* aspires instead to a kind of spatial utopia. Given the aura of utter finality that its terminal "Yes" radiates, there is probably no book to which it would be more comical to append a "where-are-they-now?"-style epilogue than to *Ulysses*. As I discussed in Chapter 2, *Ulysses* might be a kind of sequel to *A Portrait*, but *Ulysses* forecloses almost entirely on the idea of the sequel itself. A novel as self-contained as *Ulysses*, with such a strong "totality-effect,"[13] as Jameson puts it, necessarily challenges the place and functions of hope in the traditional, forward-tending novel, whose orientation is as much or even more temporal than it is spatial. While Joseph Frank famously argued that modernist novels generally retreat from time into an autonomous (or, more accurately, semiautonomous) shape that relies on an "entire pattern of internal references [that] can be apprehended as a unity,"[14] few modernist novels seem to achieve this condition as completely as *Ulysses* does. Molly's final "Yes" seems less to affirm a future than it affirms the finished artwork of *Ulysses* itself: the final brick in the edifice, the final stroke of the statue, the final brushstroke on the canvas.[15] Through its last temporal utterance, *Ulysses* becomes a thing done, a work completed, a day unfolded and enfolded into a monument, time recast as an aspiringly eternal space.

At the same time, *Ulysses* does not sacrifice its sense of nearness to and intimacy with its characters' hopes and desire. Readers are presented with extensive information about Stephen's wishes—for instance, to be included in Dublin literary circles and to self-actualize and be recognized as an artist. They learn of Bloom's anxieties about Milly in Mullingar, about Molly's infidelity with Boylan, and about Bloom's own unmet sexual, social, and financial desires. They hear Molly articulate her complex feelings about the past, Boylan and Bloom, and many other topics. *Ulysses* allows readers to enter into the privacy of these three characters to such an extent that each can be seen to be in want of a kind of touch or form of love that might compensate for their grief, their many frustrations, and their melancholy losses: "Touch me. Soft Eyes. Soft soft soft hand. I am lonely here. O, touch me soon, now" (*U* 3.434–5), thinks Stephen, alone on Sandymount Strand. Bloom composes a letter to Martha while listening to sad music at the Ormond hotel: "P. P. S. La la la ree. I feel so sad today. La ree. So lonely. Dee" (11.894). Molly thinks, "a woman wants to be embraced 20 times a day almost to make her look young no matter by who so long as to be in love or loved by somebody" (18.1407–9). The skillful and inventive naturalism and interior monologue of the early episodes of *Ulysses* and the "Penelope" episode create a convincing virtual reality in which the hopes and wishes of the characters, in light of their common loneliness and alienation, are rendered with perhaps unparalleled vividness.

Yet few novels accomplish this emotional immediacy while simultaneously calling attention to their own formal totality, or in other words, to their own status as a contrived aesthetic object as *Ulysses* does. The situation *Ulysses* presents is thus one in which hope is represented with intimate nearness and emotional intensity at the same time that the form itself eventually closes in on these very hopes and, in the end, chokes off the sense of unfolding temporality that would seem to be the very oxygen of characters' wishes. In contrast to the mode of *Dubliners* and *A Portrait*, then, which look forward to an open future of real possibility, *Ulysses* constellates hope and calls on readers to contemplate a complex configuration of hope as it exists and persists in a single day: hope at a standstill. No matter how long it actually takes to read the novel, the hope content it contains eventually exists in a relative eye blink, at a glance.

Another way to say this is that as the hope-content of the novel develops and increases, its future horizon concomitantly narrows.[16] Jameson formidably poses the challenge of imagining a future for *Ulysses*, and implicitly, therefore, of locating hope in Joyce's novel at all. Jameson startlingly argues that *Ulysses* is fundamentally closed off to the future because of its peculiar autonomy of style—"the illusion of a language that speaks all by itself"[17]—and by its conceit of being comprised of "simply ... printed sentences."[18] He describes Joyce's "radical depersonalization"[19] and "autonomization"[20] of language and style. He argues that as a result of the ways in which Joyce effaces author, reader, and point of view even the future fantasies entertained by characters within the book—like Bloom's Flowerville—or those entertained by readers—such as what happens on June 17th, whether Stephen ever becomes an artist like Joyce, or what will become of Bloom and Molly's marriage—are all somehow negated by the end of *Ulysses*.[21] For Jameson, *Ulysses* evidences little apparent need any longer for history, the future, or even for temporality itself, much less for the trivia, logistics, and domestic politics of tomorrow morning's breakfast at 7 Eccles Street.[22] The fact that the future horizon for *Ulysses* seems narrowed by the end of Joyce's epic novel to questions about breakfast indicates that in *Ulysses* the future isn't what it used to be. Instead of projecting an open future before it as Joyce's earlier work does, *Ulysses*, to again draw on Lenehan's quip about John F. Taylor's sudden death, seems to leave "a great future behind" it (*U* 7.875–6).

From the Mountains to the Celestial Rose of Hope

Ulysses is not closed off to the future to the extent that Jameson argues. It may be, as Jameson complains, that the totality effect of *Ulysses* means that the tangible future in the form of, for example, the Easter Rising "stands forever outside the text,"[23] but the future of *Ulysses* is one that looks to the unknown future rather than to the known one. One of the innovations of *Ulysses* is that in the very act of closing off traditional narrative paths to the future, it finds ways of envisioning a wider and more open future than we are accustomed to receiving from novels. *Ulysses* explores a state in which hope constantly runs up against the limitations of human life and expectations, limitations that are reinforced by the novel's very formal self-enclosure. Far from constituting a distorting violence by objectifying and dehumanizing hope, however, *Ulysses* achieves a certain existential clarity about hope precisely by isolating it at key moments from human passion and future expectations and by denying hope a human-centered scale that limits one to a single point of view. As emblematized by its single-day duration and by its densely woven narrative, *Ulysses* is a book about what hope can mean when life is cosmically small and short. Regardless of how precisely *Ulysses* registers such hopes up close, Joyce's novel is about hope when something is coming to its end, about hope in the context of "interstellar space," billions of miles removed from the individual or communal experience of hope.

It might be tempting here to default to the old paralysis view of Joyce's vision of hope and to say that from the cosmic perspective of *Ulysses* all wishes are nullified with a brutal indifference to human desire, as in the "Ithaca" episode when Bloom's intimate and deeply held hopes are suddenly seen as just so many insignificant atoms banging around in a cosmic void. However, it would be a mistake to confuse Joyce's cosmic vision of hope with hopelessness or despair. Bloch suggests a different possible direction when he contrasts Goethe's *Faust*, a temporal utopia, with Dante's *Commedia*, a spatial utopia. Whereas Goethe's heaven consists of transcendental mountains, each rising higher than the last, in which a certain restlessness persists—"Even arrival still remains a process"[24]—Dante posits heaven as a celestial rose at rest:[25]

> Dante's figures are definitely the past in the shape of eternity, and the landscape of this immortality is so constituted; whereas the immortal element in Faust is conceived in the chrysalis condition, that is: expecting sheer future in the form of eternity. Instead of spiritual hyperspace, with every soul in the place of its revealed-finished quality, a new space of influence opens up, instead of a completed utopia of space the utopia of time as well, still lasting within that space.[26]

Dubliners and *A Portrait*, with their emphasis on *Bildung* and hope for the future, correspond more to the Faustian, chrysalis structure: the process of becoming seems in principle endless, and the summit of any peak will reveal a higher peak behind it, perhaps with many troughs and valleys in between. Within the space of their modernist forms, which strive for completion or closure in a variety of ways, there yet exists in *Dubliners* and *A Portrait* the expectation or projection of sheer future.

Ulysses, in contrast with the chrysalis or transitional formations of *Dubliners* and *A Portrait*, has stronger affinities with Dante's fixed rose, in which the past has assumed the shape of eternity. In "Proteus," a chapter intent on registering flux, Stephen nonetheless walks with his eyes closed and asks, "Am I walking into eternity along Sandymount strand?" (*U* 3.18–19).[27] Not only does Stephen seem here to intuit something about the monumental kind of book in which he appears, but all of the novel's characters and even its 1904 Dublin setting are also walking in that same direction whether they realize it or not: not just into the concrete flux and future that lies before them, but also into the precise space of eternity, into eternity as space and constellation.

The *Bildungsroman* structure that secured a future orientation for *A Portrait* has for the most part evaporated by the time we come to *Ulysses*.[28] While Stephen still seems to be in the process of becoming an artist, and more generally of maturing as a person, this process is now submerged into any number of other complex textual operations that also keep it in check, including the fixed or even coercive *Odyssey* parallel,[29] Bloom's own narrative, the inventive stylistic variations of the episodes, and the wide lens that makes human lives and hopes into microscopic stuff. Just as Dante took the contemporary Florentines whom he knew and cast them into their eternal places, so Joyce shaped the Dubliners he knew and invented into changeless forms. By the end of *Ulysses* all of the characters have become like Stephen, whom Joyce described to Frank Budgen during the composition of the novel as "a shape that can't be changed."[30] It is perhaps underappreciated how much the break from the naturalistic world to be found in *Finnegans Wake* was prepared for or even necessitated by the sense of completion that prevails at the end of *Ulysses*: the realistic fictional Dublin that had been Joyce's sole and constant setting from the time of *Dubliners, Giacomo Joyce* aside, arrives at its final standstill with Molly's terminal "Yes."[31] This is the last time that readers will inhabit the naturalistic Dublin in Joyce's *oeuvre*.

Sudden Death over Time

What distinguishes *Ulysses* not just from Joyce's previous fiction but also from other examples of modernism is the extent to which it resembles the celestial rose and constructs a static landscape in which everything seems to have found its correct and final place. This also greatly complicates the question of hope within it. In Jameson's persuasive model of modernism, for instance, modernism's deep probing of consciousness—its famous interest in the stream of consciousness or even in the Freudian unconscious—was "always accompanied by a Utopian sense of the impending transformation or transfiguration of the 'self' in question."[32] Jameson views modernism as complexly motivated by an enduring hope for change born of real possibility. He points paradigmatically to Rainer Maria Rilke's "Archaic Torso of Apollo," in which the statue tells the poet, "You have to change your life."[33] For Jameson, it is because the modernizing world itself, "seems to tremble at the brink of … momentous … transformation" that the modernists' idea of "self" comes to seem mutable and ever on the cusp of change. Jameson considers the modernist self and its subjectivity as allegorical of the transformation of the world; modernists, he writes, "evoke a momentum that cannot find resolution within the self, but that must be completed by a Utopian and revolutionary transformation of the world of actuality itself."[34] Many examples seem to confirm Jameson's sense that modernism is committed to forms of change that are dizzying, profound, ecstatic, or terrifying.[35] In this sense, the modernist project is fueled by a kind of open-ended, utopian longing expressed through moments of sudden transformation and yet would rely, for its full actualization, on corresponding transformations in the social world.

Such dizzying moments of transformation are familiar from the epiphanic moments of *Dubliners* and *A Portrait*, yet they seem curiously absent from *Ulysses*. Outside of the interpolations of the "Cyclops" episode, some of the exercises in generic conventions in "Oxen of the Sun," and the quick-change transmogrifications of "Circe," *Ulysses* contains fewer moments of sudden transformation than might be expected for such an essential work of modernism. In fact, the absence of these moments is one way to characterize *Ulysses* as different from other examples of modernism, even from Joyce's own. In the "Proteus" episode, Stephen raises the specter of instant change, only immediately to negate it: "If I were suddenly naked here as I sit? I am not" (*U* 3.390–1). In "Hades," Bloom muses, "If we were all suddenly somebody else" (6.836), but in short order this too is neatly canceled when he thinks, defeatedly, in the "Lestrygonians" episode, "No-one is anything" (8.493). In

"Penelope," Molly seems to consider having another child: "supposing I risked having another not off him though" (18.166-7). Later, after her period begins, Molly reflects, "anyhow he didnt make me pregnant" (18.1123), which fulfills her desire not to become pregnant by Boylan but also closes the door on what might have been a suddenly new and transformative future. The word "future," after occurring eight times in "Ithaca," does not appear in "Penelope."

Instead, what is most likely in *Ulysses* to come suddenly is not a terrible or beautiful transformation of character or world, but merely a sudden limit, especially a sudden death. Paddy Dignam plays the key role here. Dignam's death is marked repeatedly throughout the day above all by its suddenness: "Mr Dignam that died suddenly" (*U* 13.315); "He died quite suddenly, poor fellow" (8.219-20); "He had a sudden death, poor fellow" (6.311); "—As decent a little man as ever wore a hat, Mr Dedalus said. He went very suddenly" (6.303-4). Death's primacy as the sudden transformation in *Ulysses* is a symptom of its strange and, on the face of it, even anti-modernist resistance not just to transformation and temporal utopian possibilities but even to real possibility, to all of those things that might plausibly happen in the immediate future, however likely or unlikely, given the concrete and changing conditions of the present. It is true that Stephen evokes real possibility when he contemplates the imagination's capacity to picture an individual's future as a complex relation of past, present, and potentiality: "In the intense instant of imagination, when the mind, Shelley says, is a fading coal, that which I was is that which I am and that which in possibility I may come to be. So in the future, the sister of the past, I may see myself as I sit here now but by reflection from that which then I shall be" (9.381-5). Yet Stephen's capacious meditation on the transformations of life, in the wider, trans-individual view, culminates in an ultimate vision of change as death: "God becomes man becomes fish becomes barnacle goose becomes featherbed mountain. Dead breaths I living breathe, tread dead dust, devour a ruinous offal from all dead" (3.477-80). *Ulysses* embodies the problem of how modernism can operate when transformation is halted, forestalled, negated, or finally seen at such a great distance that it is drained of immediacy and intensity.

Joyce's spatialization of hope—the manner in which he wrests emotions, but especially hope, out of time and brings them to a standstill—is one of *Ulysses*' most defining and yet underappreciated characteristics. The novel consistently looks past the temporal scope of the individual's transformations to glimpse life as a distant dot, as when the "Ithaca" episode's narrator rather comically considers the relation between Stephen's and Bloom's respective ages, culminating in the claim, "Bloom would have been obliged to have been alive 83,300 years, having been obliged to have been born in the year 81,396 B.C." (*U* 17.459–61).[36] The narrator next contemplates "events that might nullify these calculations" (17.462), which include, "The cessation of existence of both or either, the inauguration of a new era or calendar, the annihilation of the world and consequent extermination of the human species, inevitable but impredictable" (17.463–5). Not only is it utterly certain that Bloom and Stephen will cease to exist before Bloom lives to be 83,300 years old, but it is even possible that the world itself will end by that time. This huge swath of time minimizes Bloom's comparatively ephemeral lifespan and it also makes it possible to visualize that tiny span in a spatial relationship to a much larger volume of time. On this comparative scale, poor Bloom recedes into a dot.

Last Wills, Dying Wishes, and Ghosts

Ulysses' spatialization of hope is nowhere better emblematized than in its dead or dying character's last wishes. Whereas the last will and testament, which transfers wealth from one generation to the next, is the cornerstone of many Victorian novel plots, it plays a curiously negligible or peripheral role in *Ulysses*.[37] It is curious because the novel form is closely associated with a rising bourgeois class and is thus tasked in part with thinking through and finding means of representing the social implications of the bourgeois class's relatively newly created wealth. This makes the preoccupation with and frequent contestation of wills and inheritance at the heart of novels by a writer like Charles Dickens hardly surprising. But *Ulysses*' exemplary bourgeois, Leopold Bloom, does not even appear to have a prepared will, which we would expect but do not find among the financial documents and personal papers that Bloom keeps in his two locked drawers. Stephen's father, of course, has already auctioned or squandered any inheritable property, so the Dedalus family will, if it did exist, would amount to very little. We saw Joyce's father lament as much in his New Year's letter to his son. Neither Bloom nor Stephen stands to benefit from inherited property and, accordingly, wills do not take up much space in their minds during June 16, 1904. Joyce sets these two characters in contrast to Will Shakespeare, who, in Stephen's discourse in "Scylla and Charybdis," lives up to his first name by being an Englishman much concerned with his property, and who in his will ("the swansong ... wherein he has commended her to posterity" (*U* 9.682)) leaves his wife Ann Hathaway his "Secondbest Bed" (9.698–9). The substitute for this kind of will in *Ulysses* is the dying wish, which takes the will's place as a formally and structurally determining principle. In other words, the English may have their wills, but the Irish have their dying wishes. It turns out that this makes for a very different kind of novel.

Stephen and Bloom think about and are haunted, to one degree or another, by the deathbed or dying wish of a parent. Bloom remembers his father's last wish, conveyed by his suicide note, about his pet dog: "Be good to Athos, Leopold, is my last wish" (*U* 6.125–6). Stephen is haunted by the dying wish of his mother, and Buck Mulligan reminds Stephen that when he refused to pray for her soul as she lay dying, he "crossed her last wish in death" (1.212). An important key to understanding the form of Joyce's novel and its complex relationship to hope and future lies in such representations and in the concept of last or dying wishes, especially as they touch upon greater structural features of the novel. Specifically, instead of processing wish temporally through forms of prospective hope—and for the traditional novel this is embodied above all in the inheritance plot and the centrality of the last will and testament—Joyce builds a spatial form around dying wishes, around the hopes of characters on the cusp of death, at the threshold of walking off into eternity. This is a powerful expression of time transformed into a space or place. Joyce's spatial reconfiguration of the workings of wish in *Ulysses* provides a key to the modernism of the novel; the shifting of wish from time to space in *Ulysses* helps to define its difference from the realist novel. Through its spatialization, *Ulysses* recasts hope out of its typical orientation toward the future and into a form of remembrance. Instead of envisioning hope as it looks forward to fulfillment, *Ulysses* renders hope as a thing completed in the past and subject to being memorialized. Under these conditions hope is fragile, but it is capable of being remembered.

The shift of wish from time to space can be noticed in the way in which *Ulysses* intervenes in the Shakespearean discourse of the posthumous will of ghosts. *Hamlet*, for instance, quintessentially expresses the urge that stands behind the last will and testament: the urge to maintain one's desires and effects in the world after one's death. The ghost of Hamlet's murdered father seeks to redress his betrayals by Claudius and Queen Gertrude. King Hamlet's ghost returns to the world in order to realize its posthumous need for vengeance. Stephen sympathetically imagines the motivation for these posthumous wishes: "Two deeds are rank in that ghost's mind: a broken vow and the dullbrained yokel on whom her favour has declined, deceased husband's brother" (*U* 9.666–8). The play allows audiences to imagine and asks them to take seriously the idea that after death there yet remains, if not a literal ghost, at least a *position* from which the cares of the dead can be coherently organized. *Hamlet* makes available the concept that the dead, even if they are not literal ghosts, still have a perspective or position from which to care about anything at all. The will represents the legal means of imposing such desires beyond one's life in matters of property. But the will also presupposes that the dead will have the capacity to care about these matters when they are gone, that they will, in some way, not only continue to live but also to wish after death and actively to monitor or worry about events in the living world. King Hamlet embodies this state of superstition. Even though the will can only finally represent one's living wish for a future from which one will be entirely absent, the ghost represents not just the wish image behind the will that our desires might transcend death, but also the wish that the subject position or the perspective of our desires should survive and persist in some form after we are gone. To be sure, by asking whether it was wise for Hamlet to listen to the ghost, *Hamlet* also scrutinizes the illusion that the ghost is still enmeshed in time (and is capable of hoping for a better future) and space (that it occupies a position from which to wish). However, the illusion of posthumous will and wish that King Hamlet represents has continued to haunt (not just) the literary imagination.

The posthumous wishes that King Hamlet's ghost embodies are neatly parodied in *Ulysses* through Paddy Dignam. Dignam may be the best candidate for a reincarnated King Hamlet in *Ulysses*. When the "Cyclops" episode parodies a Theosophist séance, Dignam appears from beyond the grave and is shown not only still to be invested in the progression of time and to have rather urgent desires about the world he has left behind, but still to have bodily desires such as hunger as well. After requesting and drinking a quart of buttermilk, he reveals not only a high-minded spiritual "message for the living" concerning "true path" (*U* 12.357, 358), but also two more "special desires" (12.361) that prove to be quite a bit more mundane: that Corny Kelleher should not be allowed to pile on costs for Paddy's funeral, and that "it should be told to his dear son Patsy that the other boot which he had been looking for was at present under the commode in the return room and that the pair should be sent to Cullen's to be soled only as the heels were still good. He stated that this had greatly perturbed his peace of mind in the other region and earnestly requested that his desire should be made known" (12.366–71). The mixture of spiritual advice with the triviality of the lost boot provides the comedy here. Like King Hamlet, Dignam presents himself as "greatly perturbed" by events in the world; both ghosts require a worldly intermediary to redress a grievance or wrong, but they operate on comically incongruent scales. In the case of Dignam, it is as though King Hamlet came all the way back from the dead just to tell his son that there is an actual rat behind the arras.

When Dignam appears resurrected again in the "Circe" episode, in the form of a Circean dog-man, he is searching for a lamppost in order to "satisfy an animal need. That buttermilk didn't agree with me" (*U* 15.1234–5). The extraordinary fact that there is narrative continuity concerning the buttermilk between the parodic interpolation of "Cyclops" and the hallucinogenic world of "Circe" suggests that something of the parodic thrust of the former episode also carries over into the latter. Once again Dignam is shown to have a bodily need, this one a direct consequence of the earlier episode. Once again, he is solicitous about the feelings and health of a loved one and seeks an earthly intermediary: "The poor wife was awfully cut up. How is she bearing it? Keep her off that bottle of sherry" (15.1232–3). The identification between Dignam and King Hamlet is solidified when Dignam addresses Bloom in a way that echoes King Hamlet's words: "Bloom, I am Paddy Dignam's spirit. List, list, O list!" (15.1217). Dignam's partial transformation into a grisly "ghouleaten" (15.1208) dog-man emphasizes, in contrast to the guise of the "apparition of the etheric double being" (12.340–1) in which he appeared in "Cyclops," that he is now, as Mulligan described Stephen's mother, rather *"beastly dead"* (1.198–9, emphasis in original). At all levels of the parody in both episodes, Joyce uses the incongruity between conceptualizations of the spirit and the afterlife with the exigencies of the body and the temporal world to suggest how dubious it is to attribute hopes to the dead. Dignam's rather mundane wishes tend to puncture the grandiose projections of ghostly desire that King Hamlet's ghost embodies and which drive the plot of *Hamlet*. By contrast, in *Ulysses* hope is so deracinated from traditional grounds that the hopes of its ghosts are no more likely to persist than those of its intimately rendered flesh-and-blood characters. The ghosts in *Ulysses* are eminently bustable.

Ghostbusting

In parodies like the Dignam episodes in "Cyclops" and "Circe," *Ulysses* unmasks the fantasy that the will can persist past death in any other way than in the projections of the living who are willing to conjure and then listen to ghosts. *Ulysses*' dying wishes work to exorcise the illusion of the posthumous will and of the objective existence of the ghost. Wishes in *Ulysses* lack the authority of the legal will that could sustain the idea that there remains a posthumous position from which to hope for the future. Dying wishes not only lack the power to temporalize themselves but being made on the cusp of the subject's death they emphasize rather than conceal the coming extinction of the very position from which any hope could issue. Dying wishes reveal the vacancy of the hopes and positions that the dead once held as readily as the last will and testament would pursue and confirm the masquerade of presence. The dying wishes of Stephen's mother and Bloom's father expose the illusion that the legal will, designed to supplement the subject's desire and to paper over its absence, would maintain: the illusion that after death there is still a position from which the dead can hope.

But if wills are revealed to be little more than dying wishes with added illusions, they are also shown to be nothing *less* than dying wishes, which Joyce invests with value. By focusing on this form of hope at the cusp of death, Joyce emphasizes the frailty of wish. In contrast to the vision presented by wills, which represent the ways in which the testator would confidently impose a blueprint onto the future (to the extent that the future can be dictated by redistributing property), last wishes represent ideal or even utopian, but toothless, visions of the present or the future over which the dying one has no control. The last wish is pled for from a position of frank weakness and even of supplication rather than dictated from a position of authority. Last wishes are made from the perspective that at least partially recognizes that one's desires will soon be absent in the world. As distinct from the will, the last wish looks toward an outcome that one can perhaps influence but is powerless to dictate. Unlike the will, the last wish need not concern property and its fulfillment relies entirely on the unforced good will and compliance of others to carry it out after the desire itself, from the perspective of the self, will have been canceled out. It asks that the living adopt the hope of the dying, that the living occupy a position of hope that is about to disappear into the grave, and that the living honor that wish as a form of remembrance: "Poor old Athos! Be good to Athos, Leopold, is my last wish. Thy will be done. We obey them in the grave. A dying scrawl" (*U* 6.125–7).

Joyce represents the dying person's position of weakness in the "Cyclops" episode, whose cheerful Irish martyr ("in capital spirits" (*U* 12.630)), refused his final meal of "rashers and eggs, fried steak and onions, done to a nicety, delicious hot breakfast rolls and invigorating tea" (12.627–8), and then "rose nobly to the occasion and expressed the dying wish (immediately acceded to) that the meal should be divided in aliquot parts among the members of the sick and indigent roomkeepers' association as a token of his regard and esteem" (12.632–5). Among the other grotesque features of this scene, part of the ironic humor comes from the fact that the martyr's last wish is not even on his own behalf but is rather selflessly and charitably for the behalf of the sick and indigent. This is likely why the wish was immediately granted.

In *Ulysses*, Bloom and Stephen have to contend with the desires of ghosts, but these ghosts are revealed to come from their guilt for a dead parent; their guilt, and in Stephen's case torment, persists through an approximate reconstruction of a hope-position that no longer exists in the world independently of the survivors. The living keep these positions alive for the dead. *Ulysses* depicts a world in which the hopes of ghosts are neither objectively present in the world nor legally enforceable; they are only to be found within the self, projected in the mirror or encountered in the whirl of a solo dance. As a result, they turn out to be as easily smashed as a cheap chandelier in a brothel, as in the "Circe" episode, when Stephen smashes that flimsy prop in the theater of desire: "*He lifts his ashplant high with both hands and smashes the chandelier. Time's livid final flame leaps and, in the following darkness, ruin of all space, shattered glass and toppling masonry*" (*U* 15.4242–4, emphasis in original). This apocalyptic imagery pictures time dying out along with the light, like a candle. Space is left in ruins, toppled and shattered. When Stephen finally repels the specter of his mother's wishes, what is revealed behind her ghost is the absence of the temporality (time's final flame) upon which hope relies and the shattered ruins of a position in space. Stephen's mother's absence, masked all day by the ghost of her wishes as they persist within Stephen, is laid bare precisely as the negation of any position *from* which to hope and as the lack of any temporality *in* which to hope. She is outside of time and the space that she once occupied is a ruin. Stephen's mother, the smashed chandelier confirms, is simply not there. If a ghost, as Stephen earlier defines it, is "One who has faded into impalpability through death, through absence, through change of manners" (9.147–9), then Stephen is able desperately to exorcize it by unmasking the temporal absence and the spatial ruin behind it: there is no "there" from which to hope, there is no "there" outside the self from which to be haunted. We can only haunt ourselves as acts of remembrance.

But if there is weakness rather than control or self-determination attached to the dying wish, it also comes with a certain authority, and this too tells us something crucial about the meaning of hope in *Ulysses*. Dying wishes might be treated with respect because of the air of authority that, for instance, Benjamin attributes to the dying person on his or her deathbed:[38] "suddenly in his expressions and looks the unforgettable emerges, and imparts to everything that concerned him that authority which even the poorest wretch in the act of dying possesses for the living around him. This authority lies at the very origin of the story."[39] Wishes made on the cusp of death crystallize hope, at least momentarily, in a kind of epiphanic form or constellation. In the dying wish, hope, which attaches so readily to the future that it seems already to be straining toward it, comes to a standstill. If *A Portrait* and *Dubliners* measure something like the momentum of hope, then *Ulysses* networks or constellates hopes and desires that, when locked into a futureless form, have no velocity but rather stand in place. *Ulysses* offers a vision of hope spatialized, a matrix of myriad hopes that hang in suspension, never to be pursued or realized.

The novel compensates for this loss of hope's future by assuming the haunting and authoritative air of the dying wish. Not only do the hopes of characters who make an actual dying wish haunt the novel, but because of the spatial orientation and unique "futurelessness" of *Ulysses*, every aspiration, dream, and hope conveyed in the novel becomes a species of dying wish as well. We come to know these hopes intimately because Joyce's technique of interior monologue and other narrative innovations acquaint readers with the minute details of the major and some minor characters' minds and desires. At the same time, the single-day duration of the novel ensures that readers will never know whether the many hopes and ambitions of Bloom, Stephen, Molly, Gerty, and others will be fulfilled; the form of the novel in which they appear has an airtight finality that makes it fairly ridiculous to speculate for more than a minute or two about their future trajectories. Instead, their dreams hang with the finality of "The heaventree of stars hung with humid nightblue fruit" (17.1039): static and remote, but perhaps all the more dignified and enduring because of it. *Ulysses* lets readers get so close to the wishes of its characters, yet thoroughly alienates them from these characters by using distancing narrative techniques and by implanting the characters into a perfected spatial structure that makes even the next morning almost impossible or beside the point to imagine. Few books admit readers so fully into the hopes and wishes of its characters while simultaneously shrinking their significance and emphasizing their fictionality and imprisonment within a book that we can hold in our hands.

The difference between the ghostly will and the dying wish underscores the ideology of style behind the shift from realism to modernism. *Ulysses* is narrated from the position from which Hamlet's ghost can no longer speak unless it is also simultaneously unmasked as ventriloquism.[40] One way of accounting for the radical form of *Ulysses* is to say that it aspires to a fixed and closed condition in which the dead will finally be mute. This runs against a certain post-structuralist tendency to see Joyce as deconstructing a deep Western preference for presence over absence by liberally admitting ghosts into *Ulysses*,[41] but the ghost can also be a fantasy of presence so entrenched, and often enforceable by the law of the will, that it would even necessitate the narrative experiments of *Ulysses* to expunge it. The last or dying wish stands in a world bereft of the secure structures that once seemed to guarantee the stability of the world and the futures posited by its last wills. Wish now appears as a fragile speck within the cosmic chaos rather than within the worldly and temporal social order with which we habitually magnify and comprehend wish. Joyce's modernist form in *Ulysses*, with its deep sense of order and totality, if not perfection, may in fact be seen as an aesthetic utopian compensation for the loss of this order.

But its form also enables *Ulysses* to grasp thereby a thing that is otherwise difficult to imagine: the world not just without our presence in it, but without our hopes and wishes as well. This is a most difficult state to grasp, the state in which all of one's hope and wishes will have been nullified from the point of view of the self. The last will and testament may be seen as one way of trying to represent this state to ourselves, to compensate for death by asserting that a form of traffic runs back and forth between the hopes and wishes of the living and the dead. Yet if we conceive of death not just as the termination of life but also as the erasure of the subject position that once organized a particular confluence of hopes and wishes, then death is the moment when the will and testament becomes irrelevant for the very author who had so anxiously sought to impose his or her desires onto the future. While it is almost possible to convince ourselves that we can imagine the world without ourselves in it, we can still only do so from the perspective from which we also wish. Our presence returns in the form of the wish positions that we find it impossible to abandon. The difficulty is to picture our absence from the world from a perspective other than the one from which we wish. Joyce admits this absent perspective by examining dying wishes through the minds of Stephen and Bloom and through the novel's spatial self-containment. In these ways, *Ulysses* may evoke precisely the Real which on basis of the novel's depersonalization and autonomization Jameson would deny it:[42] a way of accessing and representing the world shorn of the illusions that proceed from individuation and any given hope-position.

Just as there is a utopian impulse in the myth of the posthumous will (that our wishes can survive death and maintain a certain independence, coherency, and agency in the world without us), so too is there something utopian in the demythologizing work of the dying wish. The dying wish reveals the impossibility that the posthumous will exists, but it is also a wish image of the world bereft of our own perspectives, the world stripped of the illusion that comes as the byproduct of the human conceived as an individual. Perhaps the dying wish even offers some relief from the existential burden of occupying a subject position, or from what Henry Staten calls Bloom's "great anxiety of individuation."[43] Joyce's form leads to an insight rather similar to when Proust reflects, "death, which interrupts [our old love affair with life], will cure us of our desire for immortality."[44] There is a certain utopia in being quite done with wish altogether.

In *Ulysses*, hope ceases to be solely an expectant emotion that looks to the future; it also becomes a space of remembrance. The spatialization of hope presents the opportunity for remembrance. It is not through represented or imagined ghosts that *Ulysses* remembers wish, but rather through the spatial anamnesis or remembrance of the novel itself. In a different context from the one cited earlier, Benjamin emphasizes that the unfulfilled hopes of the dead remain vulnerable to history, even long after the dead are gone: "The only historian capable of fanning the spark of hope in the past is the one who is firmly convinced that *even the dead* will not be safe from the enemy if he is victorious."[45] For Benjamin it is the historian's duty to take up the disappointed hopes of history's victims. For Joyce a comparable duty is given to readers who, after coming to the end of the novel and closing it, are implicitly charged with remembrance of the single day of *Ulysses* and of all of its intricacies and events, including what each character hoped and dreamed of, but did not receive. Hopes that once looked forward to fulfillment can now only be remembered. Even as *Ulysses* works to foreclose on a sense of its own narrative future, the novel's massive anamnestic demands, unique perhaps in the history of fiction, necessarily turn devoted readers of the novel into historians and memorializers of the characters' wishes: "We obey them in the grave. A dying scrawl." Readers memorialize *Ulysses* in the minute and obsessively detail-oriented ways that they often do because its single-day fragility turns all of the hopes it contains into dying wishes. *Ulysses* asks readers to haunt themselves with *Ulysses*. If they choose to do so, perhaps as carefully and attentively as the "Araby" narrator, readers bear the chalice of Joyce's fragile and wishful day "safely through a throng of foes" (*D* 22.63–4) or, rather like *Voyager*, through the cold of interstellar space.

In *Ulysses* Joyce demonstrates that all wishes are dying wishes, that hope is radically circumscribed by the astronomical, interstellar conditions in which it must always finally operate. *Ulysses* is a novel about what happens to hope when it is not hopeless, but futureless, when the temporal coordinates from which hope once issued have vanished altogether, into a dot or speck, in which even the ghosts that the living use to approximate and imagine vanished hope-positions no longer persist. In this way, *Ulysses* suggests that the hopes and wishes of ghosts exist solely in the minds of the living, much as literary characters exist solely in the mind of readers. Yet *Ulysses*, through its visions of sympathy and compassion, also shows that these hopes are, in the final analysis, in no way fruitless, vain, or meaningless. Instead, these wishes require the work and dignity of recollection. Remembrance is no less a presence in *Ulysses* than it is in *A Portrait*; only now remembrance is poised not against *Bildung* but against the dying wish, against death itself. *Ulysses* lets us have our ghosts and bust them, too.

Ulysses, Utopia

While *Ulysses* unmasks ghosts that stand in for and try to imagine a present existence for the dead and the persistence of their hopes, it also opens a portal for another kind of ghost in Joyce. Luke Gibbons writes, "Ghosts are best seen as premonitions, reminding us of 'infinite possibilities' that have yet to unfold."[46] Gibbons's ghosts remind us that ghosts are not only about recollection, but also about future possibility. Joyce's spatialization of hope shifts away from the temporal, but, just as it must have been for Carl Sagan, it turns out that this is only a momentary stratagem. Sagan's spatial reading of the pale blue dot admits of recollection and remembrance, but that is only the beginning: temporarily spatialized and memorialized, hope is now freed into the future. The future that Sagan imagines is one in which humans come to inhabit new planets and to look back at Earth in the manner that only *Voyager* has done:

> They will gaze up and strain to find the blue dot in their skies. They will love it no less for its obscurity and fragility. They will marvel at how vulnerable the repository of all our potential once was, how perilous our infancy, how humble our beginnings, how many rivers we had to cross before we found our way.[47]

To spatialize hope is not to banish temporality or wishes about the future forever. It is rather strategically to bracket the immediate future so that it might be less difficult to envision an astronomical shift of perspective and hope. Spatial parallax pursued as far as *Ulysses* pushes it comes out the other side as temporal parallax. As Dante and Virgil descend past the legs of Lucifer to the very center of the frozen space of Hell, they suddenly find themselves climbing upward again. When they leave the infernal space of eternity and return to the world of time, they look up to see—what else?—the stars above and ahead of them. Like Dante and Virgil on the cusp of a new journey, which will take them into *Voyager*'s territory of interstellar space, *Ulysses*, after encapsulating hope in space, also posits a future. It is a future that comes out of space rather than from time.

Bloom's "logical conclusion" (*U* 17.1137) about the constellation of stars that he sees from the backyard of 7 Eccles Street is that it is an image of Utopia:

> That it was not a heaventree, not a heavengrot, not a heavenbeast, not a heavenman. That it was a Utopia, there being no known method from the known to the unknown: an infinity renderable equally finite by the suppositious apposition of one or more bodies equally of the same and of different magnitudes: a mobility of illusory forms immobilised in space, remobilised in air: a past which possibly had ceased to exist as a present before its probable spectators had entered actual present existence. (17.1139–45)

Bloom considers that the constellation of stars he sees is not the heaventree it appears to be but rather an infinity rendered finite and the ungraspable made to appear comprehensible by the illusions of apposition, proximity, and nearness. It is Bloom's organizing perspective alone that makes stars of different magnitudes, distances, and velocities appear to stand still and cohere as a heaventree. He recognizes that he is not really seeing the stars as they are because their light has had to travel cosmically far and wildly variable distances in order to appear coincidentally before his eyes in that instant. Bloom knows he is really looking into the past, or more precisely stargazing at an uneven and staggering array of different pasts. He is even likely seeing starlight just arriving to Earth from distant stars that burned out before he was born. In this cosmic vision, *Nacheinander* (one after another) and *Nebeneinander* (side by side) appear infinitely and profoundly in the same instant. For Bloom, the vision afforded by the apparent heaventree—the infinite rendered finite, the mobile rendered immobile, and the past rendered present—makes the night sky "a Utopia."

By Bloom's logic, *Ulysses* is "a Utopia" as well; in terms of human hope, it too renders finite, immobilizes, and makes present the infinite, the mobile, and the past. By spatializing and constellating character hopes—"immobilised in space, remobilised in air"—*Ulysses* creates enough distance from them that it is suddenly easier to imagine a wider Irish world or even an interstellar future than it is to imagine the more narrow futures of Stephen, Bloom, or Molly, who, no matter with what a great sense of regret we must lose sight of them at novel's end, leave their futures behind them.[48] *Ulysses* gives a wide stage to the openness of the future: not as a utopian method or program, but as the utopian impulse innovated into a spatial and at times shockingly atemporal form. *Ulysses* holds up for remembrance a heaventree of hopes of different sizes, distances, brightness, and speeds constellated and rendered finite, immobile, and present through the suppositious apposition of modernist form: not a "method from the known to the unknown," but instead a humid nightblue dot surrounded by possibilities.

Notes

1 Jameson writes, "as Joyce's text, his language, become more and more autonomous, they can no longer be thought to be representational or to include 'characters' who 'have' various emotions and feelings," Fredric Jameson, "Joyce or Proust?," in *The Modernist Papers* (New York: Verso, 2007), 197.
2 Richard M. Kain, *Fabulous Voyager: James Joyce's Ulysses* (Chicago: University of Chicago Press, 1947), 227.
3 Ibid., 238.
4 For a detailed discussion of the latter phrase and the page proofs in which it appears, see Roy Gottfried, "'*Le point doit être plus visible*': The Texas Page Proofs of *Ulysses*," in *Joyce at Texas*, ed. Dave Oliphant and Thomas Zigal (Austin: Humanities Research Center, University of Texas at Austin, 1983), 12–27.
5 For a detailed account, see Austin Briggs, "The Full Stop at the End of 'Ithaca': Thirteen Ways—and Then Some—of Looking at a Black Dot," *Joyce Studies Annual* 7 (Summer 1996): 125–44.
6 See ibid.
7 Or, alternately, the dot may become Sinbad's point of origin, which has been left behind to recede into the size of a pinprick and eventually disappear from view.
8 Kain, *Fabulous Voyager*, 227.

9. Ellmann goes so far as to say that "the earth may be considered the point of the book, as well as of the *Ithaca* chapter," Richard Ellmann, *Ulysses on the Liffey* (New York: Oxford University Press, 1972), 159.
10. See Briggs, 134–5.
11. Carl Sagan, *Pale Blue Dot: A Vision of the Human Future in Space* (New York: Random House, 1994), 8.
12. For instance: the controversy surrounding Hans Walter Gabler's editorial decision to add "love" as Stephen's word known to all men. See, for details, Richard Ellmann, "Preface" to James Joyce, *Ulysses: The Gabler Edition* (New York: Random House, 1986), xii–xiii.
13. Jameson, "Joyce or Proust?," 179.
14. Joseph Frank, "Spatial Form in Modern Literature: An Essay in Two Parts," *Sewanee Review* 53.2 (Spring 1945): 230. See also Joseph Frank, "Spatial Form in Modern Literature: An Essay in Three Parts," *Sewanee Review* 53.4 (Autumn 1945): 643–53.
15. Indeed, Jameson argues that *Ulysses* materializes language analogously to the ways in which modern painters foreground the medium of paint, pointing to the book's uncanny sense of its own materiality. See Fredric Jameson, "*Ulysses* in History," in *The Modernist Papers* (New York: Verso, 2007), 146–7. Similarly, Kenner argues that *Ulysses* is not told in the voice of a storyteller, but is rather "mimed in words arranged on pages in space," Hugh Kenner, *Ulysses*, Revised Edition (Baltimore, MD: Johns Hopkins University Press, 1987), 63, 65. Kenner also captures something of this feeling of self-containment in what he calls the novel's "principle of pervasive indifference," Kenner, 63. While Lessing famously allotted the *Nacheinander* to poetry and the *Nebeneinander* to painting, Joyce's novel seems calculated also to accomplish the work of painting (representing the side-by-side simultaneously) through its self-consciousness about its own space. (Although it is most typical to see Joyce's source for the terms *Nacheinander* and *Nebeneinander* as issuing directly from Lessing's *Laocoön* (see, for instance, Don Gifford with Robert J. Seidman, *Ulysses Annotated: Notes for James Joyce's Ulysses*, Second Edition (Berkeley: University of California Press, 1988), 45), Wim Van Mierlo raises the possibility, using evidence from Joyce's "Subject Notebook," that Joyce found the terms instead in Otto Weininger's *Über die letzten Dinge*. See Wim Van Mierlo, "The Subject Notebook: A Nexus in the Composition of *Ulysses*—A Preliminary Analysis," *Genetic Joyce Studies* 7 (Spring 2007): 38–9. Joyce does reference Lessing by name in "Circe" (15.3609), which Gifford also glosses with reference to the *Laocoön*.) At times it seems that we are not so much falling into or becoming absorbed by a story that *Ulysses* unfolds for us temporally, but are rather consciously holding a book full of fiercely independent words and sentences in our hands, one that keeps

encouraging us to flip its pages back and forth in search of some cross-referenced object that we are sure we have encountered before—a throwaway or a three-mast schooner—as one similarly scans the visual field of a large and complex modern painting. But this quality can only mitigate the novel's sense of unfolding time and any posited future because its palpable materiality helps to affirm *Ulysses* as something accomplished, finished. The "printerly" or "bookish" quality of *Ulysses* chimes with Kenner's reading of the novel as presided over not so much by the traditional voice of a storyteller who recalls past events so much as by a presence with "access such as ours to a printed book," one who can flip back just as readers often must do to quickly check a fact or two. See Kenner, *Ulysses*, 65.

16 At least the novel's *immediate* future horizon narrows. As we have seen, "Ithaca" also forecasts an immense cosmic future that far transcends the individual life, but this only contributes to the feeling that the future of Joyce's characters is definitively small.

17 Jameson, "Joyce or Proust?," 191. This is especially true, Jameson argues, about *Ulysses*' relationship to real historical future events, such as the Easter Rising. See "Joyce or Proust?," 196.

18 Jameson, "*Ulysses* in History," 148.

19 Ibid., 146. Jameson writes,

> this is the moment to say the price *Ulysses* must pay for the seemingly limitless power of its play of reification and dereification; the moment, in other words, to come to terms with Joyce's modernism. Stated baldly, that price is radical depersonalization, or in other words, Joyce's completion of Flaubert's programme of removing the author from the text—a programme which also removes the reader, and finally that unifying and organizing mirage or aftermirage of both author and reader which is the "character," or better still, "point of view."

20 See Jameson, "Joyce or Proust?," 194.

21 Ibid., 196.

22 I will eventually contest Jameson's conclusion about *Ulysses* and the future, but its persuasive dimensions are difficult to deny: Molly's "Yes" seems more readily to offer knowledge of some cosmic variety and more plausibly to affirm all of life itself (or is it death?) or to embrace all of the past (or does it repudiate it?) than to tell us anything about the very next day. And at times, *Ulysses* even seems more interested in mysterious minutiae, such as the identity of the Mackintosh man—"Now who is that lankylooking galoot over there in the macintosh?" (*U* 6.805); "Golly, whatten tunket's yon guy in the mackintosh?" (14.1546)—than it is in the larger questions about the future and fate of its characters' quotidian but deeply felt cares and hopes. Arguably, even the unnarrated parts of Stephen's,

Bloom's, and Molly's day, or the many "alternatives" to Bloomsday that are briefly entertained by following other characters in the "Wandering Rocks" episode, do not trouble the novel's encyclopedic completeness. Nor does *Ulysses*, with its "printerly" solidity, exactly feel like a kind of accordion folder that could expand or contract to admit more or less material in the manner in which Jameson characterizes Marcel Proust's seemingly infinite elasticity. See Jameson, "Joyce or Proust?," 174, 196. In contrast to *Ulysses*, Jameson contends, is *À la recherche du temps perdu*, in which a sense of infinite expansiveness and future extensibility prevails. Jameson imagines finding a stray fragment of Proust that could shed light on the novel's future, opening Proust's massive novel outward and even changing its ending, whereas, he argues, in *Ulysses* this is almost unthinkable, because the novel is as complete as it could ever be. See Jameson, "Joyce or Proust?," 196. For Jameson, compared to Proust, Joyce is stubbornly totalizing; the discrete episodes of *Ulysses* function as units of completeness within the larger constraining enclosure of the single-day frame. See Jameson, "Joyce or Proust?," 178–9. Leo Bersani similarly complains of the tautology of *Ulysses*, which demands a kind of "affectless busyness" from readers to make connections whose end result could only be the encyclopedic restatement of *Ulysses* itself, Leo Bersani, "Against *Ulysses*," in *James Joyce's Ulysses: A Casebook*, ed. Derek Attridge (New York: Oxford University Press, 2004), 224. He writes, "*Ulysses* promises a critical utopia: the final elucidation of its sense, the day when all the connections will have been discovered and collected in a critical Book which would objectively repeat *Ulysses*, which, in being the exegetical double of its source, would express the *quidditas* of Joyce's novel, would be, finally, *Ulysses* replayed as the whole truth of *Ulysses*," Bersani, "Against *Ulysses*," 225.

23 Jameson, "Joyce or Proust?," 196.
24 Bloch, *The Principle of Hope*, 825.
25 Bloch expresses the difference between Goethe's infinite striving and Dante's repose in terms of religious difference: "The scrupulous distance is Protestant … as resolutely as the faith in attainability and contemplatable goal-form has remained arch-Catholic," ibid., 825.
26 Ibid., 824.
27 In "Ithaca," when Stephen finally does walk into eternity down the lane behind Bloom's Eccles Street house, Bloom cannot see Stephen, but hears, "The double reverberation of retreating feet on the heavenborn earth" (*U* 17.1243). According to Gifford, this configuration echoes the hidden path that Virgil and Dante use to return to Earth from the nadir of Hell, which cannot be seen but only identified by the sound of water running in it. Gifford argues that the scene evokes the glacial nadir of *Inferno*, where Satan is frozen in Lake Cocytus, when Bloom feels "The cold of interstellar space, thousands of degrees below freezing" (*U* 17.1246).

See note for *U* 17.1243–4 in Don Gifford with Robert J. Seidman, *Ulysses Annotated: Notes for James Joyce's Ulysses*, Second Edition (Berkeley: University of California Press, 1988), 586. This presages the final moment of the novel in which *Ulysses* ends with characters not so much frozen in time as frozen in space, the space of the finished book itself.

28 Not the least among these checks on the *Künstlerroman* and *Bildungsroman* processes is *Ulysses*' single day duration. As Jameson writes, "the perspective of the single day radically interferes with the temporality of the [*Bildungsroman*] which it effectively cancels, while leaving its negation behind as a trace," Fredric Jameson, *The Antinomies of Realism* (New York: Verso, 2013), 150. Jameson numbers the *Bildungsroman* among the other traditional forms whose ruins or residue can be found in *Ulysses*, including the novel of adultery, the historical novel, and naturalism.

29 Kenner characterizes the *Odyssey* parallel as coercive. See Hugh Kenner, *Ulysses*, Revised Edition (Baltimore, MD: Johns Hopkins University Press, 1987), 62.

30 See Frank Budgen, *James Joyce and the Making of Ulysses, and Other Writings* (London: Oxford University Press, 1972), 107.

31 The year 1904 was the last year that Joyce lived primarily in Ireland, so the clock on Joyce's first-hand, naturalistic knowledge of Dublin was set to expire. Could this also be a factor? Perhaps the interwoven fictional worlds of *Dubliners, A Portrait of the Artist as a Young Man,* and *Ulysses*, set in the Dublin of Joyce's youth and young adulthood, had only a certain shelf life, and as Joyce inched his fictional universe toward the pivotal year of 1904, maybe there also approached something like an expiration date on the material out of which he had created so much. His fictional world eventually had to encounter the singularity of Joyce's own departure from Ireland.

32 Fredric Jameson, *Postmodernism, or, the Cultural Logic of Late Capitalism* (Durham, NC: Duke University Press, 1991), 312.

33 Quoted in Jameson, *Postmodernism*, 312.

34 Fredric Jameson, *A Singular Modernity: Essay on the Ontology of the Present* (New York: Verso, 2002), 136.

35 The most canonical expression of the feeling that the world might or has suddenly changed may be Virginia Woolf's conceit that "on or about December 1910 human character changed," Virginia Woolf, "Character in Fiction," in *Selected Essays*, ed. David Bradshaw (New York: Oxford University Press, 2008). Similarly, Woolf's novel, *Mrs. Dalloway*, represents many moments of being in which the world seems on the brink of awful and awesome change, moments when whole new vistas or modes of being come briefly in and then out of focus, at once exhilarating and frightening. For instance, for Clarissa Dalloway: "She and Sally fell a little behind. Then came the most exquisite

moment of her whole life passing a stone urn with flowers in it. Sally stopped; picked a flower; kissed her on the lips. The whole world might have turned upside down!," Virginia Woolf, *Mrs. Dalloway*, ed. Bonnie Kime Scott (Orlando: Harvest, 2005), 35.; or for Septimus Smith: "The world wavered and quivered and threatened to burst into flames," *Mrs. Dalloway*, 15; or for Peter Walsh: "What is this terror? what is this ecstasy? he thought to himself. What is it that fills me with extraordinary excitement?," *Mrs. Dalloway*, 190. Readers know that it is Clarissa standing near him, but it is also the world on the cusp of transforming, the world changing utterly in an instant. Another canonical expression of such potential for change, and its ambiguous relation to hope and desire, is in Franz Kafka's *The Metamorphosis*, when Gregor Samsa wakes up to discover that he has been transformed into a large insect. Suddenness is also a feature of Stephen's definition of epiphany in *Stephen Hero*: "By an epiphany he meant a sudden spiritual manifestation, whether in the vulgarity of speech or gesture or in a memorable phase of the mind itself" (*SH* 211). Stephen goes on to explain, "I will pass [the clock of the Ballast office] time after time, allude to it, refer to it, catch a glimpse of it. It is only an item in the catalogue of Dublin's street furniture. Then all at once I see it and I know at once what it is: epiphany" (*SH* 211). In accordance with this idea, moments of suddenness recur regularly in *Dubliners* and *A Portrait* to mark points of significant personal transition that happen "all at once," none more dramatically, perhaps, than Stephen's vision of the bird-girl: "—Heavenly God! cried Stephen's soul in an outburst of profane joy" (*P* 150.876–7). For Irish modernism, there is probably no better expression of this modernist potential for transformation in an instant than when William Butler Yeats writes of the Easter Rising: "All changed, changed utterly: / A terrible beauty is born," William Butler Yeats, "Easter, 1916," in *The Collected Poems of W.B. Yeats*, ed. Richard J. Finneran (New York: Collier Books, 1989).

36   Robert M. Adams has noted that in this passage:

> [Joyce's] figures trail off into major inaccuracies. In 1952 when Stephen would be 70, if Bloom were 17 times older, he would be 1190, and would consequently have had to be born in 762, not 714. This is not a parodic error, Joyce has simply forgotten to count back from 1952, and has worked from 1904 instead. On the other hand, the figures in the last two lines of the calculation should be, instead of 83,300 only 20,230; and instead of 81,396 only 17,158 years. Joyce forgot his basis of comparison, and multiplied Stephen's maximum age of 1190 years by 70 instead of 17.

See Robert M. Adams, *Surface and Symbol: The Consistency of James Joyce's Ulysses* (New York: Oxford University Press, 1962), 183.

37 *Ulysses*' only scene of probate occurs in the context of a "Cyclops" parody, set in "the halls of law" (*U* 12.1114): there "master Justice Andrews, sitting without a jury in the probate court, weighed well and pondered the claim of the first chargeant upon the property in the matter of the will propounded and final testamentary disposition *in re* the real and personal estate of the late lamented Jacob Halliday, vintner, deceased, versus Livingstone, an infant, of unsound mind, and another" (12.1116–20).

38 Perhaps the dying wish commands even more authority than the will, which, as in *Bleak House*, can be infinitely interpreted and debated.

39 Walter Benjamin, "The Storyteller: Observations on the Works of Nikolai Leskov," in *Selected Writings, Volume 3, 1935-1938*, trans. Harry Zohn, ed. Howard Eiland and Michael W. Jennings (Cambridge, MA: Harvard University Press, 2002), 151. For another way of looking at hope in relation to death in *Ulysses*, one that focuses not on the spatialized hope and spatial form of the novel but rather on its narration, see my "Storytelling and Alienated Labor: Joyce, Benjamin, and the Narrative Wording Class," *Journal of Modern Literature* 38.2 (Winter 2015): 29–44.

40 The way in which the dying wish dispels the illusion of the posthumous will mirrors the functions that Jameson attributes to *Ulysses* of depersonalizing the voice and of autonomizing language. For Jameson, the traditional poles of communication between sender and receiver are disrupted when *Ulysses* "produc[es] the illusion of a language that speaks all by itself, without the intervention of human agency," Jameson, "Joyce or Proust?," 191.

41 See, for instance, Maud Ellmann, "Ghosts of *Ulysses*," in *James Joyce's Ulysses: A Casebook*, ed. Derek Attridge (New York: Oxford University Press, 2004), 83–101.

42 It is of Proust, instead of Joyce, that Jameson wonders "whether this negative sublime, this stripping away of the very connotations of language, is not the closest literature can ever come to the Real itself," "Joyce or Proust?," 200.

43 Henry Staten, "The Decomposing Form of *Ulysses*," in *James Joyce's Ulysses: A Casebook*, ed. Derek Attridge (New York: Oxford University Press, 2004), 192.

44 Marcel Proust, *The Prisoner and The Fugitive* (*In Search of Lost Time*, Volume 5), trans. Carol Clark and Peter Collier (London: Penguin, 2003), 609.

45 Walter Benjamin, "On the Concept of History," in *Selected Writings, Volume 4, 1938-1940*, trans. Harry Zohn, ed. Howard Eiland and Michael W. Jennings (Cambridge, MA: Harvard University Press, 2003), 391, emphasis in original. Many aspects of Benjamin's profound observation are not directly relevant to the present discussion. I discuss the meaning of this sentence more fully in *Hope and Wish Image in Music Technology* (New York: Palgrave Macmillan, 2017), 24–5.

46 Luke Gibbons, *Joyce's Ghosts: Ireland, Modernism, and Memory* (Chicago: University of Chicago Press, 2015), 225.

47 Sagan, 405.
48 Indeed, with respect to contemporary readers who are now 100 years removed from the publication of *Ulysses* and even farther removed from its 1904 setting, Stephen's, Bloom's, and Molly's pasts have already "ceased to exist as a present before its probable spectators had entered actual present existence."

4

Daydreams of History and Reincarnation in *Finnegans Wake*

The critical history of *Finnegans Wake* has been preoccupied with nightdreams and the past. This chapter proposes instead to view the *Wake* in relation to daydream and the future. Accordingly, our initial questions are these: If *Finnegans Wake* daydreams, what does it daydream about? If the *Wake* itself could be seen as the attempt to fulfill a certain kind of daydream, what is significant about the particular form in which its fulfillment manifests? To answer these questions, this chapter approaches *Finnegans Wake* as a consciously constructed wish image whose primary hopes attach to historical perception and to utopian wish images of the future.

Before we can consider *Finnegans Wake* as a book of hope and future, it is necessary to confront several considerable critical obstacles. The first obstacle is the critical commonplace that *Finnegans Wake* is cyclical, that it begins again immediately after ending and ever replays the same anew. The cyclical premise about *Finnegans Wake* trains attention on elements of the book that involve the past, memory, and cyclical recurrence. In contrast, this chapter presents a reading that stresses the open and definite future born of real possibility. It directs attention toward what the *Wake* posits as lying ahead and to what it represents as to be wished for of the future.

Another obstacle to confronting the hope-content of *Finnegans Wake* has been the critical analogy of the book to a nightdream. The nightdream points backward through the obscurity of the unconscious to the roots of anxiety and neurosis in the ego's ancient past. The nightdream threatens to deflect attention toward the past and to emphasize repetition at the expense of real possibility and what the future might bring. This chapter resists the unconscious Oedipal anxieties of Joyce, his characters, or his form; instead of seeing *Finnegans*

Wake as a nightdream, this chapter approaches the *Wake* as a conscious and clear-eyed form of wishing that is directed toward the future.

A final obstacle to grasping the roles of hope and future in *Finnegans Wake* is a certain species of historicism that not only trains attention on the granularity of the past in *Finnegans Wake* but is also at times hostile to theoretical approaches and to the idea of utopia itself. This chapter presents a way of reconciling the *Wake*'s undeniably rich historical particularity with hope and utopia through the formal-utopian principle of reincarnation or metempsychosis. Through this principle, *Finnegans Wake* brings varieties of real and fiction people and events from different times and places into stunning juxtaposition. The daydream and the historical wish dream of reincarnation can reinforce critical tendencies to think seriously about secular history in *Finnegans Wake* and to regard Joyce's use of history politically. At the same time, daydream and reincarnation might also correct for frustrating tendencies in contemporary approaches that discount the utopian impulses in Joyce's project and his sense of the openness of the future. This chapter presents the *Wake* as the product of Joyce's wishful and utopian daydreams about history itself.

After confronting these obstacles in the critical tradition at greater depth, this chapter pursues the wishful dimensions of the *Wake* through Bloch's conceptualization of the daydream. It regards the *Wake*'s thoroughgoing principle of reincarnation or metempsychosis as a formal-utopian expression of the desire to be present at the moment of utopia that never arrives in our lifetime. Finally, it turns to two formal features of the *Wake*—its terminal "the" and its frequent tableaux of characters—in order to explore the distinctive forms of the *Wake*'s openness, including its spatialization of historical time, its future orientation, and its formal-utopian historical yearnings.

Finnegans Wake, Historicism, and Utopia

Viewing *Finnegans Wake* in terms of historical daydream and utopian reincarnation presents an opportunity to revisit basic questions about the book: Is *Finnegans Wake* a book of unconscious dreaming or of conscious vision? Is it a book of mythic history or of secular Irish history? These have been major questions in the history of *Wake* criticism, and the critical story has largely been of a gradual shift in consensus from theses about sleeping to those about some form of awakening, often of political awakening, and from those about mythic history to those about secular history. The earliest critical views of *Finnegans Wake* and history focused on mythical history, usually concentrating on Joyce's use of mythical patterns rather than on the question of the book's historicity. It is now well accepted that the historical schema of Enlightenment thinker Giambattista Vico's *New Science* gave Joyce a conceptual means of grasping and presenting the sprawl of history.[1] Vico's four-part historical cycle is comprised of three progressive ages—divine, heroic, and human—and a *ricorso*, or return to the beginning, which became a major influence on critical views that see the *Wake* itself as recursive. While Vico's historical schema contains an idea of progress, this is tempered by a belief in cyclical reversion—an inevitable decline from the peak of democracy back to the depths of barbarianism. Vico's cyclical view is a heuristic method that enabled Joyce to order and give flesh to a history that might otherwise appear as a vast and ungraspable temporal abstraction, one that stretches much wider than can be comprehended in terms of the human lifespan and always threatens to dematerialize into what Walter Benjamin calls "homogeneous, empty time."[2] However, few critics these days believe that *Finnegans Wake* subscribes in any wholesale sense to Vico's mythical conceptualizations of history or to any other kind, nor are the *Wake*'s wish dreams about history structured around such a schema.

The 1980s and 1990s were a transitional period between historically mythical and historically particular approaches. At this time, theoretical approaches to history still played a major role in historical analyses of *Finnegans Wake* while an interest in historical particularity was also emerging.[3] Since the critical turn represented by the work of this period, critics have been much more likely to study Joyce's engagement with history in highly particular and concrete forms rather than in the mythic forms that characterize early Joyce criticism. Interest in secular Irish history has now securely taken hold in Joyce criticism, and critics view historical material in the *Wake* with lenses that are increasingly information-based, granular, and politically oriented.[4] It is now common to understand *Finnegans Wake* as deeply engaged with secular Irish history, and debates about the extent to which Joyce represents and takes positions on key

Irish-historical matters have almost entirely displaced concerns about Joyce's mythical visions of history.

Today the trend in historical work on Joyce is often to focus intensively on historical specificity, not only eschewing the lens of myth but also working from a certain position of wariness about theoretical abstraction altogether.[5] The shift has been from one extreme of high abstraction in the mythic-historical approach to another extreme of particularities in the historicist approach, one which is wary of and often resistant to theoretically oriented approaches other than a "historical materialist" one.[6] But as much as has been gained and learned through these changes in focus, something too has also been lost: the idea of the utopian impulse that was present in earlier approaches to the *Wake* was also liable to be thrown out along with theses about Joyce's aestheticism and mythic ahistoricism.[7] We thus observe the aesthetic-utopian strivings of modernist form coming into conflict with the historical particularity of the *Wake*'s material, and this rift that opened in critical views has seldom since been adequately repaired. Yet the divorce between aesthetic utopianism and historical materialism seems at odds with the obviously utopian dimensions and aesthetic ambitions of Joyce's vast and searching project of experimental historical representation and synthesis in *Finnegans Wake*. The task of the present, therefore, is to reconcile its historical material with the *Wake*'s ambitiously utopian form, to find a place for utopian hope and striving in *Finnegans Wake* in ways that do not succumb to myth but that rather emerge from Joyce's treatment of the historical past and his daydreams about history.

Another potential loss that results from focusing on *Finnegans Wake* as secular history is the loss of the future.[8] For while it is true to say that the *Wake* is obsessed with the past, there are also dangers in describing it too entirely in relation to history.[9] *Finnegans Wake* reflects on the pitfalls of prioritizing the past at the expense of the future. As Joyce writes of Finn MacCool, "though his heart, soul and spirit turn to pharaoph times, his love, faith and hope stick to futuerism" (*FW* 129.36–130.1). In the *Wake*, the past is often associated with the backside, posterior, hindquarters, or the hams. Past violence is figured as "the effrays round fatherthyme's beckside" (90.7), and Humphrey Chimpden Earwicker or HCE declares, "I have bared my whole past" (536.28). Some, like Shaun, look forward to nothing more than to looking backward, anticipating little but Proustian anamnesis: "it is becoming hairydittary I have of coerce nothing in view to look forward at unless it is Swann and beating the blindquarters out of my oldfellow's orologium oloss olorium" (410.2–5). But the *Wake* also begins with an image of youth giving age a swift kick in the ass, as when "a kidscad buttended a bland old isaac" (3.10–11). And even as the hams look back at a past behind one, don't the feet still move forward into the future?: "—The mujic of the footure on the barbarihams of the bashed?" (518.28).[10]

The Unconscious, the Future

Finnegans Wake is at all points saturated with the mad desire to bring people and events from disparate times and places simultaneously before our eyes. A sentence from the book's second page is a characteristic example: "Where the Baddelaries partisans are still out to mathmaster Malachus Micgranes and the Verdons catapelting the camibalistics out of the Whoyteboyce of Hoodie Head" (*FW* 4.3–6). Here the Whiteboys, the Battle of Verdun, and Brian Boru (according to Roland McHugh, the Vernon family is supposed to possess Brian Boru's sword) are brought together in the space of the same sentence, a sentence of the kind that is perhaps most typical of the book in containing strange historical juxtapositions. Why is this technique so pervasive and what does it mean?

It has been most typical to appeal for answer to the logic of the nightdream as conceptualized by psychoanalysis: condensation and displacement, in principle, allow for any historical material to be concentrated at a single point, which could account for the *Wake*'s outrageous adjacencies. This strategy was formulated very early in the reception of *Finnegans Wake*.[11] However, the richest and most rigorous defense of the dream proposition came in 1986 in John Bishop's *Joyce's Book of the Dark*, in which Bishop accounts for the style and language of *Finnegans Wake* by presuming that Joyce was committed to comprehensively representing the night and the full experience of sleeping, dreaming included: "Only a little reflection … will demonstrate that the systematic darkening of every term in *Finnegans Wake* was an absolute necessity, dictated by Joyce's subject."[12] Bishop sees the *Wake*'s experiments with language as a generalized form of what Joyce calls "sordomutics" (*FW* 117.14), a word combination whose Latin roots suggest deafness and muteness: "Not a single 'blanche patch' in *Finnegans Wake* fails either directly or obliquely to evoke such states of imperception as blindness, deafness, dumbness, and numbness," Bishop claims.[13]

While some, like Derek Attridge, reject the nightdream thesis about *Finnegans Wake* because of a pluralist resistance to authoritative perspectives of any kind,[14] another of the claim's liabilities is that the dream and its attendant, especially psychoanalytic, terms tend to pull backward toward infantile Oedipal conflicts. For instance, Margot Norris argues, "*Finnegans Wake* harbors at its center a myth of origins that functions as a living mystery for its figures. A secret source of guilt, like the theological Original Sin or the Freudian crimes of incest and parricide buried in the unconscious, its manifestation is an evasive and digressive narrative style."[15] Seen in these terms, the *Wake* is not simply directed toward the past, but simultaneously seeks to evade knowledge of the past in a markedly neurotic fashion.[16] It is true that, like in *A Portrait*, *Finnegans Wake* often expresses a thoroughgoing and illimitable sense of anxiety about the past. Like readers of *A Portrait*, *Wake* readers necessarily become something like detectives, dusting literary traces to try to determine, for example, exactly what crime was committed in Phoenix Park. Just as in *A Portrait*, where the "darkness at the beginning" can never finally be illuminated, in *Finnegans Wake* the core scandal never quite comes into focus, and it is perhaps all the more anxiety-provoking for its ambiguity.[17]

Although the *Wake* represents a sense of illimitable anxiety about the past, the Freudian explanation is unsatisfying for several reasons. First, attempts to locate the origin of this anxiety in the nightdream or the unconscious of a single character or of the author have never been persuasive, so it is difficult to maintain the coherence of the nightdream explanation for every part of the book and for each of its different narrators and narrative perspectives. Second, it is dissatisfying to have to account for these creative and intriguing historical juxtapositions through the mechanism of the unconscious, which suggests that these relationships are accidental, opportunistic, and symptomatic. Third, it too readily explains away the concrete reality of the juxtapositions by seeing them as merely convenient expressions for unconscious desires rather than as meaningfully visionary on their own terms.

But most importantly, as Bloch writes, "The unconscious of psychoanalysis is ... *never a Not-Yet-Conscious*, an element of progressions; it consists rather of regression," and, as Bloch puts it most succinctly, *"there is nothing new in the Freudian unconscious."*[18] Regarding *Finnegans Wake* solely or primarily as a nightdream robs it of its visionary forward-looking power. It becomes all the more difficult to see how the *Wake* might be restlessly inventive, forward-looking, and in search of the new, how its style might be driven not by neurotic evasion, as in Norris, or by systematic darkening or blindness, as in Bishop, but rather by a consciously driven constructive visionary principle. The nightdream blocks our ability to see those things about which *Finnegans Wake* daydreams. The nightdream also fundamentally colors the mood and undercurrents of the *Wake*, circumscribing what we can and cannot notice about it. We ought to abandon the understanding of the *Wake* as a massive evasion and digression from the object, committed to darkening our vision, thoroughly neurotic in fashion, and perhaps even fatally repetitive. Better is to see *Finnegans Wake* as future-oriented, single-mindedly and doggedly pursuing an object whose task it will now be for us to define.[19]

The Wake and Daydream

For Bloch, unlike the nightdream, which is rooted in the unconscious and the past, the daydream has a deliberate visionary power and is resolutely future-oriented. Bloch credits the daydream with the capacity for "a tireless incentive towards the actual attainment of what it visualizes."[20] Contrary to most nightdream accounts of the *Wake*'s relationship between form and content, the *Wake*'s magnificent historical juxtapositions should be seen as wish images that result from quite conscious historical and formal fantasies and desires. This approach is not given to universalism, though it seeks to uncover a certain utopian dimension in Joyce that historicism overlooks. Nor is it devoted to extreme historical specificity or allergic to theory, though in using the work of Bloch the theory is rooted in historical and material socioeconomic considerations.

As it happens, the only place in *The Principle of Hope* in which Bloch mentions Joyce is at the very point when he considers the intersection between nightdreams and daydreams. His subject is *Ulysses*, but his claims seem even better suited to *Finnegans Wake*: "The cellar of the unconscious discharges itself in Joyce into a transitory Now, provides a mixture of prehistoric stammering, smut and church music …. But in the midst of the monkey-chatter (from one day and a thousand subconscious human reactions strictly mixed up) there appears something clearly viewed, applied montage shows quite rational cross-connections or analogiae entis; Lot's wife and The Old Ireland Tavern near the salt water down by the docks, cutting straight through time and space, celebrate their meeting, their everyday beyond space and time."[21]

Bloch's comments on *Ulysses* capture well the way in which the *Wake* seems to resemble expressions of the unconscious in its opaque but highly synthetic juxtapositions. A short phrase, plucked at random, such as "Anthea first unfoiled her limbs wanderloot" (*FW* 354.21–2), combines material as diverse as *Alice in Wonderland* and Aphrodite (Anthea is one of Aphrodite's epithets as flower-goddess), but in such a curious way that it appears to rely less on rational connections than on some skewed dream meeting or collision, a "transitory Now" comprised of layer upon layer of displacement, condensation, and revision, whose neurotic path it would be the critic's task to patiently reconstruct and analyze. This, as we have seen, is a familiar way of thinking about *Finnegans Wake*: by now every possible variation of dreamwork and unconscious seems to have been applied to Joyce's final and densest book.

It is true that the nightdream dimension of the *Wake* calls for unraveling dense unconscious connections between things, and this interpretative necessity has also played a large role in the long and gradual deciphering and annotating of the book. However, such an interpretive imperative and preoccupation should be recognized as a form of "secondary revision," Freud's term for the way in which condensed and displaced dream content is shaped into a more or less coherent narrative. One problem with interpretation as secondary revision is that the *Wake* is notoriously resistant to the process of making-coherent. Efforts to translate the book into a smooth, naturalistic narrative have never been quite convincing.[22] Moreover, Freud himself asserts that secondary revision "seeks to construct *something* like a daydream from the material available which offers itself,"[23] signaling how subtly the nightdream shades into the territory of daydream. And while Freud dismissively likens the daydream to fantasy, Bloch sees the daydream as potentially aligned with forward-dawning and with the actively visionary. It is precisely the visionary rather than revisionary quality of *Finnegans Wake* that Bloch helps to capture: it is contained in those things that are viewed *clearly*, in the rational daydreams that reside within the analogies of being or in the correspondences between things (*analogiae entis*) that the *Wake* projects. While the nightdream resides in a cellar of the unconscious, discharging and mixing its detritus into a monkey-chatter, the daydream, for Bloch, is clear- and open-eyed; it cuts straight through time and space with a purpose, formulating a conscious wish dream rather than a censored evasion of unconscious knowledge or desires.

It is in genetic criticism of Joyce, with its focus on the process of textual composition and production rather than on the "product" of the text, that we find the best articulation of the *Wake* as creative vision. Geneticists have, among other things, made clear the disproportion between the *Wake* as a product whose effect may be a bewildering chaos of juxtapositions and the *Wake* as a process whose composition was nothing if not purposeful, methodical, and visionary. Interestingly, when geneticist David Hayman comments on the *Wake* manuscripts and on Joyce's methods of composition and revision, he loosely echoes Bloch's comments about *Ulysses*: "Muddied with ink, crayon, pencil, crossed through and written over though the manuscripts may be, there is method beneath the apparent chaos of Joyce's revisions."[24] Like Bloch, Hayman locates Joyce's writing at the intersection of muddy chaos and (re)visionary method, resembling the way in which Bloch differentiates between the nightdream and the daydream. As the highly self-referential book I, chapter 5 puts it, "No, so help me Petault, it is not a miseffectual whyacinthinous riot of blots and blurs and bars and balls and hoops and wriggles and juxtaposed jottings linked by spurts of speed: it only looks as like it as damn it" (*FW* 118.28–31). Like its fabled letter referenced here, *Finnegans Wake* only appears to be an inky riot made at the speed of unconscious thought. Hayman also writes, "The fact that Joyce's methods of composition can be categorized testifies to the orderly development of most of the chapters and to the amount of thought which in each case preceded composition."[25] Here, again, we find a methodical, constructive, and visionary quality that is more consistent with forward-dawning and daydreaming than with nightdreaming, darkening, and becoming-blind, however much the effect of reading the *Wake* as a product might suggest otherwise. The creator of the "muddest thick that was ever heard dump" (296.20–1) yet "must slav to methodiousness" (159.31–1).

For Freud, daydreams are compensatory fantasies to which unhappy people turn in order to fulfill wishes: "We may lay it down that a happy person never phantasies, only an unsatisfied one. The motive forces of phantasies are unsatisfied wishes, and every single phantasy is the fulfilment of a wish, a correction of unsatisfying reality. These motivating wishes vary according to the sex, character and circumstances of the person who is having the phantasy; but they fall naturally into two main groups. They are either ambitious wishes, which serve to elevate the subject's personality; or they are erotic ones."[26] Bloch offers two useful correctives to Freud's sense of daydream. First, Bloch emphasizes that daydreams are not just the flimsy stuff of compensatory fantasy: "How richly people have always dreamed of this, dreamed of the better life that might be possible. Everybody's life is pervaded by daydreams: one part of this is just stale, even enervating escapism, even booty for swindlers, but another part is provocative, is not content just to accept the bad which exists, does not accept renunciation. This other part has hoping at its core, and is teachable."[27] While daydreaming may involve feeble compensations, it also can be a place for provocations that help to condition new habits of thought.

Second, Bloch emphasizes that the drives of hunger and self-preservation are not only importantly prior to the sexual drive but also resolutely sociohistorical and forward-looking in nature.[28] To call the Joyce of *Finnegans Wake* a daydreamer, then, is not to inquire into his erotic fantasies or egotistical ambitions, but rather to see him as primarily dissatisfied with certain deprivations that arise from irreducible material realities in relation to historical conditions. It would be too reductive to make the counterclaim that *Finnegans Wake* actually *represents* a daydream rather than a nightdream or that it is preoccupied solely with the future rather than with the past. Rather, the *Wake* reflects Joyce himself as a daydreamer and as a forward-looking artist to whom the categories of hope and future are deeply meaningful. This is not to say that Joyce does not revisit his and others' earlier texts, that he does not exploit the idea of the nightdream and the unconscious for his purposes, or that his imagination does not often fixate on the past with curiosity and even anxiety; just as *A Portrait* would not be what it is if it were all green roses with no *Fœtuses*, so *Finnegans Wake* would not be what it is without the historical past, especially Irish history, and the nightdream with all of its attendant concepts and affordances. However, in the *Wake* history is approached not just as an unconscious symptom but also with a forward-looking and searching style, inventiveness, and restlessness that suggest that *Finnegans Wake* was conceived and written with an orientation toward hope and the future. Far better than viewing *Finnegans Wake* as a version of history would be to adopt Bloch's phrase, "a transitory Now" as emblem for it, like Shem's writing on his own body, in which "one continuous present tense integument slowly unfolded all marryvoising moodmoulded cyclewheeling history" (*FW* 185.36–186.2).[29]

Unlike in the night dream, the ego is present in the daydream.[30] Daydreams recognize and welcome their objects; they can serve as the conscious beginning for pursuing and fulfilling wishes.[31] Bloch invests the daydream with inventive consciousness: "But clearly, people do not dream only at night, not at all. The day too has twilight edges, where wishes are also gratified. In contrast to the nocturnal dream, that of the daytime sketches freely chosen and repeatable figures in the air, it can rant and rave, but also brood and plan. It gives free play to its thoughts in an indolent fashion (which can, however, be closely related to the Muse and to Minerva), political, artistic, scientific thoughts. The daydream can furnish inspirations which do not require interpreting, but working out, it builds castles in the air as blueprints too, and not always just fictitious ones."[32] The free play, inspiration, and blueprinting that Bloch correlates with the daydream are essential to understanding Joyce's approach to his material, whether it is engaged with the past or looking into the real possibilities of the future.

Finally, for Bloch, by distinguishing between nightdreams and daydreams we can identify different orders of hope and wish in which the nightdream corresponds to the past and the unconscious and in which the daydream corresponds to the future and to conscious wishing. The nightdream logic by which Aphrodite and Alice, Brian Boru and the Whiteboys, or even Lot's wife and The Old Irish Tavern might in principle be brought together by tracing the path of condensation, displacement, representation, and revision is evident enough, but what remains to be shown is how these collisions also express quite conscious historical wishes that result from future-oriented wish dreaming on Joyce's part. The daydream is a category capable of mediating between mythic and actual history, and between the unconscious and the visionary. Like paralysis readings of *Dubliners*, nightdream readings of the *Wake* are likely here to stay, but they need to be mediated by a sense of Joyce's quite conscious, rather than unconscious, visionary and utopian relationship to his material. We should differentiate between the *effect* of Joyce's dazzling juxtapositions in *Finnegans Wake*, which often seem to express the displaced and condensed logic of the nightdream, and the *process* of composition, the constructive principle that is methodical and guided by the conscious wish of the daydream.

Metempsychosis, Reincarnation, and the Being-Present of History

Reincarnation or metempsychosis has long been acknowledged as a key principle in *Ulysses*. For example, Maria Tymoczko writes, "In the repertory of mythic elements that Joyce uses in *Ulysses*, metempsychosis is in fact the mainspring; it coordinates and drives all the mythic systems of the book. Metempsychosis is the philosophical center of the reanimation of all mythologies in *Ulysses* and the rationale for Joyce's complex mythic compression; serving to bind the parallel mythic systems, metempsychosis is in fact the center of Joyce's mythic architectonics and mythic method in *Ulysses*."[33] In *Ulysses*, Joyce had experimented with narrative reincarnation through the concept of metempsychosis. Through parallels with the *Odyssey*, *Ulysses* represented characters who could be considered reincarnations of the ancient epic's characters in relationships of congruity, incongruity, or sometimes even outright irony or parody. Doing so allowed Joyce to shuttle between the ancient and the modern in innovative ways. However, like the molecules of Stephen's mole, Joyce's mode of reincarnation in *Ulysses* could only circulate within a defined shape that, as Joyce complained of Stephen to Frank Budgen, could not be changed.[34]

It has not been sufficiently appreciated how *Finnegans Wake* is not only impelled by a spirit of reincarnation similar to that of *Ulysses*, but also how the *Wake* seems designed to harness the concept in ways that Joyce could or did not within the narrative architecture of *Ulysses*. In order to take the principle of narrative reincarnation further than Joyce did in *Ulysses*, it would be necessary to make characters much more malleable, to empty them out until they amounted to little more than character-positions or even simple sigla that could allow for maximum circulation and recirculation of people and characters from different times and places. To animate them fully would require a much more extensive form of circulation, indeed a Viconian form of recirculation, which would also allow Joyce to introduce a form of historical cycling unavailable in the binary *Odyssey*-parallel structure of *Ulysses*. *Finnegans Wake* would thereby be able to embrace a greater and more flexible degree of reincarnation while also releasing the historical imagination to travel in practically any direction. If one set out to design a machine whose purpose it was to reincarnate any and all elements of history together at a moment's notice and to assemble them in an anecdotal present,[35] it would be difficult to daydream anything better than *Finnegans Wake*.

Finnegans Wake's principle of reincarnation is so pervasive that there is hardly a moment in the book when figures from secular history and literary/mythic history are not being blasted out of chronology and presented for the reader's contemplation as a formal constellation: "Our wholemole millwheeling vicociclometer ... receives through a portal vein the dialytically separated elements of precedent decomposition for the verypetpurpose of subsequent recombination so that the heroticisms, catastrophes and eccentricities transmitted by the ancient legacy of the past ... may be there for you, Cockalooralooraloomenos, when cup, platter and pot come piping hot, as sure as herself pits hen to paper and there's scribings scrawled on eggs" (*FW* 614.27–615.10). In "wholemole," there is perhaps a sense that the principle of Stephen's molecules cycling through his mole is still in operation, but now that process finally operates within a vaster purview, encompassing not just an individual's history, such as ALP's, but also the "ancient legacy of the past." In *Finnegans Wake* everything is the mole. The *Wake* figures itself here like the morning newspaper, a mole replenished daily, which contains any number of stunning though largely arbitrary juxtapositions brought together by calendrical coincidence, except that through the recombination of decomposed elements Joyce makes moments from different eras of the past absolutely contemporary with each other. The ancient past begins to coexist spatially like the stories in the morning paper and to appear just as contemporary as today's cockcrow and morning breakfast.

In *Finnegans Wake* fictional and historical figures can exchange positions with extreme fluidity. So accustomed can readers of the *Wake* become to this ubiquitous technique that it may at times take extra effort to register just how stunning its collection of characters and its spatialization of time can be, as in the very familiar passage from the first page, which offers ample evidence of the book's incredible spatialization of historical and literary history.[36] At the very start, Joyce accommodates at once and in the same space a dazzling variety of people, characters, and things from different times and places: the historical Sir Amory Tristram, 1st Earl of Howth; the mythical Tristan (and implicitly Isolde and King Mark); North America, Brittany, Europe, Howth, the Isthmus of Sutton, the Oconee river, Topsawyer's Rock, the city of Dublin in Laurens County, Georgia; Tom Sawyer and Peter Sawyer; St. Patrick, the Old Testament figures Moses, Noah, Jacob (and implicitly Esau), and Isaac; the apostle Peter; Irish politicians Isaac Butt and Charles Stewart Parnell; fiction writers William Makepeace Thackeray (*Vanity Fair*) and Jonathan Swift, along with Swift's friends Esther Johnson (Stella) and Esther Vanhomrigh (Vanessa); the Irish libations Jameson whiskey and Guinness beer; also present are Joyce's inventions, Issy, Shem, Shaun, HCE, and ALP as well as Joyce's family members, Giorgio and Nora. And there's probably more, all joined together at the wake. The *Wake* tends to cluster and to spatialize its cast of characters in constellations or tableaux of this kind that suggest a fantastic and idealized metempsychosis.

What wishes are imaginatively fulfilled by reincarnation and metempsychosis? Most obvious is the desire to overcome death. Reincarnation is easy to grasp as a wish image of life persisting after death, albeit in an altered future form. In this sense, reincarnation shares certain wish elements with the concept of heaven or with any other picture of an afterlife, yet it also crucially differs from these by maintaining an interest in the given world rather than in the beyond. In the way in which the transmigration of souls is conceptualized during the Enlightenment by Lessing, Bloch locates an additional wish image that puts reincarnation in relation to wishes about history: "above all the doctrine of the transmigration of souls afforded individuals with Lessing's longing for activity and future the gleaming prospect of an actual being-present in the epochs of history as a whole."[37] As Bloch notes, this wish image reflects both Enlightenment individualism and a certain faith in progress.

Nevertheless, it is useful to look at the *Wake* through the wish dream of reincarnation in part as a corrective to the disproportionate attention that has been accorded to Vico's circular influence. The *Wake*'s juxtapositions richly suggest ever-shifting forms of being-present in the epochs of history.

In another context, Bloch suggests an additional historical motivation for wish dreams that involve overcoming death: "Today the train of events is so very much longer than our life … that no worthy man can still die sated with life in the historical sense."[38] For everybody, except for martyrs, Bloch argues, there is "the right to complain that they will not be present at the victory, that they will not know themselves to be unbroken subjects of history."[39] Although Bloch does not explicitly say so, this desire to see the outcome of historical events should be included in the inventory of wish images that collect around reincarnation. Reincarnation, in these terms, would mean the arch-utopian overcoming not just of the finitude of human life but also of the violence and sufferings of history. It represents the desire not just to view or experience history as a being-present in all epochs but also to eventually be present at the utopian moment itself, which must elude one in life.

Like *Ulysses*, *Finnegans Wake* offers an image of time spatialized into discrete forms.[40] But spatialization occurs in *Finnegans Wake* above all in the uncanny transhistorical meetings and collisions that it stages and celebrates on its sweeping "collideorscape" (*FW* 143.28). Characters from different historical positions are constantly telescoped together into the same formal space or landscape. The structure of the *Wake* is largely defined by its unceasing tension between the temporal imperative of narrating life stories or "livestories" (17.27) and the spatial prerogative of making narrative space, or "annal livves" (340.22).[41] Anyone coming to the *Wake* expecting it to tell a story very soon recognizes that a spatial imperative consistently thwarts the desire for and disrupts any sense of narrative continuity. Like the annals, the river Liffey is both a temporal flow and a place. In *Finnegans Wake*, time and history continually become space and fossil: "annals of themselves timing the cycles of events grand and national, bring fassilwise to pass how" (13.31–2). When history is made into annals, it takes on a form and shape that can then facilitate any conceivable number of transhistorical encounters in which "one is continually firstmeeting with odd sorts of others at all sorts of ages!" (51.10–11). All of the "livestories" that the *Wake* tells become conflated, the dead and the living together. Hopes are spatialized as hoops: "For then was the age when hoops ran high" (20.28). In Joyce's version of "faith, hope, and charity," hope is again a hoop: "Keep cool faith in the firm, have warm hoep [Dutch *hoep*: hoop] in the house and begin frem athome to be chary of charity" (434.2–3).[42] When hope is a hoop, it brings time ("the age") into a space, a ring shape. It combines Vico's temporal circle with a spatial arena.

Joyce uses a technique of anachronistic juxtaposition in *Finnegans Wake* to creatively appropriate and to spatialize history, to daydream a utopian overcoming of lifespan and the transcendence of death, and to imagine an arch-utopian and unbroken being-present in all epochs of history, especially at the utopian moment.[43] Specifically, Joyce's powerful acts of simultaneity and his strange syntheses suggest a future-oriented and conscious wishing to know the outcome of historical events in a way that is necessarily denied to us given how short our lives are relative to historical processes and how vulnerable any historical outcome is to future change. In our brief and finite lifetimes, which *Ulysses*, as we have seen, defines against an astronomical scale as "a parenthesis of infinitesimal brevity" (*U* 17.1055-6), we can typically only see these larger movements as through the tiny keyhole of individual life. *Finnegans Wake* constitutes a wish image of inhabiting a vast history that has been radically tailored to human dimensions and given a fleshly reality to overcome abstraction in historical conceptualizations. The *Wake*, then, is historical not just in its mythic visions or in its presentation of secular historical material, but also and especially in its particular daydream of bringing certain moments of history together through acts of imaginative reincarnation into anticipatory and formal-utopian spatial configurations. Joyce realizes the historical wish image of history's being-present through a daydream of reincarnation and metempsychosis. These daydreams blast historical events out of their temporal historical continuum, overcoming the abstraction of homogeneous empty time, until history is finally concretized and spatialized on a single plain and becomes available for contemplation as a spatial constellation.[44]

Yet for all of its spatialization, the *Wake* never loses sight of time, especially the future.[45] A sequence in book III, chapter 4, written in a prophetic mode and driven by a number of "shall" and "will" statements, looks forward to events as near as the next day or farther into the future.[46] In the course of this passage the speaker expresses a wish: "Yet if I durst to express the hope how

I might be able to be present. All these peeplers entrammed and detrained on bikeygels and troykakyls and those puny farting little solitires! Tollacre, tollacre!" (*FW* 567.32–4). The wish here is to be present in the future, to be there in order to see the way in which all of the people's various journeys (German *Fahrt*: journey), whether by tram, train, bike, trike, or perhaps even by unicycle (solitary tires = unicycles?), turn out. This desire to see what will happen, to be present beyond our expiration dates, helps to account for the book's form, which insistently constellates different times and places until they are able to exist and to be grasped in a simultaneous present, as a being-present in history.

The "The" and the Future of *Finnegans Wake*

Finnegans Wake famously concludes with, "A way a lone a last a loved a long the" (*FW* 628.15–16). In the conventional reading, the unpunctuated "the" that ends *Finnegans Wake* invites readers to link back to the lowercase first word of the book, "riverrun," to form a continuous sentence.[47] This view understands *Finnegans Wake* as an infinite loop, "the book of Doublends Jined" (20.15–16) whose joined ends invariably replay the same strange scenes and sequences or "seequeerscenes" (556.24) over and again. And it is true that *Finnegans Wake* often seems intent on demonstrating that the past recurs in a reshuffled form. It sometimes seems pessimistic that there is anything new under the sun: "Yet is no body present here which was not there before. Only is order othered. Nought is nulled. Fuitfiat! [Latin *fuit fiat*: as it was, let it be]" (613.13–14). Seen this way, the *Wake*'s presumed structural circularity, with its suggestion of eternal return, would take us right back to the frustrating sense of cyclical "cyclewheeling" (186.2), stasis, paralysis, and hopelessness that are so commonly attributed to *Dubliners*.

Especially when seen from a great distance, as on the cosmic scale familiar from "Ithaca," the events of the *Wake* even take on a certain "aerily perennious" (*FW* 57.22) quality, as when all human ambitions and expressions of pride, generation after generation, end up buried in the earth: "Countlessness of livestories have netherfallen by this plage, flick as flowflakes, litters from aloft, like a waast wizzard all of whirlworlds. Now are all tombed to the mound, isges to isges, erde from erde. Pride, O pride, thy prize!" (17.26–30). Reminiscent of the largely fruitless and sometimes circular perambulations of characters in *Dubliners*, like Lenehan who walks in a big loop in "Two Gallants" and Gabriel Conroy who enjoys "cycling" (*D* 164.460) "on the continent" (*D* 157.189), *Finnegans Wake* shows, "A human pest cycling (pist!) and recycling (past!) about the sledgy streets, here he was (pust!) again!" (*FW* 99.4–6). Vicious circles are superimposed onto Vico's cycles, as in one of the many characteristics attributed to Finn MacCool: he "moves in vicous cicles yet remews the same" (134.16–17). With an emphasis on cycles and cycling, then, Joyce's trajectory as a writer and thinker from *Dubliners* to *Finnegans Wake* would appear remarkably consistent, and given its incredible inventiveness in other areas, paradoxically static and even paralyzed.

On the other hand, the *Wake* also imagines resistance to vicious cycles and imagines ways of halting or breaking out of them. In fact, *Finnegans Wake* is unique in Joyce's work to the extent that in it the future, in the form of the next day, actually arrives. *Ulysses* and "The Dead" present turbulent and potentially transformative nights in the lives of their characters, to such a degree that readers cannot help but speculate about what the next morning might bring for Gabriel and Gretta Conroy or for Leopold and Molly Bloom. But it is only in the *Wake* that the next morning denied to the Blooms and the Conroys is finally given.[48] In contrast to the night and early morning endings of *Dubliners* and *Ulysses*, book IV of *Finnegans Wake* shows the sun rise—"So an inedible yellowmeat turns out the invasable blackth" (*FW* 594.32–3)—and the open future emerges along with it: "It was a long, very long, a dark, very dark, an allburt unend, scarce endurable, and we could add mostly quite various and somewhat stumbletumbling night. Endee he sendee. Diu! The has goning at gone, the is coming to come" (598.6–10). As the river runs out to the sea and new waters displace the old, the final part of the book presents resurrection in the form of awakening and the coming future: "And let her rain now if she likes. Gently or strongly as she likes. Anyway let her rain for my time is come" (627.11–13). The *Wake*'s strong sense of a future belies the strictly cyclical and paralyzed view.

Even more, while it is a critical commonplace that the *Wake*'s final "the" *can* turn around and cyclically join "riverrun" at the beginning of the book, it is equally true that nothing dictates or forces readers to round out a circle or finish a circuit. Even though in many of our readings of the *Wake* the past "rearrive[s]" (*FW* 3.5), things only "seim anew" (215.23), and "the same roturns" in "cycloannalism" (18.5, 254.26), "the" might as easily point to an escape from the loop as act as a hook for the eye of "riverrun." As Jim LeBlanc puts it, "Surely, this presumption of circularity, like any reading of virtually any moment in *Finnegans Wake*, is only partially correct. Doesn't it tend to conceal, in fact, the plain-as-day truth (which is, perhaps a little *too* self-evident as we hold the book in our hands) that Joyce's final novel *ends* with 'the'?"[49] All we can be sure of is that the *Wake* ends without punctuation and that nothing but a blank vista of space stretches out ahead of its final word.

Seen this way, the end of *Finnegans Wake* is not so much a space of return as it is a space of expectation: "*the* is coming to come."[50] Just as the beginning of *Ulysses* cannot quite foreclose upon the future opened up by the conclusion of *A Portrait*, neither can "riverrun" foreclose upon the state of possibility represented by the suspended "the" and the alluring blankness to which it gives way. There is nothing to say that the *Wake* will play out the same way every time, even if it usually does, and nothing to say that the future will be "riverrun," even if it usually is. There is nothing to militate against unforeseen possibilities.

While LeBlanc reasonably stresses the anxiety inherent in this state of expectation,[51] potentiality also lies in this moment if we are able disassociate it from a reflexive return to the beginning. Less "a finger pointing at nothing,"[52] as LeBlanc has it, Joyce's final "the"—the culminating word of his writing career, as it turned out—is a finger that points at something quite definite to come (as the definite article always does), but presently unknown. Joyce's suspended "the" thus strikes the ideal anticipatory and hopeful combination of the openness of the future with the definiteness of form with which the future never fails to arrive. In suspending "the" so, Joyce leaves open every variety of real possibility—that which could occur given present conditions, however likely or unlikely. Whatever is on its way will surely be determined by these real possibilities, one of which is always the chance of "riverrun," and yet the future remains scandalously open to other eventualities as well.

In English, "the" most thoroughly anticipates something concrete and specific to follow. By leaving "the" to hang before and to preside over the expansive white space at the close of *Finnegans Wake* (excepting the paratextual notation, "PARIS, / 1922-1939"[53]), Joyce ends the book with the greatest sense of possibility that the English language can evoke. It hangs like the cosmic dot of "Ithaca," a seed rich with possibility, or like a green rose hovering in the imagination. The *Wake*'s definite article is perhaps best seen as pointing toward what Bloch calls the Not-Yet-Become,[54] that future which is unforeseeable, unconceptualizable from the standpoint of the present, and most inaccessible to memory. When the trajectory of Joyce's first sentence from "The Sisters" to his last word in *Finnegans Wake* is thought of in these terms, the potentialities and possibilities implied in the suspended definite article represent the very antithesis of the common reading of "no hope." When "no hope" is seen not as hopelessness but as non-hope, a state open to new and unforeseen states of being within the context of material conditions and real possibility, then Joyce's *oeuvre* is remarkably and consistently future oriented and open to the unforeseen. Joyce's "the" suggests every realizable hope while specifying none.

Tableaux of All the Charictures in the Drame

The tendency to spatialize characters not only attaches to a utopian ideal of metempsychosis, but it also represents the promise of a community of characters seen clearly, graspable all at once in the same space. These spatialized character tableaux are one of the ways in which *Finnegans Wake* both tantalizes with and withholds the utopia of understanding. Joyce's technique of placing or evoking characters in tableaux should be seen in relation to the utopian future. In the sequence in book III, chapter 4 examined above, for instance, we find a constellation or tableau of characters explicitly attached to the promise of morning, daylight, and awakening. We are promised the entire royal "court" of the *Wake*: "Then the court to come in to full morning" (*FW* 566.24–5). The court will include "Soakersoon," "Katya," "Those twelve chief barons," "The maidbrides all," "The dame dowager," "The two princes of the tower royal," "The dame dowager's duffgerent," and "The infant Isabella" (566.10–23). If we "Have peacience" (568.5), we will see and hear Anna Livia Plurabelle in her morning activities: "The annamation of evabusies, the livlianess of her laughings, such as a plurity of bells!" (568.4–5). In the morning, ALP will also be "Mbv!" (568.4), a rearranged BVM, or Blessed Virgin Mary. Shem,

Shaun, and Issy will be there, too: "Britus and Gothius shall no more joustle for that sonneplace but mark one autonement when, with si so silent, Cloudia Aiduolcis, good and dewed up, shall let fall, yes, no, yet, now, a rain. Muchsias grapcias!" (568.8–11). Brutus, Cassius, and Mark Antony, as well as the Brits and the Goths and the Mookse and the Gripes will be there. Naturally enough, HCE will be present—"Arise, sir Pompkey Dompkey! Ear! Ear! Weakeat!" (568.25–6)—along with Humpty Dumpty.

But the sun is not yet fully risen: "In the sleepingchambers. The court to go into half morning" (*FW* 566.7). The full sunrise, which will come in book IV, is only anticipated here. In the phases of morning that he evokes, Joyce plays on different valences at once: awakening and resurrecting (morning), but also falling and dying (mourning). Joyce puts the morning in the expected order: full morning follows from half morning in a linearly temporal progression, just as the sun rises. But by putting morning in order, Joyce necessarily puts full and half mourning out of order, because "full mourning," when one wears black, should precede "half mourning," the period that follows. This inverse tension that Joyce establishes between morning and mourning suggests that to await full morning is to anticipate resurrection and redemption: morning will reverse mourning and will bring the dead back, awaken them. Morning is hope in dialectic with mourning, which connotes above all the material world of history, hunger, and the final deprivation of death.

The anticipatory sequence between pages 566 and 570 culminates this way: "It stays in the book of that which is. I have heard anyone tell it jesterday (master currier with brassard was't) how one should come on morrow here but it is never here that one today. Well but remind to think, you where yestoday Ys Morganas war and that it is always tomorrow in toth's tother's place. Amen" (570.9–13). This passage acknowledges that the longed-for morning never arrives: it "should come on morrow here but it is never here that one today."[55] As if to explain this curious fact ("Well but to remind"), we are asked "to think" about where yesterday's mornings were (and how they warred) and about how today is yesterday's tomorrow. And yet we find ourselves no closer to the tomorrow that we imagined or for which we hoped. By evoking death through his allusion to the *Egyptian Book of the Dead* ("the book of that which is" [in the Underworld]), Joyce perhaps conjures Macbeth's "tomorrow and tomorrow and tomorrow" soliloquy: "all our yesterdays have lighted fools / The way to dusty death." When we go on waiting for tomorrow to come, we die waiting. It is "always" and perhaps only tomorrow in Thoth's other place: in death, in the underworld in which Thoth served as scribe. The idea is dispiriting: the future does not arrive as hoped for, nor is it likely to arrive in our lifetime. Perhaps we are clowns who fell for a sad joke, this "jesterday." Yet all may not be so bleak. Thoth is also the inventor of writing, and his "tother's place" is not just the underworld but also the place of writing, of fiction, of the *Wake* itself. In this other place, it is "always tomorrow": *Finnegans Wake* is the space between "half mo(u)rning" and "full mo(u)rning," that place that in the context of material history, hunger, and death looks toward tomorrow, to waking up, and to reawakening the dead. Writing is the mediating *space* between the deprivation of death and the time of tomorrow.

The tableaux in this sequence, like the one on the first page of the book, offer "All the charictures in the drame!" (*FW* 302.31–2). The frequency with which *Finnegans Wake* imagines all of its characters spatialized in tableaux suggests the frequency with which it imagines and provokes in readers the desire for certain utopian constellations: the coincidence and community of all the characters/caricatures in the drama/dream revealed and fully present at once. As much as the *Wake* tantalizes with these tableaux, which represent the promise of full presence or full clarity, these characters never quite stand still; they never come together or solidify for readers. The promised sharp-edged characters in the drama remain hazy caricatures in a dream.

But that constant motion and haziness is finally the *Wake*'s strength: the sheer capacity to imagine these characters together, along with the astonishing and splendid profusion of their historical and fictional avatars, is the *Wake*'s most creative and profound form of daydreaming. These dreamy characters who can embody historical people and literary characters with unrestricted flexibility are the very stuff of historical daydream. To attribute such collections and such unlikely communities to the unconscious and to see them as a series of displacements that actually point to something other before contending with their actual being-present together is to miss the visionary in Joyce's imaginative acts, to miss the will toward reincarnation by which *Finnegans Wake* lives, dies, and is continually reborn.[56] Nor is it possible to reduce this recycling, synthesizing, and community-making tendency to a mere compositional principle of the book without thinking about the wish images that surround the concept of reincarnation: being-present in all epochs of history beyond one's short lifespan and being-present at the moment of utopia.

The moment of utopia or final victory never comes, but what produces the new is the wishful anticipation and the daydream of tomorrow, in "toth's tother's place." Joyce's spatialization of hope in the form of reincarnation is inseparable from a certain spatialization of history itself. In *Finnegans Wake* the spatialization of history joins past, present, and future together into a continuously raveling and unraveling, expanding and contracting, continually metamorphosing historical daydream. *Finnegans Wake* represents Joyce's deepest engagement with hope and future in relation to the material world. Even as it continues the trajectory set in motion by his earlier works and furthers the process of spatializing hope that he had developed in *Giacomo Joyce* and most extensively in *Ulysses*, Joyce's final work acts as a culmination of his evolving conception of hope and future in relation to real possibility and the material world. In *Finnegans Wake*, writing becomes the full creative space of wish and vision, the space of utopian overcoming of death in the form of profuse metamorphosis and metempsychosis, the space of being present at the utopian moment itself, all in complex negotiation with the materiality of historical conditions—hunger, deprivation, mourning, and death—as well as with the resistances of literary form and language itself. Here, formal and utopian striving coincide with the full complexity of hope's dialectic with the resistances of material history, oppositions which like Shem and Shaun alternate, struggle, metamorphose, and recompose in the space before our eyes.

Notes

1 In 1941 Harry Levin wrote, "The four sections of *Finnegans Wake* approximate Vico's periods of civilization, which recapitulate the four seasons of the year and the four ages of men," Harry Levin, *James Joyce: A Critical Introduction* (Norfolk: New Directions, 1941), 146-7. William York Tindall also subscribed to this mode of mythic history: "*Finnegans Wake* is about anybody, anywhere, anytime," William York Tindall, *A Reader's Guide to Finnegans Wake* (Syracuse: Syracuse University Press, 1996), 3. Bernard Benstock noted the presence of Irish history in the *Wake*, but understood it as a microcosmic reflection of a cosmic vision of history: "History in *Finnegans Wake* is a world of its own. The entire history

of the human race flows past with the waters of the Liffey in an order logically concomitant with Joyce's structural plan ... in a Viconian circle that Joyce the Artificer has successfully squared. ... The history of man's globe is mirrored in the history of Ireland, the microcosm reflecting the cosmos, in whose invasions, defenses, struggles, absorptions, and metamorphoses Joyce saw universalities," Bernard Benstock, *Joyce-Again's Wake* (Seattle: University of Washington Press, 1965), 43. Hugh Kenner saw the origin of *Finnegans Wake* in the passing of the time of Joyce's father's Ireland "into myth," Hugh Kenner, *Dublin's Joyce* (Bloomington, IN: Indiana University Press, 1956), 268. In fact, Kenner was among the first to bring the myth and dream theses together in a tight knot: "A new book was taking shape, polarized between the dreams of his recumbent father and the phantasmagoric actualities of the Healy regime, with the legendary displacement of gods and heroes by mortals as an archetypal action," Kenner, 269.

2 Walter Benjamin, "On the Concept of History," in *Selected Writings, Vol. 4, 1938–1940*, ed. Howard Eiland and Michael W. Jennings (Cambridge, MA: Harvard University Press, 2003), 395. Benjamin writes, "The concept of mankind's historical progress cannot be sundered from the concept of its progression through a homogeneous, empty time. A critique of the concept of such a progression must underlie any criticism of the concept of progress itself."

3 For example, Emer Nolan writes, "Our task here is to attend to Joyce's unquestionable success in enabling the critical enjoyment of such a comic and cyclical history, while not neglecting the specific history which he draws into his writing in order that it might be transcended at the level of form," Emer Nolan, *James Joyce and Nationalism* (New York: Routledge, 1995), 141. Vicki Mahaffey argues, "For Joyce, history is an abstraction that is interwoven into the phenomenal (and the literal) at every point," Vicki Mahaffey, "'Fantastic Histories': Nomadology and Female Piracy in *Finnegans Wake*," in *Joyce and the Subject of History*, ed. Mark A. Wollaeger, Victor Luftig, and Robert Spoo (Ann Arbor: University of Michigan Press, 1996), 158. Margot Norris argues that, while Joyce draws on Vico's theories of history, *Finnegans Wake* is largely about the use and misuse of history and is thus deeply historicist: "I hope to argue that if—as his use of Vico seems to indicate—Joyce theorizes history within the Wakean text, he does so with an updated and ironized Nietzschean sense of the use and abuse of history," Margot Norris, "The Critical History of *Finnegans Wake*," in *Joyce and the Subject of History*, ed. Mark A. Wollaeger, Victor Luftig, and Robert Spoo (Ann Arbor: University of Michigan Press, 1996), 181. Drawing on Walter Benjamin's model of historiography and power, and working from contemporary Marxist and post-structuralist views of history as a power discourse, McGee seeks to "dramatize the historicity" of *Finnegans Wake* and to demonstrate the way in which Joyce discursively subverts dominant historical discourses, Patrick

McGee, *Joyce Beyond Marx: History and Desire in Ulysses and Finnegans Wake* (Gainesville: University of Florida Press, 2001), 11. And Charles Altieri captures something of Joyce's powerful synthetic imagination and capacity to daydream about the relationship between form and history when he writes, "Where traditional history tries to describe events and structures, Joyce extends Modernist presentational principles to project something like a holographic human mind trying to encompass in a single structure the main and the twain informing the history it has made and is still making," Charles Altieri, "*Finnegans Wake* as Modernist Historiography," *Novel* 21.2–3 (Spring/Winter 1988), 243. Altieri also casts his argument in terms of deliberate dreaming, more of the kind that Bloch associates with daydreaming than with the unconsciousness of nightdreaming: "The Promethean author clearly offers his linguistic ambitions as analogues to the synthetic dreams," Altieri, 245.

4 For a history and overview of the "historical turn" in Joyce studies, see Andrew Gibson and Len Platt, "Introduction," in *Joyce, Ireland, Britain*, ed. Andrew Gibson and Len Platt (Gainesville: University Press of Florida, 2006), 1–29. Indeed, contemporary critics are far more likely to historicize the "Healy regime" than to transform it into phantasmagoria as Kenner was so quick to do.

5 In the words of Andrew Gibson and Len Platt, this new work, "relies on a practice of historical concretion: particulars take precedence over abstractions. It also relies on a practice of historical saturation: that is, a specifically Joycean historical materialism seeks to support and/or complicate its case by introducing as much historical information as is relevant and practicable. This information has priority over everything else except the texts," Gibson and Platt, "Introduction," in *Joyce, Ireland, Britain*, ed. Andrew Gibson and Len Platt (Gainesville: University Press of Florida, 2006), 18. Gibson and Platt also write, "Historical materialism … administers the coup de grace to the universalism from which Joyce studies might be thought of as having fitfully worked themselves away. It does so in two respects: it insists on extremely specific historical factors in understanding Joyce; and it implicitly turns aside from the myth of universal explicability, the idea that any and every theoretical template or critical approach is of equal usefulness in interpreting Joyce's writings" (19).

6 If this book turns away from historical particularities and toward theoretical abstraction, it is to reclaim some of the future-orientation of Emer Nolan's forward-looking nationalist Joyce, while acknowledging that Joyce falls out of whatever category or specific political goals for the future with which we try to associate him. Cheryl Herr similarly sees *Finnegans Wake* as future-oriented, but with specific futures in mind: "I see the *Wake* as, among other things, a document produced by Joyce as an equivalent to a history book. In fact, it is a history of the future, designed to evolve with its culture and actually to authorize the size

and shape of that future's construction of histories for the various contending groups in Irish politics. ... It was through a provisional history conscious of being spied upon that Joyce authorized any number of future developments," Cheryl Herr, "Ireland from the Outside," in *Joyce and the Subject of History*, ed. Mark A. Wollaeger, Victor Luftig, and Robert Spoo (Ann Arbor: University of Michigan Press, 1996), 197.

7 This loss is hinted in the terms with which Thomas Hofheinz, a proponent of this historicist shift, rejects earlier mythical approaches to history in the *Wake* around the time of the critical pivot toward secular history in the 1990s: "Joyce's existential depiction of historical experience has been interpreted as ahistorical in nature, a systematic attempt to break free from the inertia of history through the liberating power of art. This notion of an ahistorical Joyce who replaces history with *utopias of artfully wrought language* has pervaded a remarkable range of critical responses to Joyce's work up through the present," Thomas Hofheinz, *Joyce and the Invention of Irish History: Finnegans Wake in Context* (Cambridge: Cambridge University Press, 1995), 45, emphasis added. This new rejection of the mythical and aesthetic dimension was a sign that Joyceans were ready to connect their readings of *Finnegans Wake* to the explosion of Irish revisionist histories that were being published in the 1980s and 1990s, yet it also coincides with a discarding of the question of utopia.

8 Fredric Jameson suggests that in our present moment we might need to develop an anxiety about losing the future. Fredric Jameson, *Archaeologies of the Future: The Desire Called Utopia and Other Science Fictions* (New York: Verso, 2005), 233.

9 This has become so common an approach to the book that when Finn Fordham offers a thumbnail summary to *Finnegans Wake*, he writes, "If one wants such a perspective, it is possible to say that, put simply, Joyce's music-hall version of world history concerns the comic fall of a man who had once risen," Finn Fordham, *Lots of Fun at Finnegans Wake: Unravelling Universals* (Oxford: Oxford University Press, 2007), 4.

10 Here is a forward march, though to be sure, characteristically of Joyce, it is deeply aware of the historical material of the past: as the march of the future treads on the victims of a violent past, Joyce offers a version of Walter Benjamin's famous thesis, "There is no document of culture which is not at the same time a document of barbarism," Walter Benjamin, "On the Concept of History," in *Selected Writings, Volume 4, 1938–1940*, trans. Harry Zohn, ed. Howard Eiland and Michael W. Jennings (Cambridge, MA: Harvard University Press, 2003), 392.

11 On the topics of dreaming and sleeping, Levin wrote, "The stream of unconsciousness in *Finnegans Wake* begins at the very point where the stream of consciousness in *Ulysses* left off—the point of falling asleep," Levin, 140.

Tindall argued, "the *Wake* ... is a dream .... Long interest in dream brought Joyce to the construction of his 'nightmaze' (411.8) or 'dromo of todos' (598.2), his dream of all running on a track for all," Tindall, 18. Clive Hart sought to give structural consistency and narrative clarity to the dream thesis by diagramming "three principle dream layers" in the *Wake*, Clive Hart, *Structure and Motif in Finnegans Wake* (Evanston: Northwestern University Press, 1962), 84. Hart also insisted that Joyce "was not writing anything remotely like a psychoanalytical case-history" and used the dream as a "convenient device for the exploration of personality," Hart, 82.

12 John Bishop, *Joyce's Book of the Dark: Finnegans Wake* (Madison: University of Wisconsin Press, 1986), 4.

13 Ibid., 48. But if this is so, then at the very least we might note that there is a massive and beguiling disproportion between these insensible ends and the dizzyingly sensuous linguistic means that Joyce would therefore have used to achieve them.

14 Attridge writes, "The notion of the dream as an interpretative context for *Finnegans Wake* is one among a number of such contexts which, though incompatible with one another, all have some potential value," Derek Attridge, "Finnegans Awake, or the Dream of Interpretation," in *Joyce Effects: On Language, Theory, and History* (Cambridge: Cambridge University Press, 2000), 151. Attempting deconstructively to decenter the dream thesis, Attridge tries to approach the *Wake* without any preconception that it is related to sleep and dreams. He imagines that the title alone would yield thematic cues quite antithetical to dreams and sleeping: "Read as a sentence in indicative mood without punctuation, it seems to refer to a group of people called Finnegan ending a period of sleep, with the apparent implication that this is a book about consciousness, day, the start of activity, the cleansing of perception" (135).

15 Margot Norris, *The Decentered Universe of Finnegans Wake: A Structuralist Analysis* (Baltimore, MD: Johns Hopkins University Press, 1974), 44.

16 Similarly, Kimberly Devlin writes, "The weird Wakean dreamworld is a departure from Joyce's prior 'waking' fictions, but also, more importantly I think, a reexamination of their many concerns from simply a different perspective— that of the unconscious mind," Kimberly J. Devlin, *Wandering and Return in Finnegans Wake: An Integrative Approach to Joyce's Fictions* (Princeton, NJ: Princeton University Press, 1991), ix. This claim reminds us of the ways in which the psychoanalytical categories of dream and unconscious both pull backward, not just to the ancient roots of infantile repression that bring the unconscious into being, but, when employed as textual lenses, backward into Joyce's earlier works as well.

17 Were there three soldiers involved, or were there two women, or all of the above? Was it a crime of exhibition, of excretion urinary or fecal, or of onanism? Was it a crime of illicit intercourse? And if so, was the sex straight or queer or both? Bishop uses the *Wake*'s "crime" as an example of the book's patterns of "coherent nonsense": "The story is clearly there in *Finnegans Wake* for its reader to elicit: one cannot not notice it. Were it to appear in a work like *Ulysses*, however, it would be easier to take for what it really is: ridiculous," Bishop, 27, 395 n.2. This is surely correct, but perhaps the situation resists interpretation and clarification to an even greater extent than Bishop suggests. Bishop argues, "some interpretation will have to be practiced in order to discover an underlying sense," and of the "crime" in particular, he writes, "like a dream, it will clarify with interpretation" (395 n.2). However, readers cannot even be sure that there is a definite "HCE" capable of committing a crime, rather than just a siglum under whose cover any number of fictional and historical people are invited to cycle, like the molecules in Stephen's mole, in a "continuous present tense" (*FW* 186.1). I address the ambiguity of HCE's crime in the chapter, "Scandal," in David Rando, *Modernist Fiction and News: Representing Experience in the Early Twentieth Century* (New York: Palgrave Macmillan, 2011).

18 Bloch, *The Principle of Hope*, 56, emphasis in original.

19 Another recent alternative to the nightdream approach is to see *Finnegans Wake* as a book not of dreaming but of awakening. Arriving at a similar point to Attridge through a more overtly political approach, Patrick McGee argues, "Contrary to the powerful arguments of John Bishop and many others, [*Finnegans Wake*] is not about sleep any more than it is about the waking state. It is about the process of awakening, the struggle to awaken, in the liminal field that the collective subject must pass through on the way to a new vision, a new imagination of the collective social body," Patrick McGee, "The Communist Flâneur, or, Joyce's Boredom," in *European Joyce Studies 21: Joyce, Benjamin and Magical Urbanism*, ed. Maurizia Boscagli and Enda Duffy (Amsterdam: Rodopi Press, 2011), 130. Specifically, McGee sees a route to historical awakening via *Finnegans Wake*'s voice, which, he argues, acts as a kind of *flâneur* to the extent that it "refuses monumental status" of the type so amenable to historicism, 128. McGee also approaches *Finnegans Wake* by constellating it with other texts, specifically with Benjamin's *Arcades Project* and Charlie Chaplin's *City Lights*. McGee applies Benjamin's concepts of constellation and dialectical image to *Finnegans Wake*, writing, "the dialectical image is neither ruin nor dream, for the synthesis that makes the historical image dialectical lies in the act of perception itself: not in waking consciousness but in the process of awakening," McGee, 122. In this way, McGee effectively distances *Finnegans Wake* from nightdreaming and shifts its emphasis to awakening, locating within the constellation it forms

with Benjamin and Chaplin, "the image of the sleeper who struggles to awaken to a world not yet imagined," McGee, 130. McGee's approach to opening up *Finnegans Wake* to future possibility is highly consistent with Bloch's argument that our picture of reality is incomplete without a sense of the "enormous future" that lies in real possibility, which is "inaccessible to that schematism which knows everything in advance," Bloch, *The Principle of Hope*, 223. The dialectical image and its constellations might also be thought of as a technique that the *Wake* itself employs not just in order to awaken, but also to daydream. The *Wake*'s seemingly endless meetings of periods, people, places, and things in its constantly unfolding, "continuous present tense," for instance, could also be thought of in terms of Benjamin's dialectical image and constellation: characters, times, and places blasted out of the historicist perception of history, which would otherwise have a place for everything and put everything in its place.

20 Bloch, *The Principle of Hope*, 88.
21 Ibid., 101.
22 See David Rando, "Scandal" in *Modernist Fiction and News: Representing Experience in the Early Twentieth Century* (New York: Palgrave Macmillan, 2011), 47–72.
23 Sigmund Freud, *The Interpretation of Dreams*, trans. A. A. Brill (New York: Modern Library, 1994), 354, emphasis in original.
24 David Hayman, *A First-Draft Version of Finnegans Wake* (Austin: University of Texas Press, 1963), 14.
25 Ibid., 13.
26 Sigmund Freud, "Creative Writers and Day-Dreaming," in *The Freud Reader*, ed. Peter Gay (New York: W.W. Norton, 1989), 439.
27 Bloch, *The Principle of Hope*, 3.
28 See ibid., 51–77.
29 While Bloch associates the night dream with narcotizing opium, he associates the daydream with hashish, with which he and Walter Benjamin conducted well-documented experiments for its visionary potential: "The hashish dreams of the subjects in more recent experiments are reported to be of an enchanting levity, they have a kind of elfin spirit about them, the asphalt of the street is transformed into yards of blue silk, random passers-by turn into Dante and Petrarch anachronistically deep in conversation, in short, to the talented hashish dreamer the world becomes a request concert of wishes," Bloch, *The Principle of Hope*, 89. Seen in this light, the strange transmogrifications and anachronistic collisions of the Wake are not so many displacements and condensations thrown up to semiconsciousness by the night dream, but rather wishful expressions as a form of daydream, expressions that long for certain combinations or juxtapositions unavailable yet latent in the present. Here again, Bloch uncannily

seems to evoke *Finnegans Wake*, where anachronistic conversations and dramatic transformations beguile and enchant. Perhaps it is time to think of Joyce less as a rival to Freud (Bishop, for instance, sees Joyce as in competition with Freud: "[As] a 'competent' thinker and man—a 'competitor' and not a follower—and especially as an artist whose work consistently explored the 'inner life,' Joyce was necessarily in competition with psychoanalysis, and all the more particularly because of its claims to authority," Bishop, 17) and more as a talented hashish dreamer without the hashish.

30 "The ego of the waking dream is neither deposed, nor does it practise censorship against the often unconventional content of its wishes," Bloch, *The Principle of Hope*, 90.

31 "For night-dreams mostly cannibalize the former life of the drives, they feed on past if not archaic image-material, and nothing new happens under their bare moon. So it would be absurd to take daydreams: as those presentiments of the imagination which from time immemorial have of course been called dreams but also forerunners and anticipations, and to subsume them under or even subordinate them to the night-dreams," Ibid., 87.

32 Ibid., 86.

33 Maria Tymoczko, *The Irish Ulysses* (Berkeley, CA: University of California Press, 1994), 44.

34 Frank Budgen, *James Joyce and the Making of Ulysses, and Other Writings* (London: Oxford University Press, 1972), 107.

35 I use "anecdotal" in Benjamin's sense of anecdote as intimately human-scaled and resistant to mediating abstractions:

> The anecdote brings things near to us spatially, lets them enter our life. It represents the strict antithesis to the sort of history which demands "empathy," which makes everything abstract. *"Empathy": this is what newspaper reading terminates in.* The true method of making things present is: to represent them in our space (not to represent ourselves in their space). Only anecdotes can do this for us. Thus represented, the things allow no mediating construction from out of "large contexts."

See Walter Benjamin, *The Arcades Project*, ed. Rolf Tiedemann, trans. Howard Eiland and Kevin McLaughlin (Cambridge, MA: Harvard University Press, 1999), 846, emphasis in original.

36

> Sir Tristram, violer d'amores, fr'over the short sea, had passencore rearrived from North Armorica on this side the scraggy isthmus of Europe Minor to wielderfight his penisolate war: nor had topsawyer's rocks by the stream

Oconee exaggerated themselse to Laurens County's gorgios while they went doublin their mumper all the time: nor avoice from afire bellowed mishe mishe to tauftauf thuartpeatrick: not yet, though venissoon after, had a kidscad buttended a bland old isaac: not yet, though all's fair in vanessy, were sosie sesthers wroth with twone nathandjoe. Rot a peck of pa's malt had Jhem or Shen brewed by arclight and rory end to the regginbrow was to be seen ringsome on the aquaface. (3.4–14)

To attribute this constellation to a mere representation of the unconscious is to overlook the quality of daydream that also motivates, envisions, and positively revels in the being-present of different moments of the past in this single formal space and to miss the utopian impulse that can be found at work in the *Wake*'s process and representation of metempsychosis.

37 Bloch, *The Principle of Hope*, 1145.
38 Ibid., 1106.
39 Ibid.
40 Even more than *Ulysses*, *Finnegans Wake* makes readers conscious of the material book in their hands and encourages them to notice that language is a material thing, a precise yet elastic medium that is less a transparent lens into an imaginary fictional world than it is the object of attention itself. Samuel Beckett made this point when he wrote of the *Wake*, "Here form *is* content, content *is* form. You complain that this stuff is not written in English. It is not written at all. It is not to be read—or rather it is not only to be read. It is to be looked at and listened to. His writing is not *about* something; *it is that something itself*," Samuel Beckett, "Dante ... Bruno. Vico.. Joyce," in *James Joyce/Finnegans Wake: A Symposium*. New York: New Directions, 1972, 14, emphasis in original. When virtually every edition of *Finnegans Wake* preserved the same page and line numbers, the *Wake*'s individual pages themselves seemed free to take on their own distinctive spatial character, rather like a page from the *Book of Kells*, an effect that recent editions and e-books have perhaps not entirely mitigated.
41 Derek Attridge describes *Finnegans Wake*'s form of narration as narrativity without narrative. This formulation nicely captures the way in which the *Wake* can at once be *about* a temporal narrative without sacrificing its spatialized style to the demands of temporal storytelling. Attridge writes, "The result is a certain emptiness of narrative—the stories are not new ones, and they keep coming back again and again—and a fullness of narrativity, a rich layering of stories allowing narrative echoes to fly back and forth among holy scripture, ribald joke, national history, pantomime, literary masterpiece, nursery rhyme," Derek Attridge, "Countlessness of Livestories: Narrativity in *Finnegans Wake*," in *Joyce*

Effects: On Language, Theory, and History (Cambridge: Cambridge University Press, 2000), 129.
42 I'm grateful to Lea Pao for pointing out the Dutch meaning here.
43 A thumbnail version of the *Wake* might thus see it as the music-hall wish dream of a being-present through history.
44 I draw here again on Benjamin's antidote to the progressive historicist view of temporal continuity and historical progress, which is to "blast open the continuum of history" as a constructive principle of materialist historiography. Walter Benjamin, "On the Concept of History," 396.
45 Wyndham Lewis wrote, "I regard *Ulysses* as a *time-book*," Lewis, *Time and Western Man*, ed. Paul Edwards (Santa Rosa, CA: Black Sparrow Press, 1993), 14. To some extent, Joyce embraced Wyndham Lewis's accusation that *Ulysses* was a time-book, and he seems to identify more with the temporally oriented Gracehoper than the spatially oriented Ondt. Even as the Ondt scores his victory over the Gracehoper by expanding his world domain, he is still vulnerable to time: "*Your genus its worldwide, your spacest sublime! / But, Holy Saltmartin, why can't you beat time?* (FW 419.7–8, emphasis in original). Given that no character is more associated with time in *Finnegans Wake* than the Gracehoper, it is conspicuous that his name not only contains "hope" but also points to a state of grace that can only come in some distant and better future, a Not-Yet-Become. For the Gracehoper, time is less about past history, which is constantly becoming space by being fitted into annals (and other texts) or into a grave—"we are recurrently meeting em, par Mahun Mesme, in cyclo*annalism*, from space to space, time after time, in various phases of *scripture* as in various poses of *sepulture*" (254.25–8, emphasis added)—and more about the present and the unspecified and undefined future.
46 Some of these "will" and "shall" constructions include the following: "shall cast welcome" (*FW* 567.11); "shall come on their bay tomorrow" (567.15); "Her lofts will be loosed for her and their tumblers broadcast. A progress shall be made in walk, ney?" (567.19–20); "He shall come" (567.21); "the hunt shall make" (567.25); "Ommes will grin" (567.26); "Polo north will beseem Sibernian and Plein Pelouta will behowl ne yerking at lawncastrum ne ghimbelling on guelflinks" (567.35–6); "Mauser Misma shall cease" (568.1); "Lady Victoria Landauner will leave" (568.6–7); "Britus and Gothius shall no more joustle" (568.8); "shall let fall" (568.10); "shall receive" (568.23); "'Twill be tropic of all days" (568.29); "he shall aidress" (568.30–1); "Carilloners will ring" (569.4); "Monsigneur of Deublan shall impart to all" (569.20); "will produce of themselves" (569.30–1); "their show shall shut" (570.2); and "It will give" (570.4).

47 Thus: "A way a lone a last a loved a long the … riverrun, past Eve and Adam's, from swerve of shore to bend of bay, brings us by a commodius vicus of recirculation back to Howth Castle and Environs" (3.1–3).
48 "After the Race" represents daybreak, but it is a very cold sun that shines on Jimmy Doyle's remorse and regret. It is a future that has narrowed rather than expanded.
49 Jim LeBlanc, "The Closing Word of *Finnegans Wake*," *Hypermedia Joyce Studies* 2.1 (Summer 1999), web, emphasis in original.
50 Emphasis added. In this, the ending of *Finnegans Wake* also resembles the beginning of "The Sisters," which begins in a state of expectation about the priest's imminent death.
51

> Without a noun to mask the empty space-to-be-signified that has been cleared by the article's powerful grammatical performative, the "the," like a finger pointing at nothing, comes to signify, in and of itself, signification. Put another way, we are fooled by the finger's pointing at a void. Our attention is misdirected away from the finger itself and, when faced with a semiotic situation with no apparent signified, the resulting anxiety that we experience may leave us scrambling for a referent. (LeBlanc, web)

52 Ibid.
53 The paratextual note at the foot of its final page punctuates the *Wake*'s daydreaming with a marker of the material world, the dialectical counter to anticipation and open futurity. Introducing *How Joyce Wrote Finnegans Wake: A Chapter-by-chapter Genetic Guide*, Luca Crispi, Sam Slote, and Dirk Van Hulle write, "In order to read the *Wake* as a neat Vichian loop from 'the' to 'riverrun' one must 'jump over' this witness to the text's composition. The goal of this volume is to show what might be gained from recognition of what is implied in this epigraph, that is, from reading *Finnegans Wake* in the context of its prepublication manuscripts," Luca Crispi and Sam Slote, eds., *How Joyce Wrote Finnegans Wake: A Chapter-by-Chapter Genetic Guide* (Madison: University of Wisconsin Press, 2007), 3.
54 See, for example, Bloch, *The Principle of Hope*, 141.
55 In "Circe," Bloom meditates, "But tomorrow is a new day will be. Past was is today. What now is will then morrow as now was be past yester" (*U* 15.2409–10).
56 This case for *Finnegans Wake* as a work of spatialization can help to correct the critical oversimplification that Joyce aligns Shaun with space (often as a stand-in for Wyndham Lewis, who attacked Joyce for his alleged "Time-view")

and favors the more temporal Shem. For a recent discussion of Lewis and space/time in *Finnegans Wake*, see Robert Baines, "Time and Space: The Opposition of Professor Jones in *Finnegans Wake* I.6," *Dublin James Joyce Journal* 8 (November 2015): 15–34. Baines argues that against the Lewisian division of time and space, Joyce's text is more apt to highlight their unities and connections.

5

Conclusion: Form, Utopia, and Community

Leopold Bloom is Joyce's most pragmatic and practical utopian thinker. On the morning of June 16, he meditates on urban solutions from the carriage in "Hades": "—I can't make out why the corporation doesn't run a tramline from the parkgate to the quays" (*U* 6.400–1), and this specific urban plan recurs in his thoughts throughout the day along with many other pragmatic solutions to the problems he observes around himself. In the evening, while he picks and smells his toenails before bed, Bloom dreams of a possible better world to come, when he is ensconced in his Flowerville estate as, successively, "gardener, groundsman, cultivator, breeder, and at the zenith of his career, resident magistrate or justice of the peace" (17.1609–10).[1] Nothing could be more characteristic of Bloom, or of Joyce, than this combination of dreams of a better life with the scent of toenail clippings. Down-to-earth, earthy, pragmatic, and material, Bloom is an ungual utopian. The despotic and egomaniacal utopianism exhibited in "Circe" is part of Bloom, too, of course: "My beloved subjects, a new era is about to dawn. I, Bloom, tell you verily it is even now at hand. Yea, on the word of Bloom, ye shall ere long enter into the golden city which is to be, the new Bloomusalem in the Nova Hibernia of the future" (15.1542–5). But this cartoonish utopian fantasy is less conscious or entirely unconscious when compared to Bloom's more typically grounded approach to utopia: not the fantasy of being a dictator but rather of becoming "a gentleman farmer" (17.1603).

All the same, at the end of Bloom's anxious and stressful day even Flowerville reeks of compensatory fantasy. It is rather in "Eumaeus" that we find Bloom at his most pragmatically designing and utopian. There Bloom argues to Stephen, contrary to anti-Semitic beliefs, that Jews benefit their countries because "they are imbued with the proper spirit" and are "practical" (*U* 16.1124–5). Bloom outlines his vision for giving "all creeds and classes" "a comfortable tidysized income" (16.1133–4). Such a socialist scheme, according to Bloom, would be "feasible and would be provocative of friendlier intercourse between man and man. ... I call that patriotism" (16.1136–8).

Bloom's utopia is built upon ideals, but it also connects pragmatically to his earlier violent confrontation with the citizen in the "Cyclops" episode. His utopian thinking at this late hour of the night seems motivated not just by his principles and habits of wishful thought, but also by his need to make sense of the citizen's prejudice against him and the violence that erupted from it. Bloom wonders in what ways might the world be changed for the better so that the kind of anti-Semitic verbal and physical violence he has suffered could be eradicated. When he connects a guaranteed income to "friendlier intercourse between man and man," Bloom implicitly attributes the citizen's racism and anti-Semitism to economic inequality. Bloom thinks that economic inequality must be the primary source of prejudice, because, "I'm, he resumed with dramatic force, as good an Irishman as that rude person I told you about" (*U* 16.1131–2). There is, perhaps, a certain naiveté in Bloom's analysis of why the citizen hates him, a naiveté that underestimates the strength of irrational hatred based on race or ethnicity. Nevertheless, Bloom seeks an economic solution not just to the social ills of Ireland, but also to the tangible conditions that he has seen around himself all day, from the scenes of poverty and hunger he has passed to the citizen's biscuit tin assault. When Bloom declares with dramatic force to Stephen that he is an Irishman, he echoes his earlier claim to Irishness to the citizen in "Cyclops": "—Ireland, says Bloom. I was born here. Ireland" (12.1431). Now, however, Bloom improves on his earlier claim by implying that he is as good an Irishman as the citizen is and a patriot as well.

Bloom's better world is one in which, "you can live well, the sense is, if you work" (*U* 16.1139–40). However, Stephen balks when Bloom stipulates that one must work to live well: "—Count me out, he managed to remark, meaning work" (16.1148). Bloom, anxious to accommodate Stephen in his utopia, is quick to "affirm" (16.1152) that "literary labour" (16.1153) would count as work there as well, because not just "the brawn" but "the brain," too, "belong[s] to Ireland" (16.1159). In effect, Bloom's utopia is designed practically to make a place for both Jews and artists in Ireland. He implies a resemblance and connection between his own and Stephen's forms of alienation, and he proposes a world in which both of them could be embraced by and belong to Ireland. Indeed, Bloom seems to want to make visible to Stephen their parallel forms of alienation from Ireland, to extend sympathy to Stephen and to provoke Stephen's sympathy for him, and finally to make an ally and friend of Stephen on the basis of their shared alienation. Bloom envisions utopia by combining economic idealism and pragmatic solutions to intractable social problems.

But unlike Bloom, who would class himself as a good Irishman, Stephen challenges the implication that he belongs to Ireland at all. Bloom, still trying to accommodate Stephen, says that he would "go a step farther" (*U* 16.1163) than saying that Stephen belongs to Ireland, but here Stephen cuts him off. "—But I suspect, Stephen interrupted, that Ireland must be important because it belongs to me" (16.1164–5). One wonders what Bloom was on the verge of saying. Was he going to assert that Stephen's "brain" is even more important to Ireland than its "brawn"? Would he have followed that up by proposing, too, that Jews and artists not only belong to Ireland but are, in fact, indispensable to it, perhaps even more so than nationalists like the citizen? Whatever it was to have been, Bloom certainly did not expect Stephen's retort about Ireland belonging to him, for Bloom is nonplussed by Stephen's inversion of his formula. Bloom is unprepared for the extent of Stephen's bitterness or for the way in which he rejects wholesale any role in a national project, no matter how open-handed or accommodating of literary labor Bloom's Irish utopia promises to be. Perhaps Stephen does not see that his ability to reject Ireland in this bombastic fashion is a privilege and a luxury that Bloom, as a Jew, has neither the status nor the security to afford. In the face of Bloom's confusion and in response to his delicate request for clarification, Stephen shoves aside his coffee "none too politely" (16.1170), repeats his assertion, and adds, "—We can't change the country. Let us change the subject" (16.1171). In "Eumaeus," then, Bloom proposes practical utopian solutions, but Stephen rejects a role in the utopian project and any hope at all for changing Ireland.

These poles set up a dialectical structure of wishfulness versus cynicism or skepticism that confronts any who seek to write about the way in which Joyce represents utopian idealism in the content of his fiction. Some critics move to one side or the other, or range between them. In *Utopianism in James Joyce's Ulysses*, for instance, Wolfgang Wicht argues that Joyce exposes the absurdity of all utopian idealism through a relentless comedy of negation. Wicht's

Joyce is like Adorno if Adorno had had a sense of humor: "Representing negativity through various strategies of comic disintegration, Joyce articulates a radical political stance, which is oriented toward historical practice and shuns ideological legitimations and grand concepts."[2] Wicht's radical Joyce is a familiar one from the subversive critical tradition. Alec Charles, on the other hand, argues that Joyce's texts oscillate between the poles of Joyce's dialectical structure, between utopia and skepticism or cynicism. For Charles, not strictly subversive, Joyce's writing offers "a realizable and sustainable mode of Utopianism—a Utopianism that inscribes its own opposites (the dystopian, the anti-Utopian, and the real) and its own impossibility within a continuously dynamic dialectic."[3]

Other critics seek ways outside of this polar structure by concentrating on utopian impulses in Joyce rather than on utopian projects or representations. Drawing upon Bloch and Benjamin, Hugo Azérad argues, "If there is messianism in Joyce, it is concretely represented in the texture of the book itself, and not in Bloom, who like Moses never sees the promised land of concretized hope."[4] Accordingly, Azérad finds hope in the open-ended forms of *Ulysses* and *Finnegans Wake*: "For Bloch, the world remains a project awaiting completion, and similarly *Ulysses* and *Finnegans Wake* are designed so that they remain open-ended, awaiting completion through the medium of communal human practice, a medium that could be the reading act, what I would call the aesthetic encounter."[5] Azérad's approach avoids getting caught between the poles of utopian idealism and skepticism or cynicism by focusing on utopia as it manifests in literary form rather than in idealisms or in particular castles drawn in the air. It does what Fredric Jameson suggests, which is to shift "the discussion of Utopia from content to representation as such."[6] Similarly, drawing upon Jameson's concept of the political unconscious, Cheryl Herr sees *Ulysses* as "summoning up ... an unknown sphere of inevitability and instinct" that would counter the already-known, including the already-known of the encyclopedic structure and content of the novel.[7] Part of what Herr calls the "cultural unconscious" of *Ulysses* is a submerged but palpable "desire for community (as a version of nature) from the kinds of anomie experienced by Bloom, Stephen, and Molly."[8] Indeed, it is perhaps insufficiently recognized that one utopian desire that the novel structures (especially for first-time readers of *Ulysses*) is for the lonely Bloom and Stephen to come together in some meaningful way, an end that the novel both grants and frustrates in equal measure.

Despite the only partially satisfying nature of its characters' interactions, *Ulysses* seems to recognize its own utopian longing for community between Stephen and Bloom in Bloom's imagined futures with Stephen: "All kinds of Utopian plans were flashing through his (B's) busy brain, education (the genuine article), literature, journalism, prize titbits, up to date billing, concert tours in English watering resorts packed with hydros and seaside theatres, turning money away, duets in Italian with the accent perfectly true to nature and a quantity of other things" (*U* 16.1652–6). This utopian impulse toward community is perhaps Bloom's utopianism at its best, even though readers have every reason to suspect that these plans will as little come to fruition as the fantasies of the new Bloomusalem or Flowerville will. Still, his plans represent a genuine thirst for community and would in fact concretely solve many of Bloom's problems, from his social alienation and isolation, and also perhaps his cuckoldry (as Stephen displaces Boylan on the singing tour), all the way down to his nagging worries about Molly's Italian pronunciation when she sings: "Wonder if she pronounces that right: *voglio*" (4.327).

In their different ways, both Herr and Azérad connect hope to the communal in Joyce, Herr by locating communal desires within the unconscious of the book and Azérad by locating hope in the communal practice of reading. Both avoid reducing the hopeful or the utopian in Joyce to their representations and thus to Joyce's implied attitudes about utopian programs. Indeed, the goal of this book has been to show that in order to grasp the utopian in Joyce it is necessary to look beyond utopian idealism and utopian programs, to which Joyce quite clearly cannot subscribe and tends to parody, and toward the utopian impulses that manifest in Joyce's extraordinarily inventive forms and the wish-dreams that seem to impel them. Bloom's *impulses* are more in line with Joyce's formal practices than are his variously articulated pipedreams, which are likely to go Nowhere rather than to Utopia.

Finnegans Wake confirms Joyce's skepticism about utopian programs in favor of the utopian impulse. The *Wake* contains a strong sense of the "utpiam" (*FW* 611.25) that points toward the future. Joyce's neologism "utpiam," which visually evokes "utopia" and "utopian," seems modeled on the Latin "quispiam": "a certain someone" or "anyone at all." By analogy, "utpiam" could mean "however at all,"[9] which is surely a nice formulation for utopia understood less as a finished picture of an ideal future and more as an impulse toward the better, the new, and the unknown.[10] In contrast, when *Finnegans Wake* evokes the future as a utopian program or project, it is never without irony and satire. For instance, toward the end of his sermon to the St. Bride's schoolgirls, Jaun declares, "Lo, improving ages wait ye! In the orchard of the bones. Some time very presently now when yon clouds are dissipated after their forty years shower, the odds are, we shall all be hooked and happy, communionistically, among the fieldnights eliceam, *élite* of the elect, in the land of lost of time" (*FW* 453.30–3). Joyce offers here a smorgasbord of utopian images—marital bliss or Aristophanic completeness ("hooked and happy"), spiritual communion and communist living ("communionistically"), class transcendence ("*élite* of the elect"), the redemption of the past ("in the land of lost time")—but all of these conditions are projected as an afterlife ("In the orchard of the bones"). The promised better world is as little likely to exist in the boneyard or in heaven, beyond the grave, as it is on earth. Joyce does not make us sanguine about the history to follow or the afterlife to come in the specific visions he posits. He does not offer utopian visions or programs without skepticism, irony, or outright satire. As I said in the introduction, Joyce is not even especially cheerful when it comes to such future visions. However, in contrast with the utopian program, the utopian impulse, as we have seen, is a Joycean constant. Joyce's visionary style looks forward to new forms of expression, provoking the discovery of new forms of knowledge and making possible new constructions of reality.

Most productive is when hope in the unconscious of Joyce's texts and in the act of reading meet together in the communities that Joyce excels in creating. A century after Joyce completed *Ulysses*, diverse readers routinely join forces in the hope of learning more about how Joyce's texts work and what they mean. In reading groups, university courses, summer schools, seminars, conferences, and international symposia, the paths of readers converge in ways that are far less likely than the meeting of two Dubliners with a ton of mutual acquaintances on a given spring day in 1904. Indeed, to read Joyce long enough is almost necessarily to be able to marvel at the number of strangers' faces that began unknown and blurry to one, which then slowly came into focus, and often also into the spheres of friendship and affection, over one of Joyce's open books.

To read Joyce is to hope and hunger: for clarity, for perspective, for understanding, for epiphany, for pleasure, and more. It is also to hope to learn from others, for Joyce's texts are so constructed that no single person knows enough to shine a light into every shadowy corner of them.[11] In our hope to learn from others, we often turn to the immense body of criticism and annotation published in the last eighty years by what is sometimes called the "Joyce industry" of scholars and other devotees. It is perhaps too little recognized or noticed that every time we turn to such material it is with a degree of hope. We also take or teach classes, attend conferences, and create reading groups hopefully. Our desire to understand Joyce leads to communities of hopeful participants. Reading Joyce accustoms us to looking toward others and to reading alongside others.

To read Joyce is also to look toward the future. Richard Ellmann, reflecting on the way in which readers might still feel a little bit behind Joyce (and are therefore, we might observe, of necessity tilted toward an implied future in which we do catch up), begins *James Joyce* by writing, "We are still learning to be James Joyce's contemporaries."[12] We ought more often to reflect upon the extent to which we read Joyce singly and together not simply in the present but also with an abstract sense of the future to come. We read Joyce against the backdrop of an imagined time when the shards and orts and shambles of what we have learned might be pieced together in a more perfect or at least satisfying way.

I am not thinking here about illusions of perfect exegesis of the kind that Leo Bersani sees as a symptom of the pernicious totalizing ambitions of *Ulysses*, an exegesis which would finally and merely recapitulate tautologically the truth of *Ulysses* as *Ulysses*.[13] Rather, I mean that time of personal or communal satisfaction when our understanding and pleasure reach a longed-for point of saturation, or one of many along the way, when our sense of knowledge feels right or when our curiosity has been satisfied. These feelings need not presume any odious desire for mastery, nor must they suggest that reading or interpretation will come to an end at any point. Rather than mastery or completion, they suggest a certain fullness or roundness, a species perhaps of stately plumpness. Nor must we necessarily be impatient for whatever desires with which we come to Joyce's fiction to be fulfilled. We can be content to linger, finding every satisfaction in avoiding conclusions and finality.

In any event, such final states of saturated pleasure or understanding are utopian projections, unlikely ever to materialize: they are Flowervilles, new Bloomusalems, or Nova Hibernias of the future. But that does not stop Joyce's texts from structuring and organizing wishful desires for fulfillment or from compelling readers to assume some relation to them.

When we read Joyce in communities, we take up relation to these structures and organizations of desire together. We collectively assume a relationship to an unknown and open future, one that never ceases to arrive continuously and concretely out of the conditions of real possibility, but which just as soon projects a new open future ahead of it. More direct reflection on this shared, unknown, and open future can only enrich the ways in which we conceive and practice criticism of Joyce. For instance, we might be more aware that there can be conflicts between the norms of literary criticism as an institution and practice, which even while striving to be collaborative is often individualistic and atomistic, and between Joyce's forms, which strive for the new and the unknown and seem designed to convene communities of readers who look toward the unknown and the future with mutual interest. The study of Joyce itself is a dialectic between the communal and the individual, the known and the unknown, and the past and the future. Joyce affords opportunities for reflection and experiment rather than for prescriptions, which by definition draw from the already-known.

This book has reinterpreted Joyce's claim that *Dubliners* was to be Ireland's "first step towards the spiritual liberation"[14] by removing it from the context of the already-known forms of spiritual liberation that were available at the time *Dubliners* was written, and by connecting spiritual liberation instead to a dialectic between hope and hunger that strives restlessly and with the suppleness of the stomach toward the unknown and the not-yet. The book has tracked how this dialectic operates in Joyce's content and form in order to remain open to futures that cannot always be named or known in advance. It has also shown how Joyce tends to spatialize hope so that it can be contemplated with critical distance, as a constellation at a standstill. Joyce's technique creates formal spaces from which images of the new and unknown might emerge. This is the wishful image-generating quality of Joyce's fiction.

As we have seen, however, Joyce's images dictate little but seek rather to engage readers in the dialectic of hope and hunger that pervades his fiction at all levels. Joyce's readers become his partners in vision. Joyce initially conceived these partners, at least in part, as the Dubliners about whom he wrote and for whose spiritual liberation he was apparently concerned. But as Joyce's work persists in the present and into the future, finding audiences farther and farther removed from Dublin and Ireland early in the last century, his partners are increasingly those whom Joyce could not have known or concretely anticipated. Nonetheless these readers are accommodated in Joyce's elastic fiction because of the way in which it rejects the already-known utopias of its own moment and remains open to the future. In other words, it is not just the richness with which Joyce's fiction responds to historicist inquiry that can account for Joyce's continued relevance and popularity, nor is it only his fiction's intelligent irony or its thoroughgoing subversiveness, but, even more, it is the openness of his forms to the unknown and the future that keeps Joyce in the middle of so many communities of readers. Joyce's achievement when it comes to longevity was not just, as he contended, having "put in so many enigmas and puzzles that it will keep the professors busy for centuries arguing over what I meant,"[15] but also by having created forms that keep responding to different sets of enigmas, puzzles, and questions among so many different communities of readers a century later.

For Bloch, the history of the world is only its prehistory.[16] Art matters to Bloch in part because it is correlative with the world and with the human: all are undecided, unfinished, and fragmentary.[17] Art would still be tremendously potent even if all it did was to represent the world; however, the openness in the depths of art, its immanent unfinishedness, does even more. It makes art the correlate to unfinished history and to emerging humanity. Art offers perception of the world while simultaneously remaining just as open and fragmented as the world is. Art mirrors the fragmentary "mess"[18] of the world as well as, in its formal dialectics, the experimental process of emerging from that mess. Because art offers a picture of the world while also, paradoxically, remaining as open as the world is to the unknown and the future, art is utopian.

Joyce represents the world with incredible vividness. In the introduction, I evoked Enda Duffy's phrase "will to visualize"[19] in order to characterize this representational quality of Joyce's writing. Joyce's intense perception of the world corresponds to the representational aspect in Bloch's formulation. Even if Joyce's work did nothing else, its capacity to show and to facilitate our perception of the world would make it not just remarkable, but exceptional. Much of this book has sought to demonstrate the ways in which Joyce's wishful images reveal an author who views the openness of the world with a sense of Bloch's real possibility, or perhaps with what *Finnegans Wake* calls the "PROBA-POSSIBLE" (*FW* 262.3–4, right margin). The larger purpose of this book, however, has been to establish the formal complement (as in Bloch's formulation) to these wishful images and this will to visualize: to demonstrate the open and wishful quality of Joyce's forms that correlate to the openness and unfinishedness of the human and the world. Deriving from material circumstances and produced by a dialectic of hope and hunger, Joyce's formal innovations, especially his spatialization of hope, make a space for the new and the uncharted to emerge. When we read, engage, discuss, and interpret Joyce, we become part, in Bloch's terms, of a dialectical process in which Joyce's open texts meet and generate other wishful fragments in a movement that strives toward the new and the better. It may be that the unusual capacity for Joyce's texts to attract, inspire, and sustain this dialectical process of discovery adds up to a body of work that is also still capable of being relevant to the "spiritual liberation" of readers today, even in contexts Joyce could not have anticipated. If the work is capable of spurring spiritual liberation today, it would be not solely because it gives us "one good look at" ourselves in Joyce's "nicely polished looking-glass"[20]—for we are no longer precisely the early-twentieth-century Irish people to whom Joyce referred in his letter (though neither, I suspect, are we quite alien from them)—but rather because his work still enlists readers in its wishful process of search and discovery.

Joyce was not a seer who could predict the future; nor was he a visionary utopianist who painted finished pictures of the yet-unknown. Rather, dissatisfied with and skeptical of all of the reigning paths to spiritual liberation that his nation, culture, and religion offered him, Joyce yet recognized the world as unfinished, a place where "we are in for a sequentiality of improbable possibles" (*FW* 110.15). His response to unsatisfactory utopias was not paralysis or hopelessness or cynicism,[21] but rather inventiveness. Joyce's wishful images and his open forms look toward future possibility not as it might be idealized but rather as it emerges through material conditions and as it is mediated by real possibility. With hunger at the core of this material and mediating process, Joyce populated a fictional world with characters who, though often stuck, deprived, or even crushed, yet hope, and he represented these characters within forms that are themselves restlessly innovative, striving, searching, and open. Readers of Joyce implicitly engage these levels of hope whenever they are moved to discover the new in or by the light of Joyce's works. But when we place hope explicitly and purposively at the center of our study of Joyce, when we reflect on the wishful and communal dimensions of reading and interpreting him, when we pursue the not-yet of Stephen's green rose or the non-hope of the journey westward, then we say "Yes" to the challenge posed by the definite article that stands out in front of *Finnegans Wake* and which stands implicitly before all of Joyce's work: a "the" that suggests that his readers are Joyce's wishful partners in something definite yet still unknown to come.

Notes

1 Bloch writes, "Towards evening is the best time for telling stories. The insignificant world near at hand disappears, distant things which seem better and nearer move up around us." See Ernst Bloch, *The Principle of Hope*, 3 vols., trans. Neville Plaice, Stephen Plaice, and Paul Knight (Cambridge: MIT Press, 1986), 353.
2 Wolfgang Wicht, *Utopianism in James Joyce's Ulysses* (Heidelberg: Universitätverlag Winter, 2000), 214.
3 Alec Charles, "The Meta-Utopian Metatext: The Deconstructive Dreams of *Ulysses* and *Finnegans Wake*," *Utopian Studies* 23.2 (2012): 473.
4 Hugo Azérad, "'Negative Utopia' in James Joyce, Walter Benjamin, and Ernst Bloch," in *Joyce in Trieste: An Album of Risky Readings*, ed. Sebastian D. G. Knowles, Geert Lernout, and John McCourt (Gainesville: University Press of Florida, 2007), 111.
5 Ibid., 110. Azérad views Joyce's texts as dialectical images, where hope might also be found: "language, which is the site of dialectical images, is the medium of transmission, the carrier of hope, if not its benevolent fabricator," ibid., 113. Enda Duffy also approaches Joyce from the perspective of dialectical images. See Duffy, "The Happy Ring House," *European Joyce Studies 21: Joyce, Benjamin and Magical Urbanism*, ed. Maurizia Boscagli and Enda Duffy (Amsterdam: Rodopi, 2011), 176–7, 181.
6 Jameson writes, "[Utopian] texts are so often taken to be the expressions of political opinion or ideology that there is something to be said for redressing the balance in a resolutely formalist way," Fredric Jameson, *Archaeologies of the Future: The Desire Called Utopia and Other Science Fictions* (New York: Verso, 2005), xiii.

7 Cheryl Herr, "Art and Life, Nature and Culture, *Ulysses*," in *James Joyce's Ulysses: A Casebook*, ed. Derek Attridge (New York: Oxford University Press, 2004), 67.
8 Ibid., 76.
9 I am grateful to Tim O'Sullivan for this gloss. Roland McHugh glosses the word as "anyway" in his *Annotations*.
10 Jameson makes just such a distinction between the utopian program and the utopian impulse. See *Archaeologies of the Future*, 1–9.
11 Although no single person knows everything, some people do seem to come *pretty* close. When I think about the community and dedication to knowledge that Joyce's fiction can attract at its best, I think of John Bishop. Although I did not know John well, and others closer to him have written moving and more fitting tributes to him, I would like to record two personal anecdotes that seem to me characteristic of the way in which he embodied the best in Joycean scholarly community. (1) I met John when I was a starstruck graduate student at the 2001 Miami J'yce Conference. Although I was only just starting to explore *Finnegans Wake*, when I shyly mentioned to John that I was presenting on the *Wake*, he not only attended the panel but also gave me warm and encouraging suggestions afterward. What I remember most is his kindness: John treated my unoriginal ideas much more seriously than they likely warranted. He addressed me as my smartest self, or, by being included in the kind of community that John was offering, as the smarter self that I might become. (2) In summer 2005, Jim LeBlanc invited John from nearby Auburn, New York, to visit our *Wake* group in Ithaca. On that late afternoon on Jim's back porch, John fit perfectly into our community, wore his immense learning lightly, and offered what he knew and thought kindly, humbly, and in a collective spirit. Afterward, we all braved a serious summer downpour to dine at A Taste of Thai on the Ithaca Commons. While we were huddled together under an umbrella in the drenching no-man's-land between the car and the restaurant, John decided that he had better turn back and dash uncovered through the rain to collect and bring to dinner his well-worn and extensively annotated copy of the *Wake*, which was rebound in three volumes to include plenty of extra pages for notes. These volumes were simply too precious to leave in the car. Both of these experiences stick with me as exemplars of the ways in which knowledge and community may be pursued together brilliantly, warmly, and open-handedly.
12 Richard Ellmann, *James Joyce*, New and Revised Edition (New York: Oxford University Press, 1982), 3.
13 See Leo Bersani, "Against *Ulysses*," in *James Joyce's Ulysses: A Casebook*, ed. Derek Attridge (New York: Oxford University Press, 2004), 201–29.
14 Letter to Grant Richards, May 20, 1906 (*Letters I*, 63).

15 Quoted, from a 1956 interview with Jacques Benoît-Méchin, in Ellmann, *James Joyce*, 521.
16 Bloch writes, "man everywhere is still living in prehistory, indeed all and everything still stands before the creation of the world, of a right world," Bloch, *The Principle of Hope*, 1375.
17 Bloch writes,

> Man is still not solid, the course of the world is still undecided, unclosed, and so also is the depth in all aesthetic information: *this utopian factor is the paradox in aesthetic immanence, the most fundamentally immanent paradox in this immanence itself.* Without such potency for the fragment, aesthetic imagination would of course have sufficient perception in the world, more than any other human apperception, but it would ultimately have no correlate. For the world itself, just as it is in a mess, is also in a state of unfinishedness and in experimental process out of that mess. The shapes which this process throws up, the ciphers, allegories and symbols in which it is so rich, are *all themselves still fragments, real fragments, through which process streams unclosed and advances dialectically to further fragmentary* forms. (*The Principle of Hope* 221, emphasis in original)

18 Ibid.
19 Duffy, 176.
20 Letter to Grant Richards, June 23, 1906 (*Letters I*, 64).
21 Joyce stressed to Budgen that *Ulysses* "is the work of a skeptic, but I don't want it to appear the work of a cynic," Frank Budgen, *James Joyce and the Making of Ulysses, and Other Writings* (London: Oxford University Press, 1972), 156.

Bibliography

Abrams, M. H. and Geoffrey Galt Harpham. *A Glossary of Literary Terms*, 10th ed. Boston: Wadsworth, 2012.

Adams, Robert M. *Surface and Symbol: The Consistency of James Joyce's Ulysses.* New York: Oxford University Press, 1962.

Altieri, Charles. "*Finnegans Wake* as Modernist Historiography." *Novel* 21.2–3 (Spring–Winter 1988): 238–50.

Anderson, Chester G. "Baby Tuckoo: Joyce's 'Features of Infancy.'" In *Approaches to Joyce's Portrait: Ten Essays*. Ed. Thomas F. Staley and Bernard Benstock. Pittsburgh: University of Pittsburgh Press, 1976, 135–69.

Armand, Louis. "Through a Glass Darkly: Reflections on the Other Joyce." In *Giacomo Joyce: Envoys of the Other*. Ed. Louis Armand and Clare Wallace. Prague: Litteraria Pragensia, 2006, 1–19.

Attridge, Derek. "Countlessness of Livestories: Narrativity in *Finnegans Wake*." In *Joyce Effects: On Language, Theory, and History*. Cambridge: Cambridge University Press, 2000, 126–32.

Attridge, Derek. "Finnegans Awake, or the Dream of Interpretation." In *Joyce Effects: On Language, Theory, and History*. Cambridge: Cambridge University Press, 2000, 133–55.

Attridge, Derek and Anne Fogarty. "'Eveline' at Home." In *Collaborative Dubliners: Joyce in Dialogue*. Ed. Vicki Mahaffey. Syracuse: Syracuse University Press, 2012, 89–107.

Azérad, Hugo. "'Negative Utopia' in James Joyce, Walter Benjamin, and Ernst Bloch." In *Joyce in Trieste: An Album of Risky Readings*. Ed. Sebastian D. G. Knowles, Geert Lernout, and John McCourt. Gainesville: University Press of Florida, 2007, 102–16.

Baines, Robert. "Time and Space: The Opposition of Professor Jones in *Finnegans Wake* I.6." *Dublin James Joyce Journal* 8 (November 2015): 15–34.

Bašić, Sonja. "A Book of Many Uncertainties: Joyce's *Dubliners*." In *ReJoycing: New Readings of Dubliners*. Ed. Rosa M. Bollettieri Bosinelli and Harold F. Mosher Jr. Lexington: University Press of Kentucky, 1998, 13–40.

Beck, Warren. *Joyce's Dubliners: Substance, Vision, and Art*. Durham, NC: Duke University Press, 1969.

Beckett, Samuel. "Dante... Bruno. Vico.. Joyce." *James Joyce/Finnegans Wake: A Symposium*. New York: New Directions, 1972, 1–22.

Beja, Morris. "One Good Look at Themselves: Epiphanies in *Dubliners*." In *Work in Progress: Joyce Centenary Essays*. Ed. Richard F. Peterson, Alan M. Cohen, and Edmund L. Epstein. Carbondale: Southern Illinois University Press, 1983, 3–14.

Benjamin, Walter. *The Arcades Project*. Ed. Rolf Tiedemann. Trans. Howard Eiland and Kevin McLaughlin. Cambridge, MA: Harvard University Press, 1999.

Benjamin, Walter. "On the Concept of History." In *Selected Writings, Volume 4, 1938–1940*. Ed. Howard Eiland and Michael W. Jennings. Trans. Harry Zohn. Cambridge, MA: Harvard University Press, 2003, 389–400.

Benjamin, Walter. "On Some Motifs in Baudelaire." In *Selected Writings, Volume 4, 1938–1940*. Ed. Howard Eiland and Michael W. Jennings. Trans. Harry Zohn. Cambridge, MA: Harvard University Press, 2003, 313–55.

Benjamin, Walter. "The Storyteller: Observations on the Works of Nikolai Leskov." In *Selected Writings, Volume 3, 1935–1938*. Ed. Howard Eiland and Michael W. Jennings. Trans. Harry Zohn. Cambridge, MA: Harvard University Press, 2002. 143–66.

Benstock, Bernard. *Joyce-Again's Wake*. Seattle: University of Washington Press, 1965.

Benstock, Bernard. *Narrative Con/Texts in Dubliners*. Urbana: University of Illinois Press, 1994.

Bersani, Leo. "Against *Ulysses*." In *James Joyce's Ulysses: A Casebook*. Ed. Derek Attridge. New York: Oxford University Press, 2004, 201–29.

Bishop, John. *Joyce's Book of the Dark: Finnegans Wake*. Madison: University of Wisconsin Press, 1986.

Bloch, Ernst. "A Philosophical View of the Detective Novel." In *The Utopian Function of Art and Literature: Selected Essays*. Trans. Jack Zipes and Frank Mecklenburg. Cambridge, MA: MIT Press, 1988, 245–63.

Bloch, Ernst. "A Philosophical View of the Novel of the Artist." *The Utopian Function of Art and Literature: Selected Essays*. Trans. Jack Zipes and Frank Mecklenburg. Cambridge, MA: MIT Press, 1988. 264–76.

Bloch, Ernst. *The Principle of Hope*. 3 Volumes. Trans. Neville Plaice, Stephen Plaice, and Paul Knight. Cambridge, MA: MIT Press, 1986.

Booth, Wayne. *The Rhetoric of Fiction*. Chicago: University of Chicago Press, 1961.

Bowen, Zach. "Joyce and the Epiphany Concept: A New Approach." *Journal of Modern Literature* 9.1 (1981–1982): 103–14.

Briggs, Austin. "The Full Stop at the End of 'Ithaca': Thirteen Ways—and Then Some—of Looking at a Black Dot." *Joyce Studies Annual* 7 (Summer 1996): 125–43.

Brivic, Sheldon. "The Disjunctive Structure of Joyce's *Portrait*." In *James Joyce's A Portrait of the Artist as a Young Man: Case Studies in Contemporary Criticism*, 2nd ed. Ed. R. Brandon Kershner. Boston: Bedford/St. Martin's, 2006, 279–98.

Brown, Richard. "Eros and Apposition." In *Giacomo Joyce: Envoys of the Other*. Ed. Louis Armand and Clare Wallace. Prague: Litteraria Pragensia, 2006, 304–14.

Budgen, Frank. *James Joyce and the Making of Ulysses, and Other Writings*. London: Oxford University Press, 1972.

Castle, Gregory. "Coming of Age in the Age of Empire: Joyce's Modernist Bildungsroman." *James Joyce Quarterly* 50.1–2 (Fall 2012–Winter 2013): 359–84.

Charles, Alec. "The Meta-Utopian Metatext: The Deconstructive Dreams of *Ulysses* and *Finnegans Wake*." *Utopian Studies* 23.2 (2012): 472–503.

Cheng, Vincent. *Joyce, Race, and Empire*. Cambridge: Cambridge University Press, 1995.

Cixous, Hélène. "Joyce: The (R)use of Writing." In *Post-structuralist Joyce: Essays from the French*. Ed. Derek Attridge and Daniel Ferrer. Trans. Judith Still. Cambridge: Cambridge University Press, 1984, 15–30.

Crispi, Luca and Sam Slote, eds. *How Joyce Wrote Finnegans Wake: A Chapter-by-Chapter Genetic Guide*. Madison: University of Wisconsin Press, 2007.

Culleton, Claire A. and Ellen Scheible. "Introduction: Rethinking *Dubliners*: A Case for What Happens in Joyce's Stories." In *Rethinking Joyce's Dubliners*. Ed. Claire A. Culleton and Ellen Scheible. New York: Palgrave Macmillan, 2017, 1–7.

Daniel, Jamie Owen and Tom Moylan, eds. *Not Yet: Reconsidering Ernst Bloch*. London: Verso, 1997.

Dettmar, Kevin J. H. *The Illicit Joyce of Postmodernism: Reading against the Grain*. Madison, WI: University of Wisconsin Press, 1996.

Devlin, Kimberly J. *Wandering and Return in Finnegans Wake: An Integrative Approach to Joyce's Fictions*. Princeton, NJ: Princeton University Press, 1991.

Duffy, Enda. "The Happy Ring House." In *European Joyce Studies 21: Joyce, Benjamin and Magical Urbanism*. Ed. Maurizia Boscagli and Enda Duffy. Amsterdam: Rodopi, 2011, 169–84.

Dunn, Allen and Thomas Haddox, eds. *The Limits of Literary Historicism*. Knoxville, TN: University of Tennessee Press, 2012.

Eide, Marian. "The Woman of the Ballyhoura Hills: James Joyce and the Politics of Creativity." *Twentieth-Century Literature* 44.4 (Winter 1998): 377–93.

Ellmann, Maud. "Ghosts of *Ulysses*." In *James Joyce's Ulysses: A Casebook*. Ed. Derek Attridge. New York: Oxford University Press, 2004, 83–101.

Ellmann, Maud. "The Name and the Scar: Identity in *The Odyssey* and *A Portrait of the Artist as a Young Man*." In *James Joyce's A Portrait of the Artist as a Young*

Man: A Casebook. Ed. Mark A. Wollaeger. New York: Oxford University Press, 2003, 143–81.

Ellmann, Richard. *James Joyce*, new and rev. ed. New York: Oxford University Press, 1982.

Ellmann, Richard. "Preface." James Joyce. In *Ulysses: The Gabler Edition*. Ed. Hans Walter Gabler with Walter Hettche. New York: Random House, 1986, ix–xiv.

Ellmann, Richard. *Ulysses on the Liffey*. New York: Oxford University Press, 1972.

Ellmann, Richard, A. Walton Litz, and John Whittier Ferguson, eds. *James Joyce: Poems and Shorter Writings*. London: Faber & Faber, 1991.

Felski, Rita. *The Limits of Critique*. Chicago: University of Chicago Press, 2017.

Fordham, Finn. *Lots of Fun at Finnegans Wake: Unravelling Universals*. Oxford: Oxford University Press, 2007.

Foucault, Michel. "Different Spaces." In *Aesthetics, Method, and Epistemology*. Ed. James D. Faubion. New York: New Press, 1998, 175–85.

Frank, Joseph. "Spatial Form in Modern Literature: An Essay in Two Parts." *Sewanee Review* 53.2 (Spring 1945): 221–40.

Frank, Joseph. "Spatial Form in Modern Literature: An Essay in Three Parts." *The Sewanee Review* 53.4 (Autumn 1945): 643–53.

Freud, Sigmund. "Creative Writers and Day-Dreaming." In *The Freud Reader*. Ed. Peter Gay. New York: W.W. Norton, 1989, 436–43.

Freud, Sigmund. *The Interpretation of Dreams*. Trans. A. A. Brill. New York: Modern Library, 1994.

Gibbons, Luke. "'Have you no homes to go to?': James Joyce and the Politics of Paralysis." In *Semicolonial Joyce*. Ed. Derek Attridge and Marjorie Howes. Cambridge: Cambridge University Press, 2000, 150–69.

Gibbons, Luke. *Joyce's Ghosts: Ireland, Modernism, and Memory*. Chicago: University of Chicago Press, 2015.

Gibson, Andrew and Len Platt. "Introduction." In *Joyce, Ireland, Britain*. Ed. Andrew Gibson and Len Platt. Gainesville, FL: University Press of Florida, 2006, 1–29.

Gifford, Don with Robert J. Seidman. *Ulysses Annotated: Notes for James Joyce's Ulysses*, 2nd ed. Berkeley, CA: University of California Press, 1988.

Gottfried, Roy. "'*Le point doit être plus visible*': The Texas Page Proofs of *Ulysses*." In *Joyce at Texas*. Ed. Dave Oliphant and Thomas Zigal. Austin: Humanities Research Center, University of Texas at Austin, 1983, 12–27.

Greimas, Algirdas Julien. "The Interaction of Semiotic Constraints." In *On Meaning: Selected Writings in Semiotic Theory*. Trans. Paul J. Perron and Frank H. Collins. Minneapolis: University of Minnesota Press, 1987, 48–62.

Hart, Clive. *Structure and Motif in Finnegans Wake*. Evanston: Northwestern University Press, 1962.

Hayman, David. *A First-Draft Version of Finnegans Wake*. Austin: University of Texas Press, 1963.

Heininge, Kathleen. "The Way Out of Paralysis: Joyce and the Habitual Present Tense." *James Joyce Quarterly* 57.3-4 (Spring-Summer 2020): 263-73.

Henke, Suzette. *James Joyce and the Politics of Desire*. New York: Routledge, 1990.

Herr, Cheryl. "Art and Life, Nature and Culture, *Ulysses*." In *James Joyce's Ulysses: A Casebook*. Ed. Derek Attridge. New York: Oxford University Press, 2004, 55-81.

Herr, Cheryl. "Ireland from the Outside." In *Joyce and the Subject of History*. Ed. Mark A. Wollaeger, Victor Luftig, and Robert Spoo. Ann Arbor: University of Michigan Press, 1996, 195-210.

Hobbs, John. "Are Joyce's Dubliners Paralyzed? A Second Opinion." *Papers on Joyce* 15 (2009): 17-29.

Hofheinz, Thomas. *Joyce and the Invention of Irish History: Finnegans Wake in Context*. Cambridge: Cambridge University Press, 1995.

Jaillant, Lise. "Blurring the Boundaries: *Fourteen Great Detective Stories* and Joyce's *A Portrait of the Artist as a Young Man* in the Modern Library Series." *James Joyce Quarterly* 50.3 (Spring 2013): 767-96.

Jameson, Fredric. *The Antinomies of Realism*. New York: Verso, 2013.

Jameson, Fredric. *Archaeologies of the Future: The Desire Called Utopia and Other Science Fictions*. New York: Verso, 2005.

Jameson, Fredric. "Joyce or Proust?" In *The Modernist Papers*. New York: Verso, 2007, 170-203.

Jameson, Fredric. *Marxism and Form*. Princeton, NJ: Princeton University Press, 1971.

Jameson, Fredric. *The Political Unconscious: Narrative as a Socially Symbolic Act*. Ithaca, NY: Cornell University Press, 1981.

Jameson, Fredric. *Postmodernism, or, the Cultural Logic of Late Capitalism*. Durham, NC: Duke University Press, 1991.

Jameson, Fredric. *A Singular Modernity: Essay on the Ontology of the Present*. New York: Verso, 2002.

Jameson, Fredric. "*Ulysses* in History." In *The Modernist Papers*. New York: Verso, 2007, 137-51.

Joyce, James. *Dubliners: A Norton Critical Edition*. Ed. Margot Norris. Text ed. Hans Walter Gabler with Walter Hettche. New York: W.W. Norton, 2006.

Joyce, James. *Finnegans Wake*. Ed. Finn Fordham, Robbert-Jan Henkes, and Erik Bindervoet. Oxford: Oxford World's Classics, 2012.

Joyce, James. *Giacomo Joyce*. Introduction and notes by Richard Ellmann. London: Faber & Faber, 1968.

Joyce, James. *Letters, Volume I*. Ed. Stuart Gilbert. New York: Viking Press, 1957.

Joyce, James. *Letters, Volumes II and III*. Ed. Richard Ellmann. New York: Viking Press, 1966.

Joyce, James. *A Portrait of the Artist as a Young Man: A Norton Critical Edition*. Ed. John Paul Riquelme. Text ed. Hans Walter Gabler with Walter Hettche. New York: W.W. Norton, 2007.

Joyce, James. *Stephen Hero*. Ed. John J. Slocum and Herbert Cahoon. New York: New Directions, 1963.

Joyce, James. *Ulysses*. Ed. Hans Walter Gabler et al. New York: Vintage, 1986.

Kain, Richard M. *Fabulous Voyager: James Joyce's Ulysses*. Chicago: Chicago University Press, 1947.

Kenner, Hugh. *Dublin's Joyce*. Bloomington, IN: Indiana University Press, 1956.

Kenner, Hugh. *Ulysses*, rev. ed. Baltimore, MD: Johns Hopkins University Press, 1987.

Kenner, Hugh. "Joyce's *Portrait*—A Reconsideration." In *James Joyce's A Portrait of the Artist as a Young Man: A Norton Critical Edition*. Ed. John Paul Riquelme. New York: W.W. Norton, 2007, 348–61.

Kenner, Hugh. "The *Portrait* in Perspective." In *James Joyce's A Portrait of the Artist as a Young Man: A Casebook*. Ed. Mark A. Wollaeger. New York: Oxford University Press, 2003, 27–57.

Kershner, R. Brandon and Mary Lowe-Evans. "'Grace': Spirited Discourses." In *Collaborative Dubliners: Joyce in Dialogue*. Ed. Vicki Mahaffey. Syracuse: Syracuse University Press, 2012, 323–42.

Latour, Bruno, "Why Has Critique Run out of Steam? From Matters of Fact to Matters of Concern." *Critical Inquiry* 30 (Winter 2004): 225–48.

LeBlanc, Jim. "The Closing Word of *Finnegans Wake*." *Hypermedia Joyce Studies* 2.1 (Summer 1999): web.

LeBlanc, Jim. "A 'Sensation of Freedom' and the Rejection of Possibility in *Dubliners*." In *Rethinking Joyce's Dubliners*. Ed. Claire A. Culleton and Ellen Scheible. New York: Palgrave Macmillan, 2017, 51–68.

Leonard, Garry M. *Reading Dubliners Again: A Lacanian Perspective*. Syracuse: Syracuse University Press, 1993.

Levenson, Michael. "Stephen's Diary in Joyce's *Portrait*—The Shape of Life." *ELH* 52.4 (Winter 1985): 1017–35.

Levin, Harry. *James Joyce: A Critical Introduction*. Norfolk: New Directions, 1941.

Lewis, Pericles. "The Conscience of the Race: The Nation as Church of the Modern Age." In *Joyce through the Ages: A Nonlinear View*. Ed. Michael Patrick Gillespie. Gainesville: University Press of Florida, 1999, 81–106.

Lewis, Wyndham. *Time and Western Man*. Ed. Paul Edwards. Santa Rosa: Black Sparrow Press, 1993.

Litz, A. Walton. *Method and Design in Ulysses and Finnegans Wake*. New York: Oxford University Press, 1964.

MacCabe, Colin. *James Joyce and the Revolution of the Word*. London: Macmillan, 1979.

Mahaffey, Vicki. "*Dubliners*: Surprised by Chance." In *A Companion to James Joyce*. Ed. Richard Brown. Malden, MA: Blackwell, 2011, 19–31.

Mahaffey, Vicki. "'Fantastic Histories': Nomadology and Female Piracy in *Finnegans Wake*." In *Joyce and the Subject of History*. Ed. Mark A. Wollaeger, Victor Luftig, and Robert Spoo. Ann Arbor: University of Michigan Press, 1996, 157–76.

Mahaffey, Vicki. "Giacomo Joyce." In *Giacomo Joyce: Envoys of the Other*. Ed. Louis Armand and Clare Wallace. Prague: Litteraria Pragensia, 2006, 26–70.

Mahaffey, Vicki. "Père-version and Im-mère-sion: Idealized Corruption in *A Portrait of the Artist as a Young Man* and *The Picture of Dorian Gray*." *James Joyce Quarterly* 50.1–2 (Fall 2012–Winter 2013): 245–61.

Mahaffey, Vicki and Jill Shashaty. "Introduction." In *Collaborative Dubliners: Joyce in Dialogue*. Ed. Vicki Mahaffey. Syracuse: Syracuse University Press, 2012, 1–22.

Manganiello, Dominic. *Joyce's Politics*. Boston: Routledge and Kegan Paul, 1980.

Marx, Karl. "Private Property and Communism" section of "Economic and Philosophic Manuscripts of 1844." In *The Marx-Engels Reader*. Ed. Robert C. Tucker. New York: W.W. Norton, 1978, 81–93.

McCourt, John. "Epiphanies of Language, Longing, Liminality in *Giacomo Joyce*." *Giacomo Joyce: Envoys of the Other*. Ed. Louis Armand and Clare Wallace. Prague: Litteraria Pragensia, 2006, 228–48.

McGee, Patrick. "The Communist *Flâneur*, or, Joyce's Boredom." In *European Joyce Studies 21: Joyce, Benjamin and Magical Urbanism*. Ed. Maurizia Boscagli and Enda Duffy. Amsterdam: Rodopi Press, 2011, 122–31.

McGee, Patrick. *Joyce Beyond Marx: History and Desire in Ulysses and Finnegans Wake*. Gainesville: University of Florida Press, 2001.

McHugh, Roland. *Annotations to Finnegans Wake*, 4th ed. Baltimore, MD: Johns Hopkins University Press, 2016.

Muñoz, José Esteban. *Cruising Utopia; The Then and There of Queer Futurity*. New York: New York University Press, 2009.

Newman, John Henry. *An Essay in the Aid of a Grammar of Assent*. Ed. I. T. Ker. Oxford: Clarendon Press, 1985.

Nolan, Emer. *James Joyce and Nationalism*. New York: Routledge, 1995.

Norris, Margot. "The Critical History of *Finnegans Wake*." In *Joyce and the Subject of History*. Ed. Mark A. Wollaeger, Victor Luftig, and Robert Spoo. Ann Arbor: University of Michigan Press, 1996, 177–93.

Norris, Margot. *The Decentered Universe of Finnegans Wake: A Structuralist Analysis*. Baltimore, MD: Johns Hopkins University Press, 1974.

Norris, Margot. *Suspicious Readings of Joyce's Dubliners*. Philadelphia: University of Pennsylvania Press, 2003.

Proust, Marcel. *The Prisoner and The Fugitive* (*In Search of Lost Time*, Volume 5). Trans. Carol Clark and Peter Collier. London: Penguin, 2003.

Rando, David. *Hope and Wish Image in Music Technology*. New York: Palgrave Macmillan, 2017.

Rando, David. *Modernist Fiction and News: Representing Experience in the Early Twentieth Century*. New York: Palgrave Macmillan, 2011.

Rando, David. "Storytelling and Alienated Labor: Joyce, Benjamin, and the Narrative Wording Class." *Journal of Modern Literature* 38.2 (Winter 2015): 29–44.

Sagan, Carl. *Pale Blue Dot: A Vision of the Human Future in Space*. New York: Random House, 1994.

Saint-Amour, Paul K. and Karen R. Lawrence. "Reopening 'A Painful Case.'" In *Collaborative Dubliners: Joyce in Dialogue*. Ed. Vicki Mahaffey. Syracuse: Syracuse University Press, 2012, 238–60.

Scholes, Robert. "Stephen Dedalus: Poet or Esthete?" In *James Joyce's A Portrait of the Artist as a Young Man: Text, Criticism, and Notes*. Ed. Chester G. Anderson. New York: Viking Press, 1968, 468–80.

Scholes, Robert and Richard M. Kain, eds. *The Workshop of Daedalus: James Joyce and the Raw Materials for A Portrait of the Artist as a Young Man*. Evanston: Northwestern University Press, 1965.

Sedgwick, Eve Kosofsky. *Touching Feeling: Affect, Pedagogy, Performativity*. Durham, NC: Duke University Press, 2003.

Senn, Fritz. "Book of Many Turns." In *Ulysses: Fifty Years*. Ed. Thomas F. Staley. Bloomington: Indiana University Press, 1974, 29–46.

Senn, Fritz. "Gnomon Inverted." In *ReJoycing: New Readings of Dubliners*. Lexington: University Press of Kentucky, 1998, 249–57.

Senn, Fritz. "On Not Coming to Terms with *Giacomo Joyce*." In *Giacomo Joyce: Envoys of the Other*. Ed. Louis Armand and Clare Wallace. Prague: Litteraria Pragensia, 2006, 20–5.

Shovlin, Frank. *Journey Westward: Joyce, Dubliners and the Literary Revival*. Liverpool: Liverpool University Press, 2012.

Staten, Henry. "The Decomposing Form of *Ulysses*." In *James Joyce's Ulysses: A Casebook*. Ed. Derek Attridge. New York: Oxford University Press, 2004, 173–99.

Thompson, Peter. "Introduction: The Privatization of Hope and the Crisis of Negation." In *The Privatization of Hope: Ernst Bloch and the Future of Utopia*. Ed. Peter Thompson and Slavoj Žižek. Durham, NC: Duke University Press, 2013, 1–20.

Thompson, Peter and Slavoj Žižek, eds. *The Privatization of Hope: Ernst Bloch and the Future of Utopia*. Durham, NC: Duke University Press, 2013.

Tindall, William York. *A Reader's Guide to Finnegans Wake*. Syracuse: Syracuse University Press, 1996.

Tindall, William York. *A Reader's Guide to James Joyce*. New York: Farrar, Straus & Giroux, 1969.

Tymoczko, Maria. *The Irish Ulysses*. Berkeley, CA: University of California Press, 1994.

Valente, Joseph. "Thrilled by His Touch: The Aestheticizing of Homosexual Panic in *A Portrait of the Artist as a Young Man*." In *James Joyce's A Portrait of the Artist as a Young Man: A Casebook*. Ed. Mark A. Wollaeger. New York: Oxford University Press, 2003, 245–80.

Van Mierlo, Wim. "The Subject Notebook: A Nexus in the Composition of *Ulysses*—A Preliminary Analysis." *Genetic Joyce Studies* 7 (Spring 2007): 1–46.

Walzl, Florence L. "The Liturgy of the Epiphany Season and the Epiphanies of Joyce." *PMLA* 80.4 (September 1965): 436–50.

Wicht, Wolfgang. *Utopianism in James Joyce's Ulysses*. Heidelberg: Universitätverlag Winter, 2000.

Williams, Trevor L. "No Cheer for 'the Gratefully Oppressed': Ideology in Joyce's *Dubliners*." In *ReJoycing: New Readings of Dubliners*. Lexington: University Press of Kentucky, 1998, 87–109.

Wollaeger, Mark A. "Introduction." In *James Joyce's A Portrait of the Artist as a Young Man: A Casebook*. Ed. Mark A. Wollaeger. New York: Oxford University Press, 2003, 3–26.

Woolf, Virginia. "Character in Fiction." In *Selected Essays*. Ed. David Bradshaw. New York: Oxford University Press, 2008, 37–54.

Woolf, Virginia, *Mrs. Dalloway*. Ed. Bonnie Kime Scott. Orlando: Harvest, 2005.

Yeats, William Butler. *The Collected Poems of W.B. Yeats*. Ed. Richard J. Finneran. New York: Collier Books, 1989.

Index

Abrams, M. H. 36
Adorno, Theodor W. 146
"After the Race" (Joyce) 37–8 (see also *Dubliners*)
alienation 36, 65, 83, 144–7
already-known 4, 11, 47, 146, 150–1
anamnesis 11, 56, 62–3, 98, 112–13
anti-Semitism 143–4
anxiety 11–12, 58, 97–8 (*see under* psychoanalysis)
  about origins 21, 62–5, 69–70, 109, 114, 118
  about future 68, 127
  hermeneutic 63–4
  and hunger 70–1
"Araby" (Joyce) 39, 58, 98 (see also *Dubliners*)
Attridge, Derek 114
Azérad, Hugo 146–7

Beck, Warren 35, 38–9
Beja, Morris 29, 39
Benjamin, Walter 146
  allegory 65
  dying person 95
  gambling 37–8
  homogeneous, empty time 11
  hopes of the dead 98
Benstock, Bernard 42
Bersani, Leo 149
Bildung 45, 47, 71, 85, 99 (see under *A Portrait of the Artist as a Young Man*)
Bishop, John 113–15, 154 n.11
  Joyce's Book of the Dark 113
Bloch, Ernst 3, 12, 20, 29, 146 (*see also* hope)
  art as correlative to unfinished history 151
  daydream 110, 115–20 (see under *A Portrait of the Artist as a Young Man*; *Ulysses*; *Finnegans Wake*)
  hope as process 40
  metempsychosis 122–3 (see under *Ulysses*; *Finnegans Wake*)
  music 69
  Not-Yet-Become 34, 47, 128
  Not-Yet-Conscious 13, 65, 115
  "A Philosophical View of the Detective Novel [*Detektivromans*]" 21, 56, 61–3 (see under *A Portrait of the Artist as a Young Man*)
  "A Philosophical View of the Novel of the Artist [*Künstlerromans*]" 21, 56–9, 61, 64–5 (see under *A Portrait of the Artist as a Young Man*)
  The Principle of Hope 55–8, 115–16
  real possibility 4, 11, 20, 25 n.16, 36, 55–6, 60, 69–71, 77, 83, 87–8, 109, 119, 127–8, 131, 150, 152
  self-preservation 6, 8–9, 33–4, 37, 70
  spatial versus temporal utopia 85–6 (*see under* hope)
  subject and object relations 36
Briggs, Austin 79, 81
Brown, Richard 15
Budgen, Frank 68, 86, 120

capitalism 4, 20, 36–7, 40, 43, 58–9, 89
Castle, Gregory 59
Charles, Alec 146
Cheng, Vincent 64
Cixous, Hélène 2
class 34, 58–9, 89–90, 148
classical period of Joyce studies 1–2, 8, 10, 29, 35, 38–40
"Clay" (Joyce) 41 (see also *Dubliners*)
colonialism 4, 20, 31–2, 34–5, 40, 58
community 11, 64, 67, 128–30 (*see also* readers)
Commedia (Dante) 85–6, 100
cosmic perspective 13, 17–8, 21, 77–82, 85, 96–7, 100, 125, 128

versus human-temporal scale 18, 79–80, 85, 89, 124
cynicism 63, 145–6, 152

daydream (*see under* Bloch; *Finnegans Wake*; psychoanalysis; *Ulysses*)
"The Dead" (Joyce) 8, 34, 39, 41, 45–7, 126 (see also *Dubliners*)
death 12, 93, 95, 97–9, 129–30, 131
  anti-utopia of 3, 45
  metempsychosis 122–4
  non-hope 8–9, 15–17, 45–7
Dettmar, Kevin J. H. 2, 39
Dublin 7, 12, 30, 34–7, 43, 83, 86, 122, 148, 151
Dubliners (Joyce) 2, 4, 7–8, 13, 19–20, 29–48, 95 (*see also* story titles)
  apotheosis 20, 29, 39–40, 47
  epiphany 29, 38–41, 66, 149
  "journey westward" 29, 44, 46–8, 153
  open future 77–8, 82–3, 85–7
  paralysis 2, 7–8, 11–12, 20, 29–33, 37–42, 45–8, 120, 125–6, 152
  simony 29, 41–3, 45
  spiritual liberation 8, 29, 30–3, 38, 40–8, 150 (*see under* utopia)
Duffy, Enda 11, 32, 151

Easter Rising 84
Egyptian Book of the Dead 129
  Thoth 129–30, 131
Eide, Marian 64
Ellmann, Maud 62
Ellmann, Richard 81, 149
  James Joyce 149

Faust (Johann Wolfgang von Goethe) 85
Finnegans Wake (Joyce) 4, 13–14, 21–2, 32, 78, 86, 109–31, 146–8, 152–3
  being-present in history 123–5, 131
  cyclical premise of 109, 125–8
  daydream 109–10, 112, 115–21, 124, 130–2
  history 110–13, 131
  historical juxtaposition in 109, 113–17, 120–4, 130–1
  metempsychosis 110, 121–4, 130–1

nightdream 21, 109–10, 113–20
paralysis 125
spatialization of hope (*see under* hope)
spatialization of time 110, 122–4
tableaux 110, 122, 128–31
terminal "the" 109, 125–8
Fogarty, Anne 30
Frank, Joseph 82
Freud, Sigmund 11 (*see also* psychoanalysis)
future
  anticipation of 13–14
  arrival of 126, 130
  attempts to shape 90–1, 93, 97
  challenge of imagining 82–4
  immediate versus wider 14, 21, 78–9, 84–6, 88, 99–101
  in Joyce criticism 1–4, 10–11, 31–3, 112–13, 118
  Joyce's parents 4–7
  Künstlerroman 55–60, 64–6
  not-yet 1, 4, 21, 56–7, 61–2, 64, 69, 150, 153
  openness 4, 9, 11–12, 14, 20–1, 29, 32, 34, 47, 57, 59–60, 65–71, 77–8, 83–5, 99–101, 110, 126–8, 131, 148, 150–2
  orientation 21, 29, 109–10, 119, 124–5, 147–9
  unforeseen 4, 7, 9, 12, 15, 20, 32–3, 40–1, 46–7, 64–66, 69, 71, 127–8, 150
futurelessness 14, 18, 88, 95–6, 98

gambling (*see under* Benjamin, Walter)
gender 34–5
genetic criticism 117–18
Giacomo Joyce (Joyce) 14–20, 45, 131
Gibbons, Luke 30, 99
Gibson, Andrew and Len Platt 2–3
"Grace" (Joyce) 42–3 (see also *Dubliners*)
Greimas, A. J. 43–4

Hayman, David 117
Herr, Cheryl 146–7
historicism 2–3, 10, 110–12, 115, 151
hope (*see also* Bloch, Ernst)
  connective tissue 15, 20–1, 66, 68–70
  constellation 13, 21, 82–3, 86, 95, 100–1, 124

of the dead 16, 93–4, 96–9
dialectic with hunger 1, 3–4, 6, 8–9, 12, 20, 29, 32–5, 37, 39–42, 45, 47–8, 129, 131, 150–2
educated (*docta spes*) 12, 33, 71
experience 6, 17, 37–8, 47, 67–8, 81–2, 85
forward-looking 4, 10, 13, 20, 29, 34–6, 47, 90, 98, 118–19
image 1, 4, 11, 13–16, 77, 80–2, 100, 150
intellectual 6–7, 17, 20, 146–7, 152–3
libidinal 6–7, 16–17, 19–20
liminal spaces 14–16, 20
material conditions 1–7, 11–12, 17, 20–1, 29, 32, 34, 36, 41–3, 70–1, 115, 118, 128, 130–1, 143, 152
misdirected 12–13, 33, 38, 39–42, 55, 58
non-hope 8–9, 15–17, 43–7, 128, 153
open-ended 4, 14, 46–7, 87
present conditions 4–6, 11, 13, 55, 60–1, 63, 66, 68, 78, 88, 93, 99–100, 128, 131, 149, 151
process 1, 4, 9–10, 20, 29, 40, 45, 47, 85–6, 95
redirecting 12, 32–3, 40
religion 9, 47–8, 152
restlessness of 1, 3–4, 7, 9–10, 40, 77, 85, 150
spatialization of 1, 4, 13–14, 20–1, 77, 88–90, 95, 98–101, 131, 150, 152
at a standstill 13, 16, 83, 88–9, 95, 150
stomach hope 4–7, 16–17, 33–7, 150
temporality 9, 10, 16, 46, 83, 95, 99
hopelessness
in Joyce criticism 1–2, 7–8, 10–11, 20, 29–30, 125
represented by Joyce 7, 14, 18, 33, 41, 45, 69, 98–9, 152
versus non-hope 8–9, 16, 43–6, 85, 128
hunger 16–7, 38, 92, 118, 130 (*see under* hope)
and poverty 68, 70–1, 144

"Ivy Day in the Committee Room" (Joyce) 9 (see also *Dubliners*)

Jameson, Fredric
on Bloch 56–7
modernism 87
on semiotic square 44
Ulysses and totalization 78, 82, 84, 97
utopia 47, 146
Joyce, John Stanislaus 4–6
Joyce, Mary 4–6

Kain, Richard 2, 79–80
Fabulous Voyager 80
Kenner, Hugh 8, 29, 43, 45, 59, 63
Kershner, R. Brandon and Mary Lowe-Evans 42
Kubrick, Stanley 80
2001: A Space Odyssey 80

LeBlanc, Jim 127
Lessing, Gottfried Ephraim 102 n.15, 122
Levin, Harry 1–2
Lewis, Pericles 64
literary form 1, 3–4, 13–14, 20–2, 32, 83, 121, 131, 146, 150 (*see under* modernism)
"A Little Cloud" (Joyce) 47 (see also *Dubliners*)
loneliness 83, 146–7
Litz, A. Walton 60

MacCabe, Colin 2
Mahaffey, Vicki 14–15, 19–20, 42–3
and Jill Shashaty 30–1
Marx, Karl 36, 65, 70
materialism 3, 10, 16, 33, 42, 112 (*see under* hope)
McCourt, John 15, 19
McGee, Patrick 136 n.19
metempsychosis (*see under* Bloch; death; *Finnegans Wake*; *Ulysses*)
modernism (*see under* Jameson; utopia)
formal innovation 3, 13, 112
perfection 85, 97
perspective 81
versus realism 96
spatial form 19, 80, 82, 90, 101
subversion 32
transformation 86–8
Moore, Thomas 35, 66–8
"Oft in the Stilly Night" 66–8
"Silent, O Moyle" 35

nationalism 9, 11–13, 55, 64, 145
Newman, John Henry 66–8
  An Essay in the Aid of a Grammar of Assent 68
Nolan, Emer 11, 64
non-hope (*see under* death; hope; hopelessness)
Norris, Margot 35, 39, 114–15

Odyssey (Homer) 78, 86, 120–1

"A Painful Case" (Joyce) 40–1 (see also *Dubliners*)
paralysis (see under *Dubliners*; *Finnegans Wake*; *Ulysses*)
pathetic fallacy 35–6
politics 1–2, 4, 33–4, 55
  textual 1–2, 9–11, 31
"A Portrait of the Artist" (Joyce) 61
A Portrait of the Artist as a Young Man (Joyce) 4, 7, 9, 11, 13–14, 21, 55–76, 95
  Bildungsroman 55, 63, 86
  "the darkness at the beginning" (Bloch) 21, 56, 61–4, 69, 114
  daydream 57–8
  detective novel 21, 56, 61–4, 69–70, 114
  Fœtus 21, 61–2, 64–5, 69–70, 99, 118
  green rose 21, 61–2, 64–5, 69–70, 118, 128, 153
  hermeneutically linked to *Ulysses* 21, 59–61, 71, 82, 127
  Künstlerroman 21, 55–9, 61–5, 69–71
  negotiating between material and spiritual 42–3
  open future 77–8, 82–3, 85–7
post-structuralism 2, 8, 10–11, 29, 31–2, 35, 38–41, 96, 146, 151
poverty 4–6, 12, 20, 32, 34–5, 38, 66, 68, 118, 131, 144
Proust, Marcel 98, 112–13
psychoanalysis 6, 63, 70, 113–15 (*see also* Freud, Sigmund)
  daydream 118
  neurosis 63, 109, 114–16
  Oedipal anxiety 6, 63, 66, 70, 109–10, 114
  Oedipal form 56, 63
  the Real 97

repression 12, 56
secondary revision 116
sex drive 6, 33–4, 70
sublimation 18–9
unconscious 11, 21–2, 87, 109–10, 113–20, 130, 147–8

readers
  the communal 22, 130, 147, 149–50, 153
  wishful communities of 22, 148–50, 151
realism 90, 96
Richards, Grant 30, 43
Rilke, Rainer Maria 87
  "Archaic Torso of Apollo" 87
Ruskin, John 36

Sagan, Carl 80–2, 99
  The Pale Blue Dot 81
Saint-Amour, Paul K. and Karen R. Lawrence 40–1
satire and parody 9, 12, 32, 43–4, 91–3, 120, 147–8
Scholes, Robert 59
Senn, Fritz 14–15, 32, 70
Shakespeare, William 7, 90
  Hamlet 90–3, 96
  Macbeth 129–30
"The Sisters" (Joyce) 7–8, 42, 45, 128 (see also *Dubliners*)
skepticism 145–8, 152
Staten, Henry 97–8
Stephen Hero 7, 38, 60
subjectivity 36, 97
subversion 48 (*see under* modernism; *see also* post-structuralism; satire and parody)

"Two Gallants" (Joyce) 33–7, 38, 40, 126 (see also *Dubliners*)
Tymoczko, Maria 120

Ulysses (Joyce) 2, 4, 7, 11, 13–14, 21, 36, 77–101, 126, 143–9
  "Circe" 87, 92–4, 143
  "Cyclops" 87, 91–4, 144
  daydream and nightdream 116–17
  dying or deathbed wishes 21, 77, 89–99
  "Eumaeus" 22, 143–5, 147
  ghosts 91–9

"Hades" 87, 143
interior monologue 82–3, 96
"Ithaca" 13, 18–19, 77–81, 85, 88–9, 124–5, 128 (*see also* cosmic perspective)
"Lestrygonians" 36, 87
metempsychosis 91, 120–1
"Oxen of the Sun" 87
parallax 13, 77, 79, 81, 100
paralysis 85
"Penelope" 79, 82–3, 86, 88
"Proteus" 77, 86–7
remembrance 14, 21, 77, 90, 94–5, 98–9, 101
"Scylla and Charybdis" 90
sequel to *A Portrait of the Artist as a Young Man* 21, 59–61, 71, 82, 127
spatialization of hope (*see under* hope)
spatialization of time 123
sudden death in 88
totalization 82–4, 96, 149
wills 89–91, 93–7
utopia 1, 36, 56, 64–5, 69, 71, 99–101, 109–13, 115, 120, 128, 130–1, 143–53
art 3, 57, 61

better worlds 12, 58, 77–8, 143–4, 148
dying wishes 93–4, 98
hunger 33
liberation from 13, 29, 43–8 (see under *Dubliners*)
modernism 87–8
nationalism 11
sexual fantasy 16–20
spatial versus temporal 82–6
utopian program versus impulse 6–7, 9, 12–3, 22, 97, 101, 112, 147–8
the utopian moment 22, 110, 123–4, 131

Vico, Giambattista 111, 121, 123–4, 126
  New Science 111
Voyager1 80–1, 98–100

Wicht, Wolfgang 145–6
  Utopianism in James Joyce's Ulysses 145
Williams, Trevor 29–30
wishful images 4, 11, 21, 69, 91, 97, 109, 122, 124, 150
Wollaeger, Mark 62

Printed in the USA
CPSIA information can be obtained
at www.ICGtesting.com
LVHW011650091223
766046LV00004B/168